ADVANCE PRAISE FOR

RAISING CONFIDENT READERS

"I highly recommend Dr. Gentry's *Raising Confident Readers* to any parent who wants success for their child—not just in reading, but in life.

—David W. Johnson, MD,
Fellow of the American Board of Pediatrics

"*Raising Confident Readers* is a wonderful gift and resource for parents and teachers alike! Dr. Gentry has combined best research practices with a wealth of experiences in the field to provide clear answers to common questions about developing readers. This book will stretch understandings about phonics, words, spelling, reading levels, comprehension, and much more. My favorite insight in the book: 'Create a joyful, literate environment at home, and respond to your child's natural curiosity and questions.' So true!"

— Dr. Connie R. Hebert, National Literacy Consultant
and author of *Catch a Falling Writer*

"This important book will have profound impact on how parents of young children view their role as their child's first and most important teachers."

—Antoinette Fornshell, author of *Planning for Successful Reading and Writing Instruction in K-2*

"This is a carefully crafted book that is both comprehensive and practical. *Raising Confident Readers* is a must-read for every new parent. Dr. Gentry clearly describes the stages of literary development in children and explains how parents can informally instruct their children."

—Dr. Paula Egelson, Director of the Center for Partnerships
to Improve Education at the College of Charleston, South Carolina

"This book will be useful to any parent who wonders what their young child is experiencing in learning to read. And what better way to love a child than to help him or her become a reader."

—Timothy Shanahan, Professor of Urban Education, University of Illinois, Chicago

"It is encouraging to find a literacy resource for parents that is less concerned about 'racing up the levels' and focuses more on enjoying the journey! Dr. Gentry's *Raising Confident Readers* offers parents and teachers a common language, free from educational jargon, to continue to the conversation (and the exciting journey) once formal instruction begins!"

—Suzy Quiles, Reading Specialist and Language Arts Supervisor

"Richard Gentry understands just what young children need to learn to read. He has provided an outstanding guide for parents to help their children get a jumpstart on early literacy experiences. Filled with practical advice and effective and engaging activities, this dynamic book provides the tools for parents to help their children prepare for success with reading."

—Lori Kamola, MSEd, Reading Specialist

"Brilliantly written . . . this book should be required reading for every Pre-K through second-grade teacher, caregiver, and early childhood interventionist."

—Jan McNeel, Independent Educational Consultant

RAISING CONFIDENT READERS

How to Teach Your Child to Read and Write—from Baby to Age Seven

DR. J. RICHARD GENTRY

A Member of the Perseus Books Group

Printed in the United States of America. For information, address Da Capo Press, 11 Cambridge Center, Cambridge, MA 02142.

Design and production by Pauline Brown
Typeset in 13 point Perpetua

Library of Congress Cataloging-in-Publication Data
Gentry, J. Richard.
Raising confident readers : how to teach your child to read and write-from baby to age seven / Dr. J. Richard Gentry. — 1st da capo press ed. 2010.
p. cm.
Includes bibliographical references and index.
ISBN 978-0-7382-1397-2 (alk. paper)
1. Language arts (Early childhood) 2. Early childhood education—Parent participation. 3. Early childhood education—Activity programs. 4. Individualized instruction. I. Title.
LB1139.5.L35G48 2010
372.6—dc22

2010008341

First Da Capo Press edition 2010

Published by Da Capo Press
A Member of the Perseus Books Group
www.dacapopress.com

10 9 8 7 6 5 4 3 2 1

For Bill Boswell
And in memory of Bonnie Wright Gentry
Along with heartfelt thanks to
Rosemarie Jensen and Lois Bridges

CONTENTS

ACKNOWLEDGMENTS

My mom was my first reading teacher. There is a little bit of her on every page of this book.

My career as a reading educator spans a period of over thirty years. There are so many researchers, educators, and scholars to whom I owe gratitude. Giants in the field who helped shape my thinking include Edmund H. Henderson, Marie Clay, Jean Chall, Linnea Ehri, Connie Juel, Sally Shaywitz, Lois Bridges, Sandra Wilde, Lise Eliot, Betty Hart, Todd Risley, Susan Neuman, David Dickinsen, Howard Margolis, Patrick McCabe, Tim Rasinski, Charles Read, Donald Richgels, Regie Routman, Frank Smith, Marilyn Adams, Ken and Yetta Goodman, Richard Allington, Irene Foluntas, Gay Su Pinnell, Donald Graves, Eileen Feldgus, David Pearson, Richard Hodges, Connie Hebert, Richard Craddock, Tim Shanahan, Darrell Morris, Catherine Snow, Kathleen Roskos, Jim Trelease, Keith Stanovich, Jerry Zutell, and so many others. I have great admiration and respect for the academic community in education and I am grateful for the scholarship that informs best practice.

Parents, grandparents, and their children, along with many outstanding teachers of beginning reading, guided me every step of the way in *Raising Confident Readers*. A special thank you to Rick and Rosemarie Jensen, Shea Dean, Kathleen Wright, Jean Gillet, Bill McIntyre, Kathy Rogers, Mitch and Rebekah Pindzola, Carolyn Miegs, Anne Edwards, Paula Egelson, Isabell Cardonick, Katherine Streckfus, Jan McNeel, Vickie Wallace-Nesler, Lilia Nanez, Dalia Benavides, Judy Farley, Penny Jamison, Jean Mann, Antoinette Fornshell, Suzy Quiles, Alan and Jenny Wood, Kate Brenner, Nancy Pusateri, and to hundreds of children who have shared their marvelous writing and insight.

INTRODUCTION

CONFIDENT READERS are not born, but they can be made—naturally, lovingly, and joyfully—by a child's first reading teacher: *you*. If you are holding this book, it means that you know how important reading and writing are for your child's success. As a parent, grandparent, or other type of caregiver, you want to be certain your child's literacy is developing appropriately. But unless you are a literacy expert, you probably don't know *how* to teach reading—how to move your child from listening to stories to reading and writing them independently. It's likely you don't know what your child's reading, writing, and spelling should look like from birth to age seven or how to recognize when literacy may not be developing normally. That's where this book fits in.

This is the first parent-centered book of its kind—that is, the first book to show parents or other caregivers how to teach reading and capitalize on the critical role early writing plays in learning to read. Contrary to popular belief, at the beginning levels, learning to read and learning to write are almost the same. In fact, early readers are almost always pencil-and-paper kids who write first and read later: They learn to read by writing. But while many parents read aloud to their children, few take the next step by encouraging early writing. *Raising Confident Readers* will show you how to do this and more—without subjecting your child to boring scripted lessons or detracting from the bonding experience of reading together. This is an activity-based book with writing, reading, and sound-awareness activities designed to fit effortlessly into your regular day-to-day schedule and to be enjoyable and rewarding for everyone. Helping your young child learn to read and write is likely to be one of the most amazing experiences you'll ever have.

Raising Confident Readers shows you how your child's brain is wired for reading. Well before your child can speak or read, he is absorbing language at a phenomenal pace. In the first year of life, his brain will triple in size; by the time he enters kindergarten, it will be almost as big as yours. It is during this critical period that virtually all the neural pathways establishing language proficiency are formed. That is why, as your child's first reading teacher, it is so crucial to make the most of these early years—the critical period from birth to age six. The opportunity will not come again. The brain's ability to absorb new language patterns diminishes steadily from the age of seven until puberty, and capacities such as overcoming spelling disabilities or overcoming dyslexia are virtually gone in early adulthood. At a later age, the brain may compensate for these disabilities and use different pathways or circuitry, but learning to read will be harder. As described in Chapter 1, some of the complicated reading circuitry used by normal readers will have been pruned. The literacy activities in this book, each specifically tailored to your child's current development phase, will directly and permanently alter the structure and future function of your child's brain! He'll be using the same systems you activate now when he's eighty.

IT'S AS SIMPLE AS 1-2-3!

As complicated and mysterious as language acquisition may seem, all beginning readers and writers follow one clear path toward literacy: They progress through literacy milestones in a consistent sequence of five literacy phases. In this book, which is drawn from my thirty years of literacy work with children, I describe that path to you, pointing out important milestones along the way and providing fun and easy activities to help your child reach those milestones in a timely manner. Here are three easy steps to follow as your child proceeds through the five phases:

1. Get Off to an Early Start: Enjoy Loving Literacy Interactions with Your Child

Critical formative brain activity for literacy happens early. From birth to age five, your child's brain is like a sponge, soaking up information. This is the time to set the foundations of literacy. While there is no need to resort to extreme measures—formal instruction, commercial video programs, or early phonics or flash-card lessons—you should work to provide loving literacy interactions with babies and toddlers. Rich early literacy interactions can help produce rich, literate brains.

Starting early can put your child on a path toward being a confident, expert reader and writer at a young age. Consider this: Researchers say it takes 10,000 hours to become an expert at almost anything. But under the best of circumstances, your child might get only about 500 hours of reading under his belt each year in school. Do the math—at that rate your child won't be an expert reader until college. Accordingly, you'll want to begin early to create a positive mindset and good habits. Generate energy and enthusiasm for reading and writing, and keep a close check on TV or video time, so that your child will want to pick up books voluntarily and spend time with them at every age.

How much time is required at the beginning? If you start early, not a whole lot. By spending just a few minutes a day engaging your baby or toddler in literacy activities, you can rack up many valuable hours of practice and learning before your child starts school. Think of how easy it would be to label a few objects or colors in your eighteen-month-old child's bedroom: *bed*, for instance, or the toy *cat*. Write your child's name on her photograph along with *Mom* and *Dad*. Then spend thirty seconds three times a day playing "the word game," pointing out a few words labeled in baby's room, drawing attention to the sounds in sequence, and tracking them from left to right with your finger: "See this word? It says *Mom*: /m/-/o/-/m/. Baby can read *Mom*! *Mom* loves baby!" This simple ninety-second-a-day word game can lead to word reading at about the same time the baby speaks her first words!

Spending time reading and talking to your baby pays dividends. When you read aloud to your baby with positive conversational interchanges you engender long-term gains and increase your baby's or toddler's intelligence. In a famous study, psychologists Betty Hart and Todd Risley tracked baby development in forty-two professional, working-class, and welfare families, visiting their homes for one hour each month for two and a half years to record how the families interacted with the babies verbally from the time the children were seven months old until age three. The researchers described interactions between parents and children and tape-recorded all parent-child conversations. The database included analysis of words used, parts of speech, and types of sentences. The researchers tracked use of affirmations ("You are smart!"), prohibitions ("Stop, bad girl!"), and questions ("Where's the doll?"). Their findings were astounding.

Babies and toddlers in professional families over the period heard a staggering 45 million words, compared to 26 million in working-class families and a meager 13 million for welfare children. Children who interacted with a greater volume of conversation in the first three years of life and with more word and sentence variety developed much larger vocabularies than those who interacted with a smaller volume of conversation and less word and sentence variety. The children with little conversation at home entered kindergarten with a huge word gap, having heard 32 million fewer words than some of their classmates. By third grade, the children with robust early word exposure had higher IQs and were better readers, writers, and spellers.

One remarkable finding with important implications for parenting was that positive verbal responses—praise as opposed to negative conversational feedback—resulted in better intellectual and literacy gains at all socioeconomic status levels. This remarkable study alone should convince all parents to read and talk to their newborns early and often. Reading aloud to young children increases the quality of words that they hear, introduces three times as many "rare words" not often used in conversation, and provides the repeated exposure to words that preschoolers need. One can hardly imagine a more meaningful difference in the everyday lives of young children than joyfully reading, talking to them, and bonding through books.[1]

Starting literacy at home can help to eliminate literacy problems down the road or bring them to light sooner, when they can be dealt with far more effectively than if they are not caught until the child is beginning elementary school. Dr. Angela Fawcett, a researcher at the University of Sheffield in Great Britain, recently found that just *one hour a week for ten weeks* of small-group work for language-delayed preschoolers was more effective in boosting skills than *a whole year of remediation* for seven- and eight-year-olds.[2] Government statistics show that four out of ten eight-year-olds in the United States cannot read independently. Most of these children likely never received the early intervention that could have solved their problems quickly and easily; now, many will struggle with reading for years, if not for life. The best intervention therefore begins at home. *You* are in the best position to get your child started on the right track.

But even if your child is already in school, it's not too late to intervene. This book will teach you what type of text your child should be able to read and what level of writing she should be able to accomplish at important markers in kindergarten through second grade. If your child isn't reaching those markers at the right time, you will learn how to work with your child at home and direct her education at school to get things back on track. The sooner you get help for your child, the better.

2. Know the Reading Phases: The Early Milestones for Monitoring Progress

Children learn to read in a remarkably regular way, just as they progress through motor milestones or learn to speak in a consistent sequence. There are five easy-to-recognize phases in beginning reading and writing, and knowing these can help parents lead their children in appropriate literacy activities. You can chart your child's natural literacy developmental milestones, gently prodding him to the next level. Figures I.1–I.5 below give you a bird's-eye view of the five phases. Seeing and understanding these phases will open your eyes to your child's literacy development:

Phase 0

Your child's literacy development begins at birth and develops based on the foundations set by you. Your baby shows interest and joy in being read to, and later shows interest in marking, drawing, and scribbling—the precursors of writing and reading.

Figure I.1: Phase 0

Phase 1

Your toddler learns to write her name and read some words. She explores writing by attempting to write messages and stories using random letters and attempts to imitate the reading of easy books.

Figure I.2: Phase 1

Phase 2

Your toddler begins learning the alphabet, matching beginning and prominent letters to sounds, and labeling drawings or writing messages with a few letter-sound matches. You can sometimes read them. He reads some easy books from memory.

Figure I.3: Phase 2

Phase 3

Your beginner REDS (reads), RITS (writes), and SPELS (spells), using one letter for each sound. She can read quite a few books from memory and recognizes scores of words on sight.

Figure I.4: Phase 3

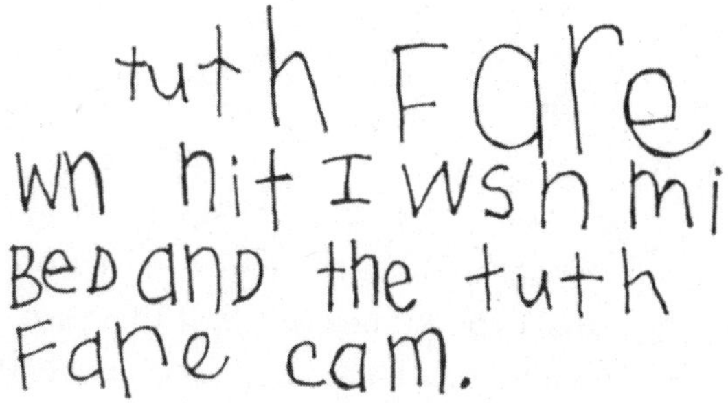

tuth Fare
wn nit I wsh mi
BeD anD the tuth
Fare cam.

Figure I.5: Phase 4

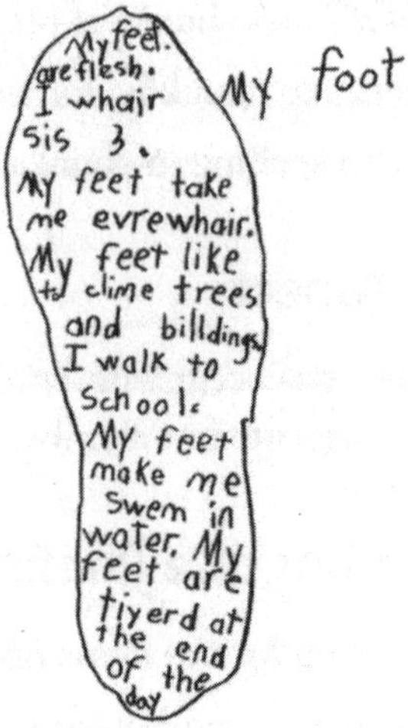

Phase 4

Your child reads easy chapter books, recognizes more than one hundred words on sight, and begins to spell many words correctly. She shows A-WAR-NIS of FON-ICS PAT-URNS (awareness of phonics patterns), spelling words such as EVREWHAIR (everywhere), BILLDINGS (buildings), and TIYERD (tired) in "chunks." She moves into fluid coding ability. Mature reading kicks in as reading becomes automatic.

3. Engage Your Child with the Right Literacy Activity at the Right Time

The best teachers of reading in school have specialized training and expertise. They know how to match children with the right books at the right time, what levels of text to use, and how to motivate and engage children with reading. They understand that reading is an interactive process, so they read aloud to children and have book talks. They know that reading entails comprehension, but they also acknowledge the importance of phonics (how letters are associated with sounds) for learning to read. They make sure that children have access to lots of books and encourage them to choose ones on topics they are interested in. They make easy books available so children can read independently. They also introduce children to the best children's literature. In short, expertly trained teachers know *how to teach* reading. Parent teachers of reading need some tips on these same areas of expertise.

You may worry that you are not an expert and fear that you might steer your child the wrong way or confuse him. That's why this book is important. I'll show you *how* to teach reading, writing, and spelling to little ones in a nurturing environment. The activities and tips I provide will be matched with your child's natural phase of development. I'll help you to choose the best books and activities at the right time for lap or side-by-side reading, to understand what to expect from your child during his first attempts as a writer and speller, and to know when to intervene to correct problems. I'll show you why introducing your toddler to drawing and early writing are as important as reading aloud.

Confident and competent teachers make confident readers grow and blossom. If you understand how reading develops in your child and are confident that you are introducing appropriate activities and techniques at the right time, you'll feel good being your child's first reading and writing teacher—it may, in fact, be one of your most positive parenting experiences.

Knowing the five phases and what type of activities to provide during each phase makes it easy for you to help your child move from one developmental level to the next. Remember, follow these three steps and your child will grow into a confident reader:

1. Start early.
2. Monitor phase development.
3. Match activities to your child's needs.

HOW TO USE THIS BOOK

This book shows you how to create a stimulating literacy environment at home with absolutely the best activities available to teach your child to read. All of the activities are specifically targeted to your child's current level of functioning, and all of them will allow you to teach reading successfully and informally through bonding, exploration, and play. They are drawn from the most current literature on research-based practices for teaching reading professionally.

But this is not a set of lockstep lessons for formal instruction—in fact, early formal instruction at home is inappropriate. Rather, in Chapters 4 through 8, each chapter focuses on one of the five phases, providing a set of choices for ensuring that print becomes a dynamic and significant part of your young child's everyday life, and ultimately leading to the ability and desire to read and write. The activities do not require you to spend a lot of time on any given day on literacy activities, but over the years you will have spent a lot of time with your child sharing literacy. Keep this book throughout the first years of your child's life and refer to it often as a guide to literacy development. It shows you how to be your child's first reading teacher and awaken him or her to literacy.

In the chapters ahead you will learn how to raise a confident reader by determining your child's current phase quickly and easily and then providing the right teaching activities at the right time as you monitor progress and celebrate accomplishments. In Chapter 1 you'll be amazed by the new discoveries from brain science. This summary of the findings will help you to understand how your child's brain learns to read. Chapter 2 shows you how easy it is to raise a confident reader by following a simple brain-based formula, which takes its name from the acronym "READ." The chapter also introduces the concept of keeping a simple Literacy Milestones Diary to track your child's progress. Chapter 3 will enable you to determine exactly where your child currently is on the developmental ladder and direct you to the chapter later in the book that covers that phase.

Each chapter in Chapters 4 through 8 provides just the right activities to move your child forward in reading, writing, and spelling when he or she is in the particular phase being covered. The activities suggested for each phase all work together. Choose from these recommendations for targeted teaching, keep your child's Literacy Milestones Diary up to date, and celebrate his or her accomplishments. Chapter 9 shows you what to expect once your child enters school and explains how to troubleshoot if things get off track. *Raising Confident Readers* guides you every step of the way as your child makes the journey to proficiency and confidence in reading, writing, and spelling, showing you *how* to teach reading with the right activities at the right time to develop your child's "reading" brain.

THE PYRAMID MODEL FOR TEACHING READING

Although learning to read is a complex process, teaching your child at home doesn't have to be. It only requires a little focused attention easily spread over the early years. Your child's literacy development begins at birth and builds on the foundations set by you. Paying attention to your child's reading development and being your child's first reading teacher is like building a pyramid—stone by stone—with foundational layers of construction supporting the climb to the top. Figure I.6 shows the "Pyramid of Beginning Reading Growth" outlined in this book that your child will be ascending. Starting with the appropriate foundations,

Figure I.6: The Pyramid of Beginning Reading Growth

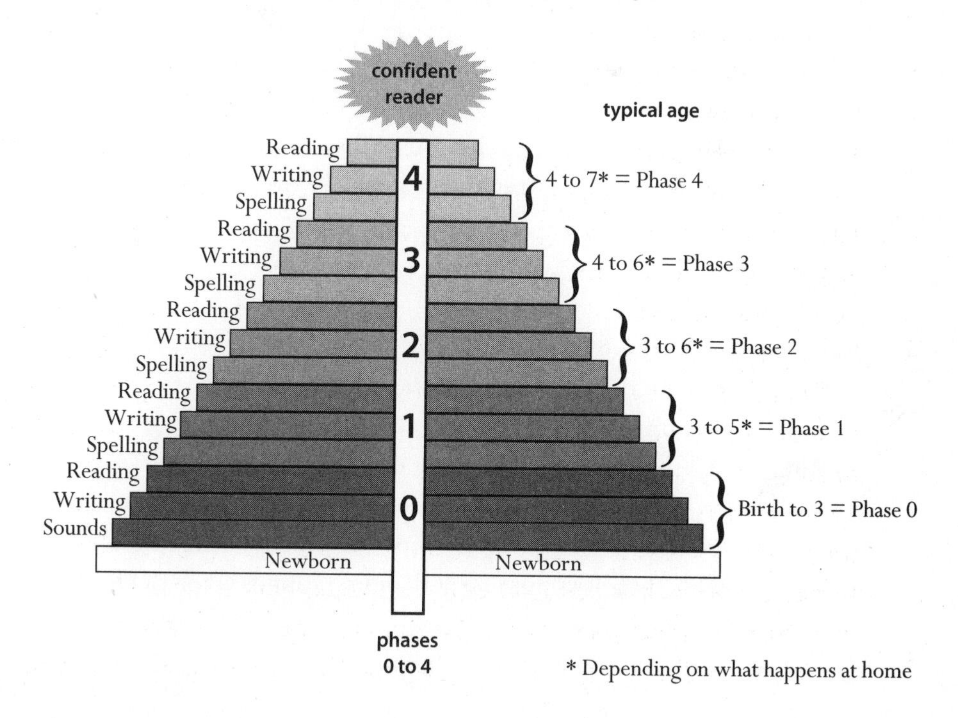

your child will grow while moving toward peak performance, enhanced capability, and confident lifelong reading. *Raising Confident Readers* makes the climb to the top easy.

Phase 0

Reading: Responds to reading aloud; pretends to read; memory reading is possible
Writing: Draws and scribbles; pretends to write; distinguishes writing from drawing
Sounds and Spelling: Masters the speech sounds of English; learns to speak; draws and scribbles; distinguishes spelling from pictures

Phase 1

Reading: Reads a few words on sight; memory reads after repetition; reads kindergarten level A
Writing: Attempts to label; attempts to write phrases or messages; writes in random letters
Sounds and Spelling: Recognizes rhymes; claps syllables; attempts to spell words with random letters; spells name and a few other words correctly; has no phonemic awareness; lacks conscious knowledge of sounds in words; may think random letters spell a given word

Phase 2

Reading: Reads up to thirty words on sight; memory reads after repetition; masters kindergarten/first-grade reading levels A–C
Writing: Writes simple stories (three to six lines or sentences); attempts several genres (lists, commands, messages, directions, labels, writing on maps)
Sounds and Spelling: Recognizes rhymes; claps syllables; spells a few sounds in words, such as beginning and ending sounds (B or BD for *bird*,

for example), but spells a few words correctly; has partial phonemic awareness; is conscious of some but not all letters in words; cannot make analogies, such as spelling *mat* from the known word *cat*

Phase 3

Reading: Reads thirty to fifty or more words on sight; reads after support of repetition and memory; masters first-grade reading levels C–G
Writing: Writes simple stories with a beginning, middle, and ending; uses various genres
Sounds and Spelling: Spells most sounds in a word with a single letter; gains full phonemic awareness; is conscious of each speech sound in a word; learns to spell words by analogy to known words; may skip vowels when a consonant such as "r" carries the vowel sound (for example, using BRD to spell *bird*)

Phase 4

Reading: Moves into independent reading; reads one hundred or more words on sight; masters first-grade reading levels G–I or begins second-grade levels
Writing: Writes more elaborate stories, such as first-then-next-last; writes in varying genres with book language
Sounds and Spelling: Spells words in chunks of phonics patterns; spells by analogy to known words; spells many words correctly; shows greater understanding of how letters combine in chunks to make up words, but may not always choose the correct combinations (for example, BERD or BURD may spell *bird*)

You need not wait to begin. Before moving forward, here are six parental goals that you can commit to *now* to ensure your child's future success. You are already on your way!

SIX PARENT GOALS FOR LITERACY

1. I can teach my child to read with simple and fun activities at home to develop literacy early, naturally, and joyfully.

2. I can bond with my child through books and nurture positive reading attitudes that last a lifetime.

3. I can encourage early writing—moving from scribbles, to name writing, to labeling, to little stories—to help my child begin to build the integrated neural circuits necessary for reading.

4. I can replace reading "to" my child with reading "for," "with," and "by" my child.

5. I can ensure that critical formative brain activity for literacy happens at home by choosing reading and writing activities—and having expectations—appropriate for my child's phase.

6. If my child has difficulties with literacy, I can intervene early in a meaningful way.

1

START EARLY

Nurture Your Child's Brain as It Grows into Reading

YOUR BABY'S BRAIN is ready for exposure to literacy activity as soon as he is born: He came into the world with a brain hardwired for communication, including aspects of communicating in print. The *critical period* for brain development for communication is between birth and six years of age. Reading can come easily and naturally for him if you introduce the right activities to stimulate specific neural systems during this critical period. You simply start early, take your time, stimulate the right neural systems—often with targeted literacy activities—and have fun with it.

Even in babyhood, introducing rich, baby-appropriate literacy activity—talking to her, showing her illustrations, responding to her smile, bouncing around her room with her in your arms pointing to a few word labels you have posted—can stimulate tremendous brain growth and initiate foundational reading connections. You can lay down the wiring for the reading system early on by injecting talk about print and by giving your baby or toddler opportunities to engage in listening, viewing, exploring, feeling, touching, and movement activities related to print in her everyday routines. You will even interject smelling and taste by cuddling your baby close and letting her grasp and explore the first board books with her mouth. Your baby is learning about books, and in a few months, she'll be turning the pages!

Starting early is important. Your baby's brain will strengthen the language and literacy connections that are used early on and eventually prune or override the connections that aren't activated. Pruning is directly related to later capacities for language learning. For example, he has the capacity to learn both English and Swahili if you were to introduce both languages before age six and strengthen those connections, but due to brain-cell pruning, he'll never learn to speak or read Swahili or thousands of other human languages (there are approximately 7,000!) without an accent if he starts learning the language beyond puberty.

Your toddler's early writing and reading strategies will be replaced with more efficient strategies as he moves up the developmental ladder. The early beginnings set the foundations, start the process, and establish a strong framework on which academic scholarship can be built.

Grab onto the 32-Million-Word Advantage

The easiest and most natural time to start laying down reading circuits and wiring up the powerful language systems in your child's brain is during the first four or five years of life. The brain's reading systems are intricately connected to its systems for learning language, with both, ideally, developing together. That means that getting started with reading early will make the most of what is already happening naturally.

For optimal development, these systems are both codependent and mutually beneficial. During the early years when your young child's brain is ripe for learning language, reading aloud stimulates and accelerates your baby's speaking skills. Studies show that when parents enrich a baby's environment by talking to her often and reading aloud, the child will have heard roughly 45 million words by age four—which gives her roughly a 32-million-word advantage in words heard over children who are not talked to in this way and exposed to early literacy.[1] Your child's brain can convert this exposure into a vocabulary of 13,000 words by age six.

Babies are smart! Beginning early with Phase 0 activities, you'll not only reap the benefits of activating the reading system, but also activate hearing, visual, social, and emotional systems and foster a love for books.[2] Here are some established facts showing what babies can do with early literacy:

- Babies can see illustrations at about three months of age and can remember bold colors such as red, blue, green, and yellow by four months of age.
- Between six and nine months of age, babies can link sounds with objects and concepts.
- Babies can understand the words you read five months before they can speak them.
- Babies can start pencil-and-paper activity before twelve months of age if you help them.
- Babies can draw pictures and create narratives at between two and three years of age.

When you start early, you benefit too. Studies show that you are strengthening bonds with your child when you read aloud to him and engage in other literacy activity, and that these bonds make you a better parent.

All of the above happens in the first phase alone—Phase 0. If you continue into Phases 1, 2, and beyond, the complex beginning-to-read circuits will fully connect to robust brain circuits for language, and before you know it you will have raised a confident reader. If you start at birth, it can happen between three and five years of age.

Choose Informal Versus Formal Instruction

Parents should make the distinction between formal versus informal reading instruction. Your baby's or toddler's brain is ripe for reading through informal activities like the ones found in this book, but not from formal reading instruction. According to brain science, the best brain-based age for *formal reading instruction* is between the ages of six or seven. In a comprehensive overview of current scientific knowledge about brain development from birth to age five, neurobiologist Lise Eliot reported that the young child's frontal lobe isn't fully developed until six years of age (or later). Until then, the child is not ready for the higher-level thinking required for formal reading instruction. Moreover, children are only able to "follow an adult's reasoning, use their memory in a deliberate fashion, begin to grasp abstract concepts, and have the self-control to sit still and really absorb what's being taught" in formal instruction *after* their frontal lobes are sufficiently developed. Eliot also concluded that there was no scientific evidence that children benefit from early *formal* reading instruction either at home or in preschool.[3] The early advantage—setting the foundations for success with reading at home and making learning to read natural and easy—comes through *informal* teaching.

A nurturing preschool with informal literacy activities can support and extend what you do at home. These preschools are not factories where literacy is forced on children through rote memorization and direct instruction. Rather, teachers are reading aloud and providing other knowledge-building experiences, engaging in higher-level conversations with children, and encouraging children to discover, question, evaluate, and use higher-order thinking skills. Children are joyfully drawing and writing about their discoveries. In fact, there is much that a good preschool teacher can do through fun activities to familiarize children with letters and sounds and to engage them in storytelling, art activities, and early drawing and writing.

Schools have raised the bar for literacy expectations in kindergarten, and as a result, most parents feel that their children must go to preschool. There is even competition to get into the "best" preschools in some cities. Whether you enlist the help of a good preschool or go it alone, what is important is that your child gets the informal types of literacy activities presented in this book early in life. If you choose not to send your child to preschool, that makes it all the more important to lay the foundation for literacy at home; even if your child does attend preschool, however, home literacy activities are crucial to literacy development.

More formal instruction is appropriate once a child is six or seven, and there is no doubt that older children do learn to read with formal instruction. In the United States, we used to wait until first grade to begin to teach reading, and even today, in some countries, such as Finland—which boasts one of the highest literacy rates in the world—*formal* reading instruction does not begin until age seven. That is not necessarily the direction that we should go in. The Finnish model does not work well in many English-speaking countries. The societal demands in Finnish schools—very few immigrants, for example—and the fact that Finnish may be easier to read than English, may explain why the "wait-for-formal-instruction model" works in Finland while it may be unsuitable for English-speaking countries.

Perhaps you didn't get the preschool jumpstart yourself and you feel quite confident with your current reading ability. Perhaps even the home activities seem unnecessary to you because your own parents did not engage in them with you. "What's different for my child?" you may ask. One difference is that kindergarten is now the new first grade. Beyond that, you are likely a product of the last century in which the general practice was to wait before beginning formal reading instruction. But perpetuating that model—waiting—may explain, in part, why four out of ten American children can't read proficiently by fourth grade. While it is true that some waiting is appropriate for formal instruction, informal instruction is another story altogether.

Want to Overcome Dyslexia? Don't Wait!

Your very young child's brain is plastic, malleable, and able—if need be—to reroute reading circuits when there are problems. This will change after the first few years of schooling, when the window of opportunity for rewiring will be diminished. According to neuroscientists, one in five American children encounter some form of neurologically based reading disability due to misfiring in the lowest level of the brain's circuitry for reading—the level where alphabetic decoding takes place.

The misfiring may be caused by the way the wiring was laid down before birth when there can be a disruption of the basic circuitry for linking letters to sounds. This condition, called dyslexia, is often hard to detect in school because the higher levels of reading circuitry, such as the abilities necessary for comprehension, are intact. Additionally, many schools do not have anyone on staff with expertise in identifying and responding to early signs of dyslexia. There is growing evidence, however, that due to the malleability and plasticity of the very young brain, if children get the kind of teaching activities presented in this book—especially the kinds of activities that I have included in each phase that address sounds, breaking the alphabetic code, and spelling—the dyslexic brain may fix itself.[4] The danger in waiting is that learning disabilities are often left undetected until the ages of eleven to seventeen in American schools, and that's too late.[5]

There's another reason not to wait. English is harder to read and write than many other languages. Here's just one example: English has 44 sounds and over 1,000 letter combinations for spelling them. By contrast, Italian only has 25 sounds and 35 letter combinations and is much easier to read and write. While parents of English speakers shouldn't push formal reading instruction too early or fret if their child isn't reading independently before kindergarten, it is important to take advantage of the malleability of the young child's brain to make sure this wiring is beginning to be put into place. The brain is ripe for it. That is precisely why teaching reading at home may be better than waiting for your child to learn to read in school.

When teaching at home, your goal is to ensure that your child has a successful beginning. The best insurance is to take action when your child's brain is ripe for learning: Teach beginning reading at home.

WATCH FOR EARLY DEVELOPMENTAL PHASES: NURTURE READING TADPOLES AND THEY TURN INTO READING FROGS

The Tadpole Reader Timeline

As a beginning reader and writer, your child will go through a series of five tadpole-like literacy phases before automatic, mature reading can evolve. It is as if the neural circuits slowly begin to light up or unfold. The sequence is the same for every child. When you start reading and writing with your child at home, the tadpole phases are stretched out over a very long period of time—as much as a year or more for some phases—but your child will move to the next phase easily, without formal instruction, by engaging in appropriate literacy activities. Children who are introduced to reading at home generally reach independent and mature brain functioning for reading just before or during kindergarten and have a successful academic beginning in school.

When children come to kindergarten with little preparation for beginning reading, such as not having learned to write their names, the tadpole phases generally take two years of formal schooling to unfold, and even if things go well, these underprepared children may not be reading independently until well into grade two or later. Too often, things *don't* go well for children who first encounter beginning reading through formal reading instruction in American schools: Some 40 percent of American eight-year-olds have not advanced through Phase 4 and cannot read independently. This may be a result of both poor reading instruction in school and a disadvantaged language environment at home.

Research over the past thirty years, including my own, reveals visible changes in a child's tadpole reading and writing phases based on the sound and letter choices children make when they begin to write. Seeing these beginning reading phases in early writing is as easy as seeing the five phases of tadpole development: (0) egg phase, (1) leg-growing phase, (2) tail-losing phase, (3) lung-development phase, and (4) insect-ingestion phase. Watch a beginning writer and you will see him make choices in what he puts down on paper to represent words. His letter choices and categorizations of speech sounds will reflect the representation he has in his brain for how the English alphabetic code works. His choices will change qualitatively at each phase level. Seeing these changes in early writing and spelling and following your child's tadpole-reader timeline is the best way to choose learning activities and monitor progress at home.

A Nurturing Literacy Environment: The Right Activities at the Right Time

Just as tadpoles need the special nurturing environment of a pond, your young tadpole reader requires special nurturing for reading and writing at home with the right literacy activities matched to his phase of development. This book makes it easy to select exactly the right activities at the right time for informal instruction at home.

Tadpole Readers and the English Spelling Code

A beginning reader must link letters to sounds, pay attention to spelling patterns, and figure out how these patterns work. The process is slow and analytical at the beginning. Ironically, the mature (frog) reader's brain can override the spelling code and read quickly and automatically, paying very little attention to the spelling. In other words, a mature reader's brain is functioning differently from a beginning reader's brain when looking at the spellings on a page of text.

Here's an example: A frog reader like you can RAED PIRNT ADN MKAE SNECE OF IT EEVN IFTHE SEPLILNG IS ALL SRCABMLED UP BCEASUEYUO'RE UISNGTHE HGIHER LVELS OF PORCSES-NIG ASYUOR BARIN SMAPELS JSUT A LTITLE OFTHE SEPLLILNG TO RCEGONZIE THE WRODS ATUOAMTCILALY. Tadpole readers do just the opposite: They slow down and *attend* to spelling because they don't yet have a full understanding of the alphabetic code. Their higher levels of automatic reading aren't fully activated, and they are lacking some neural connections, such as the ones that allow them to recognize hundreds of printed words automatically. Spelling analysis during reading competes with comprehension for the beginning reader's attention.

Repetition and reading from memory aid the beginning reader and facilitate both decoding and comprehension as the novice reader begins to integrate these systems. Consequently, while reading with your child in the tadpole phases you will do a lot of repeated readings of the same material, and you will often draw your child's attention to the letters in words even though you are not paying focused attention to the individual letters when you read yourself. You will also ask questions, elaborate, and draw attention to meaning with beginners at every phase. Eventually your child must go through all five phases and engage in appropriate learning activities matched to each phase to get to mature processing, just like the tadpole must go through five phases before hopping away from the pond.

But what do phase changes look like in the brain, and what are the implications for teaching?

HOW SAMPLE ACTIVITIES FROM THIS BOOK WILL STIMULATE YOUR CHILD'S BRAIN: FROM RHYMING TO FINGER SPELLING TO AUTOMATIC PROCESSING

You are about to see which brain areas neuroscientists say are most active during reading and how activities in this book likely stimulate specific areas. The brain responses to the activities that follow—rhyming, finger spelling, and automatic word recognition—are all integrated in the brain during the complex process of reading. Each activity is strategically targeted in particular phases to gently nudge your child from one phase level to the next.

What Do We Know from Brain Research?

Research in neuroscience, cognitive psychology, child development, and education is beginning to show where the brain's reading neural systems are located, when they become activated, and what needs to happen to activate them. This has implications for reading teachers and for parents like you. Once you understand some of the scientific findings on the neurobiological basis for reading, you will be able to see how the recommendations in the chapters ahead relate to your child's natural development. In fact, in this chapter we will begin to connect the dots between brain-development research and appropriate literacy activities.

Neuroscientists are using Positron Emission Tomography (PET) scans and functional Magnetic Resonance Imaging (fMRI) studies to watch the brain read and map out the neural systems for reading in both children and adults. PET scans introduce a radioactive tracer chemical into the bloodstream for tracking how the brain uses energy. By tracking energy use the researchers can see where neural circuits are firing off during reading. The fMRI scans measure changes in blood flow and use of oxygen in neural tissue to record changes in magnetic properties. The images that result show pictures of the brain "lighting up" during reading.[6]

Based on my synthesis of the research and my own thirty years of experience as a reading teacher, I have created the following hypothetical scenario to help you see how sample activities are likely stimulating regions of your child's brain. Since brain imaging is still in its infancy, drawing specific conclusions and designing specific reading interventions based on the reading neural systems is far from being an exact science. Neuroscientists have not yet specifically identified a set of active cerebral regions for each phase of reading development,[7] and much work remains to be done. Perhaps this book will not only help parents, but also aid neuroscientists and other researchers who may be interested in collaborating with educators and parents to more specifically map reading in the brain and link brain-imaging research with good teaching and good parenting.

Figure 1.1 highlights three areas in the left hemisphere: A, B, and C. These are the main areas that neuroscientists have identified in what they call a "left-hemisphere reading system" that is prevalent in roughly four out of five mature readers across languages.[8] Good readers have highly connected neural systems mainly encompassing Area A in the front of the left side of the brain and Areas B and C in the back of the left side.

Figure 1.1: Left Hemisphere Reading System

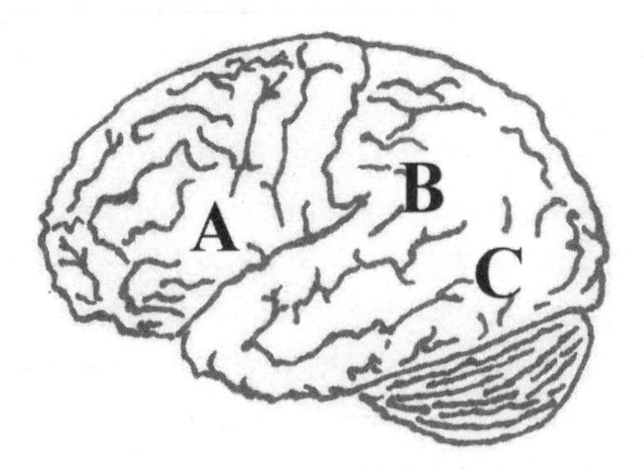

Activate Area A with Rhymes

Activities with rhyming words, according to neuroscientists, activate Area A, an area called "Broca's area" that is located in the front of the left hemisphere in a region called the "inferior frontal gyrus." If you put your finger on your temple on the left side of your head, you are pointing close to this area. This is an important area in your child's brain for beginning reading. The inferior frontal gyrus has a neural system for articulating spoken words. Sharing nursery rhymes with your child will help to activate her awareness of the shared spoken components of rhyming words. This ability, along with the ability to clap out syllables, is called "phonological awareness."

Phonological awareness comes before the more complex ability to notice, distinguish, identify, and manipulate the individual sounds in a spoken word, which is called "phonemic awareness." Phonemic awareness is recognizing that both *cat* and *night* have three phonemes: (/c/, /ă/, /t/) in *cat* and (/n/, /ī/, /t/) in *night*. Importantly, phonological awareness with rhymes and syllables helps your child develop phonemic awareness. Developing these abilities early—using rhymes, clapping syllables, and later manipulating the individual sounds in words—has been shown to be critical for beginning reading success and even predicts success with reading in later years.[9] Though it might sound complex, it's really quite simple: Your child activates Area A and sets foundations for reading simply by having fun with sounds in words.

If you are repeating a nursery rhyme with your toddler—"Jack and Jill," for example—he'll no doubt enjoy shouting out the rhyming word when you emphasize the word *hill*. "Jack and Jill went up the *hill*." Perhaps this is easy for your toddler because you started reading to him as a newborn. You can remember how you repeated the rhyme softly with him cradled in your arms, your face close to his so that he could see your lips and watch the smile on your face as you softly emphasized *hill* and sweetly smiled to see if you might get a smile back. You may have given him a soft tickle on the tummy along with your smile to match the rhythm. These weren't "lessons"; they were just fun ways of sharing the rhyme and talking to your baby. At the same time, you were activating Area A and developing pre-reading skills.

Activate Area B with Finger Spelling

Now put your pointer finger on the left side of your head next to and a little behind the left ear. This is Area B, the parieto-temporal area. Neuroscientists report that this is a word analysis area where words are pulled apart and put back together. Like processing phonemes, pulling words apart and putting them back together is most important in the beginning phases (or tadpole phases) of learning to read. You might activate this word analysis area of your child's brain using an activity called "finger spelling," which is recommended when you are helping your child move from Phase 2, which is characterized by partial phonemic (sound) awareness, to Phase 3, which is characterized by full phonemic (sound) awareness.

Finger spelling uses a tangible object (the hand), and physical movement (holding up fingers), to signal the number of sounds, or "phonemes," in a word. Try this finger-spelling exercise with me: Say the word *rat*. Now put up your thumb and say the first sound of *rat*: (/r/). Next hold out your pointer finger and say the second sound of *rat*: (/ă/). Then put out the next finger and say the third sound of *rat*: (/t/). Finally, reach out and grab the sounds and pull them back into the word as you say it again—"rat." *Rat* has three sounds, which is a pretty abstract concept for a beginning reader. Finger spelling makes it easier for the beginner to grasp how sounds work in words.

Teaching your child this simple little finger-spelling technique makes it easier for the Phase 3 child to recognize that a word like *rat* has three sounds that he can *read* (decode) by sounding out the sounds that go with the letters r–a–t, or write (encode) by creating the letters that go with the sounds /r/, /ă/, /t/.

Finger spelling likely activates Area B, the parieto-temporal region for word analysis. This kind of word analysis is extremely important in the beginning stages of learning to read when children are figuring out the alphabetic code before reading becomes automatic.

Automatic Reading—Activating the Dictionary in Your Child's Brain

Now put your pointer finger on the left side of your head, a little to the back and slightly below the ear. You are pointing to Area C, the occipito-temporal area. According to neuroscientists, this is where words are recognized automatically. It is in an area that links language to visual cues and is probably where neural representations of perfect spellings, phonics knowledge, and spelling chunks are located.

After learning to read a word correctly and processing it over and over during reading, the eyes see the word or spelling chunk and the brain recognizes it automatically. Here in the occipito-temporal area, the brain has formed a permanent and exact neural trace for that particular word or chunk. This "word form" can now be retrieved automatically by seeing the word (when reading) or by thinking of its exact spelling (when writing). Here's an example. Look at the word shown below:

hippopotamus

Just now when you read the word *hippopotamus*, constellations of neurons in your occipito-temporal area fired off in less than 150 milliseconds, registering the meaning, sound, and even the correct spelling in Area C of your brain. It's the express pathway to reading and spelling and the area most activated by proficient mature readers.[10] It's not until Area C lights up consistently for reading in your child's brain, and he recognizes hundreds of words and spelling patterns, that he has activated the express pathway and become a mature reader—just like you.

2

THE BRAIN-BASED FORMULA

Repetition-Enthusiasm-Attention-Drawing

THE BRAIN-BASED techniques and activities that guide you as a teacher of beginning reading can be summed up in four easy-to-remember words in the acronym READ: Repetition-Enthusiasm-Attention-Drawing. These are the capstones that form the basis of early reading and they underlie every action you take as your child's first reading teacher. They are the essence of good teaching for beginning readers.

REPETITION

The R in READ is for *repetition*. Joyful repeated readings of favorite books are a hallmark of early reading success. Long after you are exhausted rereading favorite books, your baby or toddler will thrill in reading them over and over again. Hang in there. Your child is still learning. Her brain loves repetition, revels in the familiarity of a favorite book, and makes new discoveries with every rereading. The repeated firing of neural circuits and the establishment of new synapses as she responds to familiar text is growing her mind as a reader.

Mimicking

One type of repetition will come naturally to your baby: She will often mimic and repeat what you do without any prompting. Even when a child is just a few months old, researchers can determine what language a baby is babbling because the baby is already repeating the sounds that her parents make when they talk or read to her. At around six months of age, your baby will increase her babbling response to you if you imitate or respond back to her when you read a children's book. Your repetition of sounds—and her repetition of sounds—are wiring her brain for English. By the time she is one year old she will understand about seventy words.[1]

Babies not only mimic the sounds of the language they hear when a parent reads aloud but also mimic *feelings* during book sharing. If you are smiling, laughing, or expressing surprise or joy at what you see on a page, your baby will respond in the same way and learn to remember and anticipate these feelings. After repeated readings of favorite storybooks, she will know what funny or delightful event or character is coming up at the turn of a page. Among other benefits, repeated readings develop memory, feelings, and thinking strategies, such as making hypotheses about what's coming next. Early, repeated, happy experiences with books are important because these joyful times together enhance the likelihood that your child will grow up with positive feelings about books that lead to lifelong reading.

Mimicking and engaging in repetition over time allow your beginner to reorganize and integrate information surrounding a side-by-side book-sharing event with higher-order concepts and understandings as she notices new aspects of print and applies new learning to what she already knows. Through repeated readings of favorite books, your baby or toddler learns new concepts about print in a kind of piling-on-concepts effect:

- How to hold the book
- Where to start

- How to turn the page
- How the print is orientated
- How English print moves from left to right and so forth

At this age, your child will likely develop favorites that she will want you to read again and again. And because repetition during this phase is appropriate, you can feel free to go ahead and read those favorites to her repeatedly. Variety is good, but so is repetition. Your baby will revel in the sublime beauty of *Good Night Moon* as you enjoy reading and rereading the classic bedtime story over and over, beginning soon after birth and continuing through the preschool years if it becomes one of her favorites. After repeated readings, she will mimic your delight in the story, feel the same soothing comfort of its rhythm that you feel, mimic the sounds that you say, and hear the same musicality that you hear—even before she recognizes the objects in the pictures or knows the meaning of the story. At the same time, she is piling on many foundational concepts of print from these repeated readings, such as the ones listed above.

Memory Reading

Your child's first "reading" is a result of repetition. You can use a repeated reading technique at home that is often used in school with kindergarteners and first-graders. It is called the "for-with-and-by technique." The technique begins with selection of an easy text with three to five words on the page. First you model by reading the text *for the child*. Then you read the same material again and again *with the child*, allowing the child to mimic every aspect of your reading—word pointing, expression, phrasing, fluency (the speed and flow of words), and response to meaning. You will repeat this process again and again with the same text. At times you pause to draw the child's attention to individual words and sounds. ("See this word, it starts just like your name! Let's read that line again.") At home this repeated reading process happens naturally because your child will want to reread favorite books over and over. After many repeated readings, the text is memorized *by the child*.

This *for, with, and by the child* repetition technique is called "memory reading." Memory reading in the early phases is one of the best ways for the beginner to integrate neural reading systems and connect to the language systems in the brain. Your baby is remembering more than you think during memory reading. Studies show that even eight-month-old babies recognize specific words repeated in storybook reading for up to two weeks after hearing them repeatedly.[2]

Repetition in Later Phases

At later phases, repetition is used in a plethora of teaching activities for learning spelling and word patterns. For example, Chapter 8, which covers Phase 4, includes a game called "Speed Sorting" for sorting words of contrasting vowel patterns, such as *hop* and *hope*, or *rat* and *rate*, into short vowel versus long vowel columns until repeated recognition and physical sorting of the patterns help the child recognize the spelling patterns automatically. Remember, all of these activities based on repetition are presented in the following chapters as options that you may choose from for teaching reading informally rather than as lessons for formal reading instruction. As you will see in the next section, part of your challenge as a reading teacher is to *entice* your child to use them.

ENTHUSIASM

The E in READ is for *enthusiasm*. You have great incentives to be enthusiastic about your child's literacy development. Many experts agree that talking to your child and having frequent read-alouds surrounded by talk about books during book sharing are the most important brain-stimulation activities in parenting: You are activating her social, hearing, emotional, and linguistic systems all at once.[3] Books have been called the most effective tools for teaching babies and toddlers language. But reading aloud doesn't work by itself. The most important ingredient for success when engaging your child in reading aloud—and in *all* the literacy activities in this book—is *enthusiasm*.

The Other E's: Enticement, Exploration, Engagement, Explosion!

Your own enthusiasm for literacy activity will create your child's motivation to engage in literacy and add up to a successful formula for teaching literacy:

> Enthusiasm = (Enticement + Exploration of books + Engagement and natural curiosity) = Explosion of vocabulary, knowledge, and fun

Your enthusiasm inspires and instills your child's internal desire to write and read by surrounding literacy activity with positive feelings. Your enthusiasm makes every literacy activity fun, interesting, sociable, and enjoyable. The ultimate key to your success as a literacy teacher is recognizing that *feelings come first*!

Sometimes being enthusiastic for literacy activity in the home requires stamina on your part. Here are some tips for setting a tone for amusement and merriment, and for avoiding negative feelings.

How to Put Feelings First

Know what your child is capable of doing.
Tune in to what's enjoyable.
Turn off what's not interesting.
Step away and hold off on literacy activities that your young child seems to resist.
Avoid extreme measures—scripted lessons, video programs, learning DVDs for babies.
Turn off the TV and videos and read with your child.
Compliment your child often.
Avoid correcting your child.
Let your child read any book that engages his or her attention.
Encourage exploration with drawing and writing.
Celebrate art and illustrations.
Read in front of your child so that he or she knows that you value books and reading.

Snuggle with your child and let him or her hold the book and turn the pages.
Avoid scripted formal lessons—they kill your child's desire to read.
Express joy and merriment in literacy activities.
Tune in to your young child's cues and moods.
Don't overdo reading and writing.
Respond with sensitivity.
Nurture literacy—don't force it.
Remember, a good reading activity is about connecting—not correcting.
Don't feel anxious or too ambitious about your baby or toddler's literacy development.
Maintain your enthusiasm and make sure you are having fun, too.
Make reading a reward.
Remember that early reading with babies and toddlers is all about actions and feelings.

"Feelings Come First": A Breakthrough for the Twenty-First Century—From *Dick and Jane*, to *Why Johnny Can't Read*, to *Raising Confident Readers*

This book's emphasis on enthusiasm and feelings is a breakthrough in the twenty-first century. Over the past one hundred years, reading educators have vociferously debated two competing theories of how to teach beginning reading. Educators call this phenomenon "the reading wars." Theory 1 is that *meaning comes first*. It is most recently represented in an educational philosophy called "whole language," a term referring to keeping language learning meaningful and whole from the beginning of instruction as opposed to starting out by reducing beginning reading to small phonics-based skills lessons that divide words into parts. The reading wars debate started early in the twentieth century with the 1908 publication of Edmund Burke Huey's influential book, *The Psychology and Pedagogy of Reading*,[4] and it was still raging when you and your parents learned to read with whole language's precursor, "the whole-word" method. Sometimes called "Look and Say," the whole-word style of teaching was popularized in a famous set of beginning readers called the *Dick and Jane* series that dominated beginning reading instruction for thirty years.[5]

The competing theory said that *phonics comes first*, and it took root in the nineteenth century. Beginning reading instruction focused on teaching how letters matched up with sounds. This technique was forebodingly and passionately renewed and presented to parents in a wildly popular 1955 parent classic, *Why Johnny Can't Read* by Rudolf Flesch.[6] The pendulum of favor for one or the other of these theories swung back and forth for over one hundred years.

Today, phonics-first method is preferred in most schools for formal instruction, largely because of the government's No Child Left Behind Act. A National Reading Panel in 2000 ostensibly touched on the need for "Balanced Literacy" by including both meaning-first and phonics-first explanations in the report, but the report ultimately sided with the phonics-first advocates, resulting in early tests in phonemic awareness and phonics and an attempt to put "research-based" phonics-first reading programs in all American schools.[7]

Phase observation and the activities in this book bridge the meaning-first and phonics-first debate, recognizing that both methods have extensive supporting evidence and important implications for teaching beginning reading. As we learn more about how the brain is wired for reading, my own hope and prediction for the twenty-first century is that America will move to better parenting at home and effective literacy education in preschool by recognizing not only that reading begins with babies and toddlers, but that *feelings come first*!

ATTENTION

The A in READ is for *attention*. When you read or write with your child, you are constantly making decisions about how to direct his attention. Since reading and writing are complex, at various times the reading teacher must focus the beginner's attention to the many different aspects of language, reading, writing, or spelling. You are constantly switching off between attention to sounds, attention to meaning, attention to the rhythm or musicality of language, attention to expression, attention to feelings, attention to letter naming, and attention to letter formation, to name a few. The list seems endless and perhaps daunting for a parent. Each phase chapter to follow offers a smorgasbord of activities organized around writing and reading, including some on speech sounds and spelling to provide appropriate balance.

It's not necessary to do all of the activities, but you should try a variety of them to see what works for your child. He may seem to enjoy some more than others. Some will require more time and effort than others. You will know when an activity deserves to be repeated based on his responses. The guiding principle for choosing what activities to concentrate on and how to direct your child's attention during reading or writing is to be a good "kid watcher." If your child is having a lot of fun with a particular activity, then this is a good one for the stage he is in right now. If he is distracted or bored, he may not be ready for that activity. Choose the activities that engage his interest and attention.

You'll learn what to expect at each phase and how to view an activity from the child's unique perspective in his particular phase of development. Ask yourself, "What is he thinking?" "How can I respond in a way that is warm, nurturing, responsive, stimulating, and supportive?" Sometimes you will recognize that he's not interested in an activity, and you'll put it on the back burner and maybe try it later. You'll have plenty of time to present the activities you choose in little doses in a nurturing environment.

Many of the decisions regarding how to direct your child's attention will be easy because the activities and recommendations in the phase chapters will guide you directly. For example, did you know that looking at illustrations in books can help your baby develop vision? But when do you start holding the book so that a baby can see the colorful illustrations? You will learn in the Phase 0 chapter (Chapter 4) that the answer is not until after three months of age. Color vision is poor during the first weeks, so illustrations don't need baby's attention. Likewise, you'll learn that Phase 3 is the best time to focus on the short vowel pattern, since that's when your child begins to demonstrate full phonemic awareness and attends to all the sounds in a word both as a reader and a writer.

The organization of this book into phase chapters is designed to guide you in directing your child's attention to what he needs at the right time. For example, when your baby begins to grasp objects at around fifteen to eighteen months of age, that's a good time to let her hold safe coloring or writing tools, make paper available, and see if she is ready to explore drawing and writing independently.

Of course, one of the big mysteries of teaching children to read is when to start drawing attention to letters and sounds. Phase observation unlocks most of the mysteries of pattern recognition and provides guidelines for when to teach various sound and phonics concepts. Let's see how pattern recognition for printed language works in phases.

Read this line:

SEIKOOCDNAMAERCECI

It's likely that you cannot read it because you don't see the patterns of English print, although they are present. Now try reading the same eighteen letters in a line of print with the order of the letters reversed:

ICECREAMANDCOOKIES

As a mature adult reader, your brain automatically converts the second line of eighteen letters into English speech by recognizing the parts of the sequence that match known sounds and meanings. Your brain isn't processing the individual letters. It is paying attention to the *chunks*, or spelling patterns. Breaking the English alphabetic reading code actually requires pattern recognition involving chunks of letters, and your child's brain can move into automatic processing once he is able to recognize roughly one hundred high-frequency, one-syllable words and hundreds of spelling patterns instantaneously. Beyond Phase 4, your child sees many words that he already knows without having to slowly and analytically sound the word out letter by letter the way beginners do. His brain has already formed a neural trace, or constellations of neurons, enabling him to see a learned word and know the meaning, sound, and even the correct spelling instantly, just as you recognize *ice cream* instantly at this moment and probably see something wrong with *ice creem*.

The brain's response to patterns in print develops in the early phases of reading and writing in the following sequence:

- No pattern recognition (Phase 0)
- Recognizing some letters but no sounds (Phase 1)
- Recognizing beginning letters and sound correspondences (Phase 2)
- Matching a letter for each sound (Phase 3)
- Recognizing chunks of spelling patterns (Phase 4)

Discovering the sound patterns and spelling patterns of English is critical for fluent, proficient reading and writing. When reading starts at home, bringing these patterns to your child's attention is one of your most important jobs as your child's first reading teacher. Remember, the phase chapters show you how to teach the right patterns at the right times.

DRAWING

Pencil-and-Paper Kids

The D in READ is for *drawing*. Your child might be ready to scribble on paper before you thought.

At thirteen months of age, Danielle was already keen on making marks with different colors of pens on paper. In the weeks that followed, she began drawing with inexhaustible curiosity, demonstrating a love for artistic expression. Soon she was drawing pictures and talking about them in baby talk. Danielle was communicating by constructing narratives from memory, representing them both symbolically and two-dimensionally, and then talking about them.

These drawings set the beginnings of literacy in motion. Her self-selected drawing sessions stretched her mind and began to expand her creativity and, even at so tender an age, kindle the stamina to stay with something that was engaging to her and come back to it after a break doing something else. She had begun her journey to reading with these symbolic, two-dimensional representations using tools for making marks on paper.

She had an internal desire to communicate, showed joy in expressing ideas, and clearly experienced the urge to make meaning. But no one had asked Danielle to take up drawing. Her mom had simply made pencil and paper available and showed her how to have fun with it. Danielle seemed to take to it naturally. Her parents gave her little doses of encouragement, talked with her about her accomplishments, and answered her questions.

Look at the following early descriptions of drawing and writing taken from Danielle's and her brother Connor's Literacy Milestones Diaries and you'll see how drawing paved the way for an astonishing path to writing to reading—the same beautiful path that your child can take. (You will be keeping a similar diary as you teach your child to read.)

Danielle's Early Drawing and Writing

Phase 0

Makes marks on paper with different colors of pens. Seems to like drawing. (13 months)

Continues to draw and scribble. Begins to distinguish between drawing and writing and signs a greeting card with her "mark." (1 year, 8 months)

Scribbles a "letter" to grandparents describing a day at the beach and eating at Boston Market. (1 year, 11 months)

Pretends to make a grocery list. (2 years, 4 months)

Colors a fish independently, choosing colors to create a pattern. Attempts to sign her artwork. (2 years, 10 months)

Danielle's early Phase 0 drawings and writing topics preserved in her Literacy Milestones Diary included happy faces, a house, a rainbow, Halloween, an airplane, fish, family members, the sun, and Mommy bouncing a ball—there were numerous others during spurts of interest when she chose to spend a lot of time drawing and pretending to write.

Phase 1

Writes her name for the first time. (2 years, 10 months)

Holds the pen while her mom guides her hand in writing "PARTY TIME." She then adds her own message with letters and letter-like forms. (2 years, 11 months)

Writes "From Danielle to Mom," with all the words spelled correctly from memory. (3 years, 1 month)

Draws a picture of herself and writes, "I love you, Connor," six times in speech bubbles—a total of twenty-four words on the page—powerful spelling practice for a three-year-old! (3 years, 4 months)

Phase 2

Writes DANIELLESRABO for "Danielle's rainbow." In this sample Danielle illustrates that she is beginning to break the alphabetic code. She gets the beginning sounds in *rain* and *bow*. (3 years, 8 months)

Connor and Danielle showed the expected normal variation in timing for starting early literacy development, but both of them began with drawing. Here are examples of Connor's early drawing and writing taken from his Literacy Milestones Diary:

Connor's Early Drawing and Writing

Phase 0

Paints watercolors with a brush. (2 years)

Makes a painting and announces in a two-word utterance that it's "By self." (2 years, 3 months)

Shows interest in "signing" his painting, perhaps demonstrating early discrimination between drawing and writing. (2 years, 6 months)

Holds his finger stiff as Mom guides it to write his name on a finger painting. (3 years, 1 month)

Phase 1

Practices writing his name on Halloween art projects. (3 years, 8 months)

Writes his name independently on a picture he makes of a pumpkin face. (3 years, 9 months)

Connor demonstrated his ability to write his name independently soon after the family moved into a new house. He used a dry-erase marker and wrote his name all over the playroom—on the cabinets, chair, train table, walls, and doors. After praising his efforts his mom was gentle but firm in directing future writing to paper.

Phase 2

Writes THAK you FR my PRTY for "Thank you for my party." (4 years, 9 months)
Writes IW M B for "I ride my bike." (5 years, 6 months)

These samples, both lovingly distinctive and remarkably similar, show two children in the same household who were allowed to develop literacy naturally and on their own schedules: Drawing opened their gate to literacy.

A Century of Reading Experts Agree: Draw—Write—and Read!

Experts agree that drawing almost always opens the gate to early literacy. Documentation of the role of drawing for early reading goes back more than one hundred years. Maria Montessori, an Italian educator who lived from 1870 to 1952 and founded the world-renowned Montessori schools, recognized that writing precedes reading and advocated early drawing and use of activity-based literacy tools such as sandpaper letters, alphabet blocks, and movable alphabet letters. She wrote, "Contrary to the usual accepted idea, *writing precedes reading*." Montessori wrote about preschoolers' early critical periods for literacy development and observed that very young children could easily put the skills of reading together after "an explosion of writing."[8]

The classic study of how very young children learn to read by writing was published by Delores Durkin in 1966, *Children Who Read Early.*[9] Virtually all of the 205 early readers that Durkin studied learned to print before they learned to read. She called them "pencil and paper kids" whose parents answered lots of questions about sounds and spelling during their "interest binges" in early writing.

The late Marie Clay, a giant in the twentieth century in the research and teaching of beginning reading, advised that even though the child is interested in books and having stories read to him, his earliest reading behaviors can best be observed by his teacher or parent in drawing and early writing.[10] This sage advice predicted the power of phase observation in children's early writing. Clay recommended that educators and parents capitalize upon the young child's urge to write, pointing out that writing often comes first, before reading.[11] Decades of solid research that informs this book have confirmed that prediction.[12]

The earliest readers not only start out by drawing, they continue to allow their drawing to support the writing process. At higher phases children often draw a picture to plan the stories they want to write. Their drawings can have elaborate details even though the first written stories may be a one-word label, phrases, or a few lines. Using artwork as a cue, three-, four-, and five-year-old beginning writers construct and tell wonderful, amazing, meaningful narratives with elaborate detail.

Early writing makes the reading process less abstract. Writing and reading are both complicated brain activities requiring the orchestration of a symphony of learned skills all at once. But writing is more concrete than reading. The child can slow the writing process down, ponder, think, and see what he's doing. His early writing requires stamina, as do later academic pursuits.

Beginning writers deliberately work in slow motion as they analyze and think about each word they put down on the page. If you watch a Phase 3 child writing a word such as *flowerpot*, he likely makes each sound in the word deliberately, sometimes slowly and painstakingly putting down a corresponding letter as he says each sound out loud and rendering a spelling such as F for /f/, L for /l/, O for /o/, W for /w/, R for /r/, P for /p/, O for /o/, T for /t/: FLOWRPOT.

Over time your young child will move from markings and scribblings to writing complete stories. Your child will go through a series of developmental phases as he learns to read, each delineated in the chapters to follow. In the next chapter, I'll help you identify your child's current phase, so that you can pinpoint his needs and start working on appropriate activities at home. Don't forget to use READ (Repetition-Enthusiasm-Attention-Drawing) techniques during every phase.

3

FIND YOUR CHILD'S PHASE

Determine Where to Go and What to Do Next to Raise YOUR Confident Reader

WHAT IF you could administer a short spelling test or do a quick analysis of your child's current writing and find out exactly where he or she was on the developmental literacy scale and what activities to choose to move him or her forward? This chapter shows you how easy it is to identify your child's current level and determine what to do next when you embrace the power of phase observation. You don't have to be a literacy expert. Any parent can do it!

TWO EASY OPTIONS

There are two easy options for identifying your child's current reading and writing level or phase of development. The first option, which I'll call "Seeing the Phase in Your Child's Writing," involves collecting recent writing samples your child created over the past several weeks and matching them with prototypes from other children who were in the same phase. (If your child is too young to scribble or write, she's in Phase 0, so go directly to Chapter 4.) The second option, which I'll call "The Monster Spelling Test," is really not a monster at all: It's quick and easy to administer. You may choose one or both procedures to find your child's current phase of reading and writing development. Before choosing an option, I recommend that you read this chapter in its entirety to get an overview of both procedures and a clear understanding of what each phase looks like.

Laying Some Groundwork—Getting Comfortable with Your Child's Early Natural Explorations with Letters and Print

Sometimes parents worry that a child's first writing is bad for him or her because the spellings are incorrect. That's not the case. These attempts are natural first steps in a long process of learning the complex system of English spelling. Children move from early low-level spelling strategies to more sophisticated strategies over time, aided by spelling instruction.

Expert spelling is the result of both a developmental process and being taught correct spelling. Just as a large wave overlaps and takes over earlier smaller waves, your child will replace the lower-level spelling strategies with more sophisticated strategies in good time. Eventually, word-specific knowledge and automatic recognition and retrieval of conventional spelling will replace the early low-level strategies. Just as sophisticated speech grows out of babbling and first words, early attempts to spell build a foundation for correct spelling that comes later. Hypothesis testing and error making precede perfect production in both speaking and writing. Your child's early explorations of letters and print encourage thinking and set foundations—adult-like correctness comes later.

Early Explorations with Spelling: A Window into Your Child's Mind

Long before your child is able to spell conventionally, she will "invent" her own early system of spelling by attempting to spell as best she can (given early natural exposure to print along with pencil-and-paper activity). This early attempt to spell words before correct spelling is mastered is called "invented spelling." Children invent spellings when they first begin to explore language from a natural curiosity and desire to write that is sparked by drawing. As you learned in Chapter 1, early invented spelling is one of the best ways for your child to begin activating the brain circuitry for reading during critical periods when the brain is ripe for language learning.

Inventing a spelling is a slow and analytical process that requires your child to really think about how reading and writing work. It helps if you encourage this activity, respond to your child's questions, show tolerance for the early lack of conventionality, and offer lots of praise during early periods of "kid writing," a concept that will be explained in detail in Chapter 5. You'll marvel at the changes you see in your child's spelling—it's like watching the changes from babbling, to first words, and then to speaking. And in your enthusiasm for seeing these first steps toward reading, you'll find yourself reassuring your young kid writer by saying "Wow! This is great kid spelling!"

Early invented spellings follow a highly researched and stable developmental sequence in the five phases of beginning reading.[1] The phases are closely linked and build on each other. Phases 0 and 1 come before your child discovers that letters represent sounds. From Phases 2 to 4, your child knows that spellings represent the *sounds* in words, but figuring out exactly how English spelling represents sounds is a gradual process. At each successive phase your child will choose a more effective invented spelling strategy, demonstrating a growing awareness of how letters spell the sounds. In this step-by-step process, she's a codebreaker, and the code she is breaking is the complex English alphabet code.

As she moves through the phases her categorizations of speech sounds and choices of letters to spell them become more and more sophisticated and move toward accurate conventional spelling. Your child's invented spelling shows the interface of her knowledge of speech sounds with what she is thinking as she chooses letters to spell a word. It's possible for you to identify her phase if you know what to look for in the choices she makes for invented spellings. Indeed, your child's invented spelling is a window into her literate mind.

Exploring Print and Inventing Spelling Is Good for Your Child

A new awakening regarding the positive impact of early writing for reading began about thirty years ago when a linguist named Charles Read coined the term "invented spelling" while conducting research in how beginners categorize speech sounds and represent the sounds with letters. Just as recent brain research has shown that babies are a lot smarter than we think they are, Read's educational research demonstrated that, when preschool teachers or parents encouraged invented spellings, rather than holding children back from writing until they learned all the conventions, preschool writers could do much more than we had ever thought possible.

Before the advent of invented spelling, there was virtually no writing in preschool, and kindergarten and first-grade writing consisted of penmanship drills, copy exercises, and fill-in-the-blank worksheets. Over the past twenty years, encouraging invented spelling in schools has become accepted as best practice. A revolution in emergent literacy instruction took place in successful schools as it became more and more apparent that allowing very young children to write prolifically in invented spelling was a natural and powerful tool in helping them learn to read. By writing, they were activating the same brain areas that are activated for reading. Early writers were learning and demonstrating reading skills! As one of the pioneers in this research, I helped to legitimize invented spelling through my own work, proving that it does indeed help children transition to the conventional system. The stages, or phases, that I discovered thirty years ago, with the help of other researchers, are still very much in use in today's successful school systems.[2]

In the past, a few phonics-first advocates took an extreme position and branded invented spelling as something bad, idiosyncratic, or eccentric, declaring it to be in opposition to direct and systematic phonics instruction for school-age children. An accurate portrayal of young children's exploration of phonics through invented spelling is just the opposite: Invented spelling with appropriate response from the parent is the *best way to teach phonics informally* before children are ready for formal reading and spelling instruction. Invented spelling teaches the logic of phonics.

Children who invent spelling are in fact using what they know about phonics to write words they are not old enough to know how to spell like an adult, and they are showing the parent exactly how much phonics they know or do not know. Watching how your child invents spelling helps you know if her knowledge of phonics is growing, and it will guide you to select the right kinds of activities to build phonics skills at exactly the right time.

Recognition of the powerful, positive, instructional, and assessment implications of children's early exploration with spelling was closely scrutinized long before it was accepted as best practice. After linguist Charles Read discovered systematic categorizations of speech sounds and consistent spellings in his research with preschool writers and coined the term "invented spelling" in 1975, he provided positive implications for spelling and writing instruction.[3] Building on Read's research, I described five stages, or phases, in 1982 with additional positive implications for teaching.[4] In 1997, Linnea Ehri showed how my phases matched phases of word reading, thus powerfully connecting the phases of learning to write with learning to read.[5]

The turning point in the educational community for advocating invented spelling as a desirable means for learning to read and write came in 1998, when a team of researchers headed by Catherine Snow at Harvard University released one of the most important research syntheses in reading education of the decade, *Preventing Reading Disabilities*. This work recognized that the act of inventing spelling helped very young children learn to read. The following year, the same group published explicit recommendations for parents titled *Starting Out Right: A Guide to Promoting Children's Reading Success*.

> It's important for parents and teachers to understand that invented spelling is not in conflict with correct spelling. On the contrary, it plays an important role in helping children learn how to write. When children use invented spelling, they are in fact exercising their growing knowledge of phonemes, the letters of the alphabet, and their confidence in the alphabetic principle. A child's "iz" for the conventional "is" can be celebrated as quite a breakthrough. It is the kind of error that shows you that the child is thinking independently and quite analytically about the sounds of words and the logic of spelling.[6]

The same year that *Preventing Reading Difficulties* was published, two highly regarded professional teacher organizations, the International Reading Association and the National Association of Education of Young Children, issued a joint position statement endorsing the use of invented spelling in preschool, kindergarten, and first and second grade, when balanced with appropriate instruction for correct spelling.[7] These revolutionary breakthroughs—recognizing the power of early writing and invented spelling and embracing phase observation—may be the most important new discoveries for improving the teaching of beginning reading in decades and will change the way reading and writing are taught in the twenty-first century. You can use these powerful discoveries to assess your child's literacy development at home.

Option 1: Seeing the Phase in Your Child's Writing

Finding your child's phase means zeroing in on the specific strategy your child uses for spelling a word before the accepted spelling has been learned. Phase 0 is characterized by scribbling with no spelling. There are four different invented spelling strategies for Phases 1–4. Whether children learn to read informally before entering school or learn through formal instruction in kindergarten and first grade, they progress through these same phases with particular strategies for inventing spelling, as shown in Figure 3.1.

The Timeline for Moving Through the Phases

Your child's timeline for moving through this step-by-step progression is a highly individual matter with a wide range of normal variation, just as when he took his first step or spoke his first word, but the sequence

Figure 3.1: Spelling Strategies for Each Phase

Phase	*Your Child's Spelling Strategy*
Phase 0	Scribbling—no spelling
Phase 1	Using random letters with *no sound matchers* (A Phase 1 child may not yet know the entire alphabet or distinguish between upper- and lower-case letters.)
Phase 2	Using beginning and ending letters *with sound matches*
Phase 3	Using one letter for each sound
Phase 4	Using chunks of spelling and phonics patterns

does not vary. The timeline for phases can vary by as much as two or three years depending on a child's literacy experiences and learning. That is why it makes so much difference whether you teach your child to read informally at home, by immersing him in literacy activities from birth until he enters kindergarten, or choose to wait until kindergarten and first grade, when the classroom teachers will begin to teach him through formal instruction. For children who arrive at kindergarten at Phase 0, unable to write their names, the expectation is that they will progress through the five phases by the end of first grade. The same progress is accomplished by the middle of kindergarten, or before, by children whose parents provided lots of informal literacy at home.

You can see phase development in any child by observing his or her invented spelling. There is one easy question associated with each of the five phases that will help you to determine what to make of those observations. In brief, you will be examining how he is using the alphabetic code to invent spellings for unknown words when he writes.

Seeing Phase 0

Look at Figure 3.2. In each of these samples of Phase 0 writing, the writer is "writing" but not using letters. Phase 0 children cannot write their names independently and do not use letters when pretending to write. They write by scribbling or use wavy or loopy writing. Sometimes their writing approximates letter-like forms.

Question for Identifying Phase 0: Can your child write his or her name? If your child scribbles, does not write with letters, and is not yet able to write her name, or if she is a baby and at an even earlier level of development, go to Chapter 4. If she is just learning to write her name, she is moving into Phase 1.

Seeing Phase 1

Look at the samples of Phase 1 writing in Figure 3.3. In each of the samples, the writer is operating with letters, but the letters do not match with sounds. Phase 1 writers use letters in a random or arbitrary fashion for representing a message in writing. Their knowledge for naming and forming letters is likely incomplete.

Figure 3.2: Two Samples of Phase 0 Writing

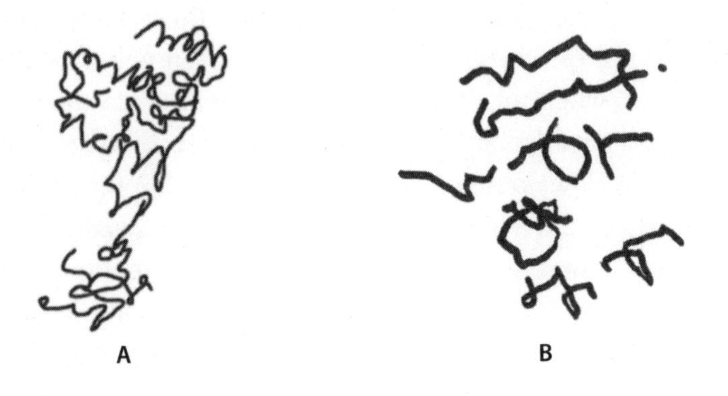

Figure 3.3: Two Samples of Phase 1 Writing

Question for Identifying Phase 1: Is your child writing with letters but not attending to sounds? If your child can write his name and a few other important words, but spells unknown words with what appear to be random letters, go to Chapter 5, the Phase 1 chapter. Children move into Phase 2 when they begin matching the letters to sounds.

Seeing Phase 2

Look at the samples of Phase 2 writing in Figure 3.4. In each of the samples, the writer is operating with beginning letters, beginning and ending letters, or abbreviated spellings that leave out some sounds in the word being spelled. Phase 2 writing may be hard for you to read unless you know what your child is writing about. If you see examples of more than one phase in your child's sample, look at a larger number of samples and choose the phase that defines the *majority* of your child's invented spellings.

Question for Identifying Phase 2: Is your child using letters and getting mostly beginning and ending sounds? If mostly beginning and ending sounds are represented but some sounds are missing, go to Chapter 6, the Phase 2 chapter. If your child is getting virtually all of the sounds in words and spells quite a few words correctly, she may be moving into Phase 3.

Figure 3.4: Two Samples of Phase 2 Writing

Seeing Phase 3

Look at the samples of Phase 3 writing in Figure 3.5. In each of the samples, the writer is operating with one letter for each sound when spelling unknown words. With very few exceptions, all of the sounds are represented in each word. The writing is pretty easy for you to read even though sometimes it doesn't look like English spelling. Sometimes

Figure 3.5: Three Samples of Phase 3 Writing

eggs MIK (milk) JOS (juice) SOD (soda)	CHIKN (chicken) fish	COLE FLOWR (cauli- flower) CON (corn) PERS (pears) LEDIS (lettuce) APPLS (apples)	BED (bread) DONUS (doughnuts) cookies
DARE (dairy) (Aisle) 4	MET (meat) (Aisle) 3	FROTES (fruits) (Aisle) 2	BAKRE (bakery) (Aisle) 1

A

EF U KAN OPN KAZ I WILL GEV U A KN OPENR

If you can open cans I will give you a can opener.

B

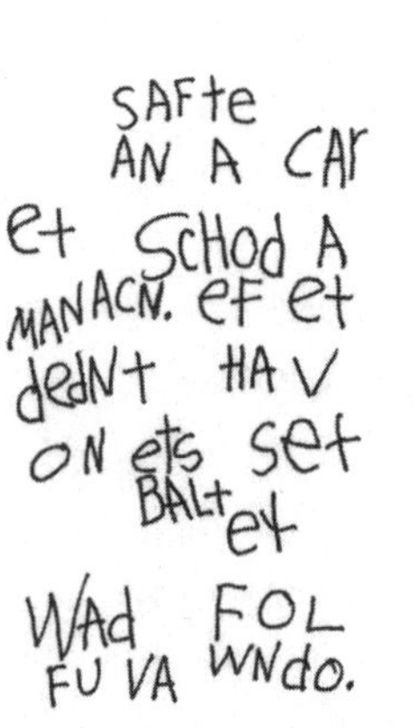

Safety

In a car

It showed a mannequin. If it

didn't have

on its seat

belt, it

would fall

through the window

C

Phase 3 writing includes quite a few words that are spelled correctly. As at earlier phases, if you see examples of more than one phase in your child's sample, look at a larger number of samples and choose the phase that defines the *majority* of your child's invented spelling.

Figure 3.5A is Danielle's map of a grocery store showing the aisle and location of various foods. By four years, eight months of age, Danielle had advanced from partial to full sound representations in her invented spelling. Most of the words on this map are pure Phase 3 spellings, with one letter for each sound in the word.

Question for Identifying Phase 3: Is your child spelling most sounds in words with one letter, such as three letters for three sounds (as in EGL for eagle, TOD for toad, and RAN for rain)? If most of the unknown words are spelled with one letter for each sound, go to Chapter 7, the Phase 3 chapter. Once your child begins spelling in chunks of phonics patterns, she will be moving into Phase 4.

Seeing Phase 4

Look at the samples of Phase 4 writing in Figure 3.6. In each of the samples, the writer is operating with chunks of spelling patterns. Vowels are represented in every syllable. Phase 4 writing is easy to read and often contains many words that are spelled correctly—often more than are invented. If you see examples of more than one phase in your child's sample—for instance, if some of the spellings are Phase 3 and some are Phase 4—look at a larger number of samples and choose the phase that defines the *majority* of your child's spelling.

Questions for Identifying Phase 4: Is your child using a chunking strategy to spell unknown words? The Phase 4 child has moved from using a letter for each sound in the word to spelling some sounds in chunks—for example, going from EGL to EGUL or EGAL for *eagle*; from TOD to TODE or TOED for *toad*; and from RAN to RANE or RAYN for *rain*. If mostly chunking spellings are represented and your child can already spell many words, go to the Phase 4 chapter.

In addition to or in place of finding your child's phase by "Seeing the Phase in Your Child's Writing," you may wish to try "The Monster

Figure 3.6: Four Samples of Phase 4 Writing

THES AFTERNEWN IT'S
GOING TO RAIN.
IT'S GOING TO BE FAIR TOMORO.

This afternoon it's
going to rain.
It's going to be fair tomorrow.

A

My Babe store

I was baon on
Janurre the 4. I
Git baon At 5-0-10
I Waod Arod I Pand.
ThE farst time I
weat to Weastn SALn
I dead a stekee in
my MOMS Lap. I
War a wiet dres
Weth Las ON eat.
And at had ABCs
ON at. I ate ham
And Grren Bens meat.

B

My foot

My feet
are flesh.
I whair
sis 3.
My feet take
me evrewhair.
My feet like
to clime trees
and billdings.
I walk to
School.
My feet
make me
Swem in
water. My
feet are
tiyerd at
the end
of the
day

C

Good THING to Eat
I like STRALBARES and I like ORRANGE.
I like tomato SUPE and I like PECHIS.
I like apples and I like BROCULE (broccoli).
I like COLEFALWORE TO, you know.
I like corn and I like green BENES.
I like FRIDE CHEKEN and I like BARBO Q
CHEKEN TO.
But most of all I like HO MAED SOPGATE.
THOSS (those) things are good for you.
THAT why I put them down.

D

Spelling Test," which is a quick and easy way to see how your child invents spellings for unknown words. Once you read the section below and understand how the test works, it will take you about ten to twenty minutes to administer the test in a "playing school" setting, and then I'll guide you in scoring it. Save the test results. You will administer the same test several months from now to see if your child is moving into the next phase. You will also want to save results and share them with your child's teachers once he enters school to show his remarkable movement through the phases. This should help your child's teachers make sure that his placements in a school curriculum are appropriate.

Option 2: The Monster Spelling Test

Test Description: The Monster Test is a quick and easy-to-administer informal spelling test consisting of five words for very young children and ten words for more advanced writers. Children will naturally spell this set of words differently at each phase of their literacy development. The words are likely words your child has in his speaking vocabulary but probably has not seen often or attempted to write, so the test words aren't expected to be spelled correctly unless your child is spelling on a second-grade level or above. Your child will categorize the sound features within each word with a particular spelling that reveals his phase. The words were scientifically selected and contain technical sound features, such as the retroflex "r" in the word *bird*, which results in the different spellings at different phases, as shown below:

Phase 1: *Bird* is spelled JLEM (or other random letters).
Phase 2: *Bird* is spelled B or BD (the retroflex "r" is left out, and the /d/ may be left out).
Phase 3: *Bird* is spelled BRD (the "r" carries the vowel sound and all three sounds are represented).
Phase 4: *Bird* is spelled BURD or BERD with chunks as in *fur* and *her*.

As you can see, each of the spellings is more sophisticated and closer to the correct spelling than at the previous level. Now you are ready to administer the test.

The Monster Spelling Test[8]

Materials Needed

The Monster Spelling Test wordlist and sentences provided below; a pencil or marker and unlined paper. (At the conclusion of the test you will consult the Monster Test Scoring Guide provided in this chapter in Figure 3.8 to assign a phase level, either 0, 1, 2, 3, or 4, for each word your child spells.)

Basic Steps

1. Call out the word and give a sentence.
2. Give your child plenty of time to write the word.
3. Locate the Scoring Guide Charts.
4. Score each word your child attempted with a 0, 1, 2, 3, or 4.
5. Note which phase gets the most spellings. That's your child's current phase. (Five 3's and five 4's would indicate a child who is in Phase 3 moving into Phase 4.)

Time Required

About ten to twenty minutes.

Administering the Test

When you administer the Monster Spelling Test, couch the activity in a game-like atmosphere—like playing school—and make sure your child feels comfortable and has no anxiety about spelling the words correctly. Keep in mind that inventing a spelling is a challenging intellectual feat for a very young child requiring time, concentration, and stamina. Your encouragement, enthusiasm, and patience will largely determine whether or not your child completes the activity successfully. You may want to start by challenging a very young child with only one word and coming back later to "play the spelling game" with the next word until you have completed the first five words. If you get off to a bad start, step back and try the test at a later date.

Your focus is on the letter choices the child makes, not on correct letter formation. If you are not sure what the letter is, ask "What's this letter?" If the child doesn't know the name of a letter he has used, make note of it but don't correct him. Say, "That letter works fine in a kid spelling." Don't make an issue of uppercase or lowercase letters. Accept whichever your child produces. Remember, the point of the Monster Spelling Test is to find out what he knows or does not know, not to correct or teach on the spot. That comes later.

Often you can tell what phase your child is in after the first few words. If the spellings are random letters, for example, your child is in Phase 1, so you can stop the test, or continue if he finds the activity amusing. Children who are in Phase 3 and Phase 4 will write all ten words. It's perfectly normal for children to sound the words out audibly as they write down letters, but don't coach the child—for example, by sounding out the letters for him and emphasizing each sound.

Sit next to your child, sitting on the left side of right-handed writers or on the right side of left-handed writers so that you can see what your child's spelling attempts as he is writing each word. Begin with these instructions:

> PARENT: Can you write your name on this paper? Let's write it here at the top.
> (If your child cannot write his name, he's in Phase 0. Discontinue the test and go to Chapter 4. If your child writes his name or gets some letters, continue with the first word.)
> PARENT: Today let's play school and pretend we're having a spelling test. I'll be the teacher. Let's try some words that are really hard. You aren't supposed to know how to spell them, just spell them the best you can. I'll bet you'll be surprised at what you can do! Remember, just think about each word and spell it however you think it should be spelled. Take your time. We'll write them in a column starting right here. (Point to the top of the left side of the page and show your child where to start each word so that they are in column formation. If your child has difficulty orienting words on the page, put a small number beside each word so you can score it later.)
> PARENT: Are you ready? Now this is a fun word. The first word is *monster*. "That big spider looks like a monster!"

Watch as your child attempts to write the word. Give prompts such as "You're doing great." "Look at what you can do! You're a fantastic 'kid writer'!" If your child is hesitant, say, "Just try it. You can use any letters you like. I think you're doing great!" Don't give cues such as "sound it out," and avoid giving the correct spelling even if your child asks for it. Just say, "Yes, that's a great kid spelling. I didn't know you could do that!"

Once you have completed the test—five words for very young children and all ten words for more advanced spellers—offer your child lots of praise. Tell him, "We'll try this again in a few months to see how much progress you are making!"

Now you are ready to begin. Give the word and the sentence listed below for each word. If you think the sentence may be confusing for your child, make up one that you think is appropriate. It's often helpful to have your child say the word before he starts to write it. Here's an example: "The next word is *united*—The *United* States is a big country. Say the word, *united*, for me, as in United States." (Child says "United.") "That's it, now write *united*."

Scoring the Monster Spelling Test

Use the word charts below to assign a phase number from 0 to 4 beside each word in the Monster Spelling Test list: Assign 0 for Phase 0, 1 for Phase 1, 2 for Phase 2, 3 for Phase 3, or 4 for Phase 4. Some of your child's spellings may seem idiosyncratic. If you are not able to score a word, don't assign a number. If your child has a correct beginning letter mixed with random letters, score it as a 2. Remember, you are looking for patterns, trends, and how your child is thinking about the logic of spelling. You are not assigning a grade. When you have completed the scoring process, count the number of 1's, 2's, 3's, and 4's. The number that is in the majority is your child's phase. For example, if your child has three 2's and eight 3's, he's in Phase 3. Generally, the scores will cluster around one or two phase numbers as opposed to being spread across four or five. If your child has five 3's and five 4's, he's moving from Phase 3 to Phase 4.

The scoring charts in Figures 3.8A through 3.8J make it easy for you to quickly score each word:

Figure 3.7: Monster Spelling Test Wordlist and Sentences

Start with the first five words for very young children:

1. **monster**—That spider looks like a *monster*!
2. **united**—The *United* States is a big country.
3. **dress**—The girl wore a new *dress*.
4. **bottom**—A big fish lived in the *bottom* of the lake.
5. **hiked**—We *hiked* to the top of the mountain.

If your child is doing well and is in the upper phases, continue with these words:

6. **human**—Sponge Bob Square Pants is not a *human*.
7. **eagle**—An *eagle* is a powerful bird.
8. **closed**—The girl *closed* the door.
9. **bumped**—The car *bumped* into the bus.
10. **type**—*Type* the letter on the computer keyboard.

Figure 3.8A: Scoring *monster*

Word	*Your Child's Strategy*	*Possible Spellings*	*Phase Score*
1. monster	scribbles, squiggly marks, wavy lines, loopy lines, letter approximations but no recognizable letters	any attempts at pretend writing	0
	letters appear but no matches with the sounds in the word	any combination of letters	1
	partial but incomplete letter-sound matches, very abbreviated spellings, sometimes a few correct letters mixed with random letters	M; MTR; MS; MR and the like	2
	complete letter-sound matches; a letter for each sound; (Exceptions: Your child may leave out letters for a few special sound features such as the "preconsonantal nasals" in monster so even if the N is omitted it's a Phase 3 spelling.)	MOSTR; MOSTOR; MOSTER; MOSTIR; MASTR (these Phase 3 spellings omit N due to preconsonantal nasal); MONSTR; MANSTR; MUNSTR or the like	3
	vowels and chunks are present in each syllable; syllable chunks may include known spellings such as stir or star in MONSTIR	MONSTUR; MONSTAR; MONSTIR; MONSTOR; MUNSTER or the like	4

Figure 3.8B: Scoring *united*

Word	*Your Child's Strategy*	*Possible Spellings*	*Phase Score*
2. united	scribbles, squiggly marks, wavy lines, loopy lines, letter approximations but no recognizable letters	any attempts at pretend writing	0
	letters appear but no matches with the sounds in the word	any combination of letters	1
	partial but incomplete letter-sound matches, very abbreviated spellings, sometimes a few correct letters mixed with random letters	any spelling beginning with a U or a Y; U; UTD; YOUTD (/nī/ sound is omitted) or the like	2
	complete letter-sound matches; a letter for each sound; (Exceptions: Your child may spell the last syllable as TD or DD in Phase 3.)	UNITD; YOUNITD; UNIDD;	3
	vowels and chunks are present in each syllable; syllable chunks may include known spellings such as you or night in YOUNIGHTED	UNIGHTED; UNIDID; YOUNIDID; YOUNIGHTED; YOUNITED or the like	4

Figure 3.8C: Scoring *dress*

Word	*Your Child's Strategy*	*Possible Spellings*	*Phase Score*
3. dress	scribbles, squiggly marks, wavy lines, loopy lines, letter approximations but no recognizable letters	any attempts at pretend writing	0
	letters appear but no matches with the sounds in the word	any combination of letters	1
	partial but incomplete letter-sound matches, very abbreviated spellings, sometimes a few correct letters mixed with random letters	Dress begins with D or J and may contain other partial matches; D; J; JR; DR; DS; DRS; DRC and the like DRPTI or the like	2
	complete letter-sound matches; a letter for each sound; (Your child may substitute J or JR for the beginning sound.)	DRAS; JRAS; JRES; JRES; DREZ; DREC	3
	the correct short vowel e and chunks are present	DRES; DREZZ	4

Figure 3.8D: Scoring *bottom*

Word	*Your Child's Strategy*	*Possible Spellings*	*Phase Score*
4. bottom	scribbles, squiggly marks, wavy lines, loopy lines, letter approximations but no recognizable letters	any attempts at pretend writing	0
	letters appear but no matches with the sounds in the word	any combination of letters	1
	partial but incomplete letter-sound matches, very abbreviated spellings, sometimes a few correct letters mixed with random letters	B; BTM; BT; BM; begins with B or contains partial but incomplete letter-sound matches	2
	complete letter-sound matches; a letter for each sound; (Your child may substitute D for T at Phase 3 due to a sound feature called the alveolar flap for /t/ and /d/. Short o may be spelled with an I in Phase 3 because the /ŏ/ sound as in hot and the letter name I sound a lot alike.)	BOTM; BODM; BITM; BIDM; BODDM; BOTTM	3
	vowels and chunks are present in each syllable; syllable chunks may include known spellings such as stir or star in MONSTIR	BOTTUM; BODDOM; BOTDUM; BOTOM or the like	4

Figure 3.8E: Scoring *hiked*

Word	*Your Child's Strategy*	*Possible Spellings*	*Phase Score*
5. hiked	scribbles, squiggly marks, wavy lines, loopy lines, letter approximations but no recognizable letters	any attempts at pretend writing	0
	letters appear but no matches with the sounds in the word	any combination of letters	1
	partial but incomplete letter-sound matches, very abbreviated spellings, sometimes a few correct letters mixed with random letters	H; HT; HCT and the like HBOPOF and the like	2
	complete letter-sound matches; a letter for each sound; (Your child may spell the -ed ending with T or D in Phase 3.	HIKT; HICKT; HIKD; HICT	3
	vowels and chunks are present in each syllable; syllable chunks may include known spellings such as high in HIGHKED	HICKED; HIGHKED; HIKICKT or the like	4

Figure 3.8F: Scoring *human*

Word	*Your Child's Strategy*	*Possible Spellings*	*Phase Score*
6. human	scribbles, squiggly marks, wavy lines, loopy lines, letter approximations but no recognizable letters	any attempts at pretend writing	0
	letters appear but no matches with the sounds in the word	any combination of letters	1
	partial but incomplete letter-sound matches, very abbreviated spellings, sometimes a few correct letters mixed with random letters	Begins with H, Y, or U and contains incomplete letter-sound matches; H; HM; YOUM; U; YM; M and the like HBOPOF and the like	2
	complete letter-sound matches; a letter for each sound; (Your child may leave out the vowel in the second syllable of human in Phase 3 because the sonorant l carries the vowel sound.)	HUMN; YOUMN; UMN	3
	vowels and chunks are present in each syllable; syllable chunks may include known spellings such as you in HYOUMAN	HUMUN; HUMIN; HYOUMAN; YOUMAN; HUMEN or the like	4

Figure 3.8G: Scoring *eagle*

Word	*Your Child's Strategy*	*Possible Spellings*	*Phase Score*
7. eagle	scribbles, squiggly marks, wavy lines, loopy lines, letter approximations but no recognizable letters	any attempts at pretend writing	0
	letters appear but no matches with the sounds in the word	any combination of letters	1
	partial but incomplete letter-sound matches, very abbreviated spellings, sometimes a few correct letters mixed with random letters	E; EG; EL and the like EBOPOF and the like	2
	complete letter-sound matches; a letter for each sound; (Your child may represent the sonorant l in the –gle syllable with GL at Phase 3.)	EGL; EAGL; EEGL	3
	vowels and chunks are present in each syllable; syllable chunks may include known spellings such as stir or star in MONSTIR	EGUL; EGAL; EEGUL EAGUL or the like	4

Figure 3.8H: Scoring *closed*

Word	*Your Child's Strategy*	*Possible Spellings*	*Phase Score*
8. closed	scribbles, squiggly marks, wavy lines, loopy lines, letter approximations but no recognizable letters	any attempts at pretend writing	0
	letters appear but no matches with the sounds in the word	any combination of letters	1
	partial but incomplete letter-sound matches, very abbreviated spellings, sometimes a few correct letters mixed with random letters	begins with C or K; C; K; CSD; KLD or the like CBOPOF and the like	2
	complete letter-sound matches; a letter for each sound; all sounds plus the –ed ending are represented	CLOSD; CLOZD KLOSD; CLOZT or the like	3
	vowels and chunks are present in each syllable; syllable chunks may include known spellings such as low in CLOWSED	CLOSSED; CLOZZED; CLOZED; CLO[illegible]TED CLOWSED or the like	4

Figure 3.8I: Scoring *bumped*

Word	*Your Child's Strategy*	*Possible Spellings*	*Phase Score*
9. bumped	scribbles, squiggly marks, wavy lines, loopy lines, letter approximations but no recognizable letters	any attempts at pretend writing	0
	letters appear but no matches with the sounds in the word	any combination of letters	1
	partial but incomplete letter-sound matches, very abbreviated spellings, sometimes a few correct letters mixed with random letters	begins with B; BM; BMT or the like BJROF and the like	2
	complete letter-sound matches; a letter for each sound; (At Phase 3 your child may leave out the m when spelling the preconsonantal nasal /m/ even though he hears this sound.)	BUPT; BOPT; BUMPT; BOMPT; BUMD; BUMPD or the like	3
	vowels and chunks are present in each syllable	BUMPPED; BUMMPPED BUMPDED or the like	4

Figure 3.8J: Scoring *type*

Word	*Your Child's Strategy*	*Possible Spellings*	*Phase Score*
10. type	scribbles, squiggly marks, wavy lines, loopy lines, letter approximations but no recognizable letters	any attempts at pretend writing	0
	letters appear but no matches with the sounds in the word	any combination of letters	1
	partial but incomplete letter-sound matches, very abbreviated spellings, sometimes a few correct letters mixed with random letters	T; TP; TI; TY TBOPOF or the like	2
	complete letter-sound matches; a letter for each sound	TIP; TYP	3
	vowels and chunks are present in each syllable; syllable chunks may include known spellings such as tie in TIEP	TIPE; TIPPE; TYPP TIEP or the like	4

Now that you have administered and scored the Monster Test, you have successfully identified your child's current phase of development and are ready to go to the appropriate phase chapter to find targeted activities to meet his needs:

Go to Chapter 4 for Phase 0
Go to Chapter 5 for Phase 1
Go to Chapter 6 for Phase 2
Go to Chapter 7 for Phase 3
Go to Chapter 8 for Phase 4

4

TEACHING READING IN PHASE 0

Building Foundations—From Reading Aloud at Birth to Teaching Your Child to Write His or Her Name

PHASE 0 IS the beginning of your baby's early critical period of literacy development. Your child's brain can literally build the foundational neural connections for reading and writing during this period. It's the longest phase—beginning at birth and lasting two or three years or more. Phase 0 is filled with firsts—first babbles, first links of speech sounds to concepts, first words, first books, and first reactions to illustrations and stories. Your child's first love for books can be developed in Phase 0, and she will demonstrate the first understanding of narratives, pen her first scribbles, and craft the first representational drawings as well as the first pretend writing. It's the only phase with age-based markers, because what you do in Phase 0 hugely impacts the timing of all the other phases of literacy.

Phase 0 is also the phase most directly connected with speech development—so unlike the other phase chapters, where we advocate more fluid age-based expectations, this chapter is organized with age-appropriate benchmarks for many foundational aspects of literacy. It's even possible that your child will learn to read her first words in Phase 0.

"Zero" is a good moniker for this phase because even though the foundations of literacy are being set, your child cannot yet make the transition from arbitrary marks to meaning, except perhaps logographically (that is, by processing a few words visually as pictures). Children in this phase do not process letters and sounds the same way that mature readers do. That does not mean it is not an important phase. Paradoxically, this phase of "zero" letter-sound processing may be the most important phase for literacy development of all. The groundwork is being laid for later phase development.

Figure 4.1 reproduces a drawing done by a two-year-old named Kendall. Throughout this chapter, we'll see the types of activities that inspire drawings such as this one, and you'll come to understand why drawing is so important for literacy later in life. We'll see how confidence in reading emerges in Phase 0: how babies think, what their capabilities are, and how reading aloud and word play can lay a strong foundation for learning to read. Phase 0 is a time for parents to enjoy interacting with their children with rhymes, poems, songs, stories, words, and art in everyday play. When parents embrace the simple activities in this chapter, they become loving teachers of reading and writing, and they enable children to explore and learn reading naturally, easily, informally, and confidently.

Figure 4.1: Kendall's Phase 0 Drawing

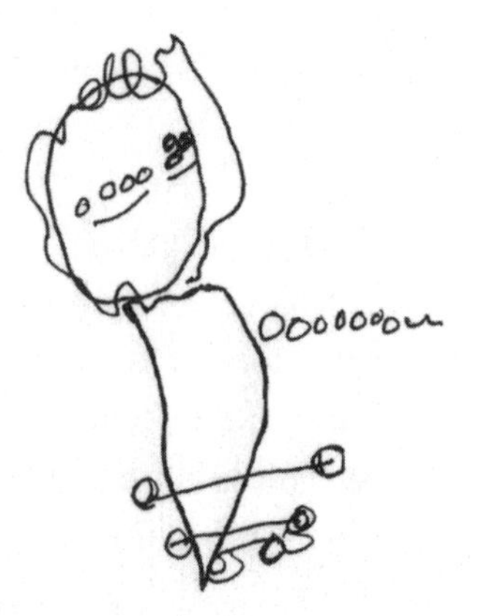

HAVE FUN WITH YOUR BABY, BUILD INTELLIGENCE, AND JUMP-START READING!

Phase 0 begins at birth and lasts until your child can write his or her name. It's the longest phase, perhaps the easiest time for teaching reading, and maybe the most important one in terms of its impact on your child's intelligence and future academic success. These are the brain-building years. It's just a marvelous time to be the child's first reading teacher because you get so much in return for such little effort.

But the thought of teaching reading to newborn-to-four-year-olds can sound daunting to any parent. This chapter shows you what activities to begin with and when to start. You could read reams of books on how to teach reading to babies and toddlers, preschoolers and kindergartners, but I want to make it easy by describing the four essential activities that are best practices for Phase 0: (1) reading aloud, (2) labeling and reading around the room, (3) art or pencil-and-paper activities, and (4) specialty techniques for teaching sounds. This makes teaching reading and raising confident readers E-A-S-Y!

TEACHING READING IN PHASE 0 IS E-A-S-Y!

Teaching babies and toddlers in Phase 0 is E-A-S-Y. Just remember:

E is for Early start.
A is for Activities.
S is for Stimulation.
Y is for You.

Early Start

You baby's brain is ready for reading at birth. Even before birth, if you are reading a children's storybook aloud, baby's brain responds to the musical quality of the sound, which she can already hear from inside the womb. If you are her mother, she will recognize your voice within a few days after her birth. You will soon begin to see hints of response and sparkles of recognition during read-alouds and other literacy activity because your baby is already learning: For example, your baby may begin babbling away with *cooooo's* and *oooooh's* and *aaaaah's* during read-alouds at around two months of age. By five months she will have quite a babbling repertoire. Babbling comes naturally and is part of how the baby learns language. But her babbling development—which is so important for learning to speak—can be positively impacted and increased during reading aloud activity: If you imitate and show delight in her babbling while reading to her cradled in your arms, she will babble more and more.[1]

Parents naturally start speaking to their babies as soon as they meet them, and the baby's specialized brain is already wired to recognize human speech, pay attention to word boundaries, and focus on categorizing the phonemes of the language the parent speaks. As it turns out, phoneme categorization is a major factor in reading and writing. Since many of the strongest connections forming in the child's brain from birth to age four have to do with language, reading aloud during this period simply enriches the language data your child's brain is processing naturally, increases repetition during a critical period of learning when repetition is helpful, and provides more words and a richer grammar for your child to hear so that your baby lays down more elaborate circuits than if you just talked to her.

When you read aloud, you provide data that your child's brain can process not only for sounds but also for words, concepts, and the grammatical structure of the language your child will eventually speak. Reading aloud broadens the vocabulary you use and presents more variation in grammatical structures than speech alone. Your baby is taking in more than you realize. Reading aloud and having baby conversations will permanently shape the function and structure of her brain. In fact, reading aloud is like fertilizer for the brain. It will make those language synapses grow bigger, stronger, faster, and better, allowing your baby's literacy to blossom and come to literacy fruition easily and beautifully—all beginning in Phase 0.

There is overwhelming evidence that starting early with language is an advantage. Printed language is a visual form of communication—

just as sign language for deaf children is a visual language. Did you know that deaf children have to be immersed in fluent sign language *before age four* to grow to be maximally competent as a signer? And that if they are immersed in it, they "babble" by signing at roughly the same time speaking babies babble? If they are introduced to signing *after* age four, studies show that they will always sign with "grammatical errors."

The same early advantage holds true for learning a second language. If the second language is introduced after age seven, studies show that the speaker will never likely achieve the perfect grammatical competence and flawless pronunciation of a native speaker.[2] He may communicate effectively, but second-language nuances will be detectable and he will not sound exactly like a native speaker. The best time to immerse children in signing or a second language is during the brain's critical language-absorbing period from birth to age four, and the same is true for immersing them in print language with Phase 0 literacy activities. But what kind of activities are appropriate?

E-Activities-S-Y

The developmentally appropriate, playful, "hands-on" language activities for Phase 0, all presented in this chapter, are *reading aloud* to your child, *book handling*, *hearing and seeing how words are made*, *incorporating rhymes* into everyday activity, and, eventually, *pencil-and-paper activity*. Reading aloud begins at birth and continues into elementary school. But early reading aloud need not be relegated to books. By six months of age you can label a few common objects in the baby's nursery and introduce an activity called *Reading Around Baby's Room* for hearing and seeing how words are made.

The reading around baby's room activity in this chapter shows you how to teach your baby or toddler to read labels or words. At the same time you are focusing your baby's attention on these words, you are drawing attention to speech sounds and showing how English reading tracks from left to right, but it will seem so natural you will not even know you are teaching. Sometimes reading around the room enables babies to learn to read some words even before they can say them. In

Phase 0 you will also begin working with sounds in rhyming activities and other sound play and introduce art activity. You will be encouraging your child to be a pencil-and-paper kid, which will lead to writing and eventually to reading as outlined in Chapter 1.

In creating an activity-based literacy-rich environment at home, you can set an example, too, by reading yourself. In Phase 0 you demonstrate that reading is a source of pleasure, not work. You make board books and fabric books a part of the joy of everyday life. Phase 0 is the time to start taking toddler to story-time events at the local library. It is also the time to start a well-stocked home library—not to forget your child's own personal book box collection—with a variety of types of books, supported by frequent trips to the public library and books given as presents for special occasions. You will know you have been successful when by two years of age your baby is perfectly content to entertain herself happily flipping through a pile of books for twenty minutes while singing and chatting to herself.

E-A-Stimulation-Y

Speech is the most important form of stimulation for your baby, and you can provide no better stimulation in Phase 0 than by reading aloud and dialoguing in a conversation with your baby or toddler about what you are reading. Reading aloud enhances the *quality* of the aural stimulation and allows you to watch her responses and respond back. Being talkative and having conversations with your baby—enhanced by reading aloud—enable your baby to hear millions of words in the first year of life alone. This exposure to a wide variety of words is needed for optimal literacy development.

Book activity and reading aloud stimulate more than just language; they stimulate many areas of your child's development. These hands-on activities stimulate hearing, vision, page turning for motor control, and, of course, social and emotional development. Look at visual development alone: It's likely that book activity and talking about illustrations can be helpful in wiring up depth perception, color vision, fine acuity, and controlled eye movement, all of which emerge by six months of age. You are stimulating vision by pointing out illustrations and stimulating the intellect by developing color concepts when you talk about the red bird, the yellow duck, and the blue horse in Bill Martin's wonderful Phase 0 book, *Brown Bear, Brown Bear, What Do You See?*

One parent I know stimulated large motor skills by walking around with her toddler like a penguin because they were reading about penguins. Creative parents turn reading aloud into game-like activities by acting out parts or taking on roles. If the label on the page in a picture book is *ball*, you can make the book more fun by stimulating motor activity such as a kicking motion as you say, "This says *ball*. Weeee, baby can kick the ball!"

Likewise, you are stimulating memory when you read aloud and dialogue to help the three-year-old Phase 0 child focus on the who, what, when, where, why, and how facts in a story; help him make links to what he already knows; or expand his growing body of general knowledge. How better to stimulate cognitive development, which is the growth of intelligence, than through book sharing and other literacy-based activities?

E-A-S-You

The Y in EASY is a reminder that you are your child's first reading teacher. *You* start early, *you* provide literacy-rich activities, and *you* provide the hands-on stimulation. EASY teaching of Phase 0 reading will not happen without you. One can't simply plop a baby in front of a video or talk on the phone in the baby's presence. You need face-to-face contact so that your baby can see your lips as you speak and watch your smiles and expressions.

Your baby must both see and hear how words work and later be able to look back and forth from the page and illustration to your face. You must take turns—you don't just talk. You listen and observe his responses—starting with coos, body movements, smiles, lip movement—and you respond back. Listening and watching what he does is your cue for what to say next. In essence, you are having a happy conversation with your child while engaging delightfully with print.

The Y in EASY is also a reminder that *you* benefit. Early literacy activities promote parent-infant bonding. Early cuddling contact with your baby as you read to her promotes mothering and parenting skills in the parents. *You will love your baby more by reading to her!* Bonding studies agree that early contact—touching, skin-to-skin contact, the parents' smells (and baby's pleasant scent), which are all part of early read-alouds, improve feelings of love and attachment and make *you* a better parent.[3] Remember, the most powerful enticements for early reading are feelings.

To recap, teaching reading in Phase 0 is EASY: You start *early*, introduce developmentally appropriate literacy *activities*, *stimulate* your emerging reader's mind, and take charge, because *you* are your child's first reading teacher.

GET SET FOR PHASE 0 BY GATHERING MATERIALS AND PREVIEWING ACTIVITIES

Books

Wordless picture books
Nursery rhyme books
Books you can chant
Books you can sing
Pattern books (easy-to-read books with predictable, repeated patterns of text)
Board books (sturdy cardboard books that withstand baby handling)
Soft cloth books
Story books
Information books

Materials for Writing and Book Making

A variety of papers, baby-safe pencils, markers, and crayons
Glue, tape, scissors, stapler, construction paper, paste, safety scissors

Materials for Letter Learning, Word Games, and Sound Play

Blocks, letter tiles, magnetic letters, magnetic boards, 3×5-inch index cards for labels
Specialty books for rhyming and word play
Picture cards

Overview of Activities and Techniques for Phase 0

This list will help you anticipate the activities and techniques ahead for teaching your child in Phase 0. It will also show you when to start each activity based on your child's brain development.

Activities and Techniques for Reading

Reading aloud (starts at birth)
Labeling and reading around the room (starts at six to twelve months)

Activities and Techniques for Drawing and Writing

Getting muscles ready to draw and write (starts at birth)
Art activities (starts soon after birth)
Name writing
Book making (homemade books your baby will enjoy and later read)

Activities and Techniques for Sounds and Pre-spelling

Using rhymes and predictable pattern books (starts at birth)
Blocks and letter tiles (starts at eight to twelve months)

ACTIVITIES FOR PHASE 0 READING

The two major activities for Phase 0 are *reading aloud* and *labeling and reading around the room*.

Reading Aloud

Materials

Choose books from "Great Books for Phase 0 to Get You Started," listed later in this chapter, or similar titles.

Skills Learned

Social and emotional bonding; all language skills; speech sounds; words; visual and hearing development; intelligence.

When to Start

At birth.

Directions

Some of the best advice available for parents on how to read aloud to babies from birth to age two is found in *Baby Read-Aloud Basics: Fun and Interactive Ways to Help Your Little One Discover the World of Words* by Caroline J. Blakemore and Barbara Weston Ramirez,[4] a book that I highly recommend for every parent of a child in Phase 0. They suggest a daily read-aloud routine involving both father and mother or other primary caregivers to build the baby's language and intelligence, but more importantly, to create a bond of comfort and love that begins with the intimacy of being held close, cuddled, and read to. These early feelings of love and attachment establish a family book-sharing habit that lasts for years. Remember, in teaching reading at Phase 0, feelings come first. Reading aloud is all about affection and attention.

Rules for Reading Aloud

Keep books simple and provide lots of repetition.
Use face-to-face contact.
Make conversation with your baby/toddler about the book.
Use elaborations, make connections.
Use affirmations but don't make corrections.
Have fun!

Answers to Questions Parents Ask About Reading Aloud to Children in Phase 0

Q: When is the best time to read to a newborn?

A: Blakemore and Ramirez suggest that almost anytime is an appropriate time to read to a newborn. At birth, babies detect the sound of your voice even when they are asleep. These authors recommend reading during nursing and, after three months, when babies are alert and awake. Read a few minutes at least twice a day, and stop reading when the baby gets restless.

Q: What should you read to young babies?

A: Reading almost anything will help your baby get familiar with your voice. I think it's best to read something you've chosen especially for the baby and give him your full attention. While you are reading, have a "conversation" that makes the experience personal and intimate.

In the first six months, reading aloud focuses on modeling sounds. Choose a book that is delightful for you and one that you would love for your child to read to you some day. It should also be one that can help create an intimate experience between you and your baby. The language in the book should be simple, clear, and happy. Since repetition is important for laying down the neural tracks of language, choose a book that you will enjoy reading over and over again. Your child may want you to read his favorites to him literally hundreds of times in the years ahead and will read them from memory himself after he starts speaking. Because sound categorizations are being wired into your baby's brain, nursery rhyme books and books that can be chanted or sung are good choices. Their simplicity and repetition of sounds is perfect for Phase 0.

Q: How should I hold my baby when reading aloud?

A: Make sure you are both comfortable. Choose a quiet environment without too much background noise or distractions so that you have your baby's attention and he can hear you. Hold him in your arms so that your arm supports his head and so that he can see your lips. His eyes should be within eight or ten inches of your face so that he can both hear and see how the words are made. After about two months hold the baby so that he can see both your face and the illustrations. After several months you can hold your baby in your lap, prop him between your legs as you sit on the floor, or read lying next to him with baby lying on his back. Read in bed propped by pillows. If you are sitting in a chair with the book in your outstretched hand, toddlers sometimes like to read standing braced against your legs in a position making it easy for them to turn pages.

Q: When should a baby start looking at illustrations?

A: Your baby's vision and visual-recognition memory limit what she can gain from looking at illustrations during the first months after birth. Though she sees black-and-white designs, she will not likely be able to see or remember illustrations until three to five months of age. It's not necessary that she see the illustrations in the first few weeks, because her vision is fuzzy and two-dimensional. She can see color in about three months, and she likes bold colors such as red, green, blue, and yellow.[5] Shape, detail, depth perception, and spatial location will emerge within about six months.[6] Focusing attention and talking about illustrations while reading aloud may help babies refine vision. Some experts feel that it's good to provide stimulation before certain abilities are apparent.

Q: How do I know baby is responding to read-alouds?

A: Your baby's reactions within the first month will include body movements, grasping, sucking, kicking, smiles, and lip movement. Babies begin to smile at about three weeks of age. She'll respond not only to your voice but also to your touch, to skin-to-skin contact, and to smell during read-alouds. She's really getting to know you and love you, and she loves this attention. Your Phase 0 Literacy Milestones Diary (located at the end of this chapter) guides you in tracking literacy development over time.

Q: How can I make reading aloud more active and interesting?

A: Babies love to be rocked. It's soothing and beneficial to the baby's mind. They will love rocking to the rhythm of a rhyme or poem. Turning the page and seeing what comes next is similar to peek-a-boo, a natural baby thrill. Baby smiles when you read, "This little pig went to the market," and wiggle his toes. Later, when you are reading around the room, giggle, bounce, and spin when you read and point to words. Baby will be delighted by this active addition to reading words because it makes it more fun. Make reading more interesting by calling attention to illustrations, using motions to fit what's on the page, changing your voice with different characters, adding animal noises, or adding gestures and sound effects.

Q: What about book handling and turning the pages?

A: Book handling begins early with baby's grasping. Baby's touch sensitivity is first developed in the mouth, so expect babies to explore board books and soft fabric books with their mouths *and* their hands. By one month of age a baby can recognize objects visually that they have explored with their mouths. Babies can point to pictures, turn pages, and pull books out of the book box by around eight months of age. They love cause-and-effect features such as lifting flaps, touching different textures, or pushing noise buttons in books.

Q: How should I read when I read aloud to babies?

A: A high-pitched, highly intonated, singsong style of speech called "motherese" is favored by young babies and should be spoken by caregivers, including fathers. Motherese is slower and slightly louder than regular speech, with wider contrasts in pitch and contrasts between syllables and words, making it easier for the baby to perceive than adult speech. Motherese comes naturally to caregivers and is cross-cultural. When speaking motherese, remember to use simple words that are enunciated clearly and correctly to provide a model for the pronunciation of the word. Avoid speaking in muddled "baby talk," such as, "U da weetist wiwo aaangell inva wowuld." Keep the reading content simple, and remember, the R in READ is for *repetition*. Babies love hearing the same story or nursery rhyme over and over again, and the repetition strengthens the neural pathways for particular sounds, words, and phrases.

Q: What about teaching sounds?

A: Do a lot of vocalization and playing with sounds during early read-alouds. Listen to your baby, and after two months, when your baby starts babbling, repeat the babbles during a read-aloud, showing delight in her and in the sounds. The babbles and back-and-forth interactions are part of the conversation you are having. Make sure your baby can see your lips when you babble back. In the months to come, move to focusing attention to syllables and rhymes. When you talk about the alphabet, teach the *sound*, not the name of the letter. That is to say, you introduce the sound of a letter before a letter's name.

Q: What is dialogue reading?

A: Dialogue reading is when you create a dialogue as you read the story with your child. Use both text and illustrations as a cue for talking about what's happening in the story and what's on the page. Ask your child questions and encourage his responses. Elaborate and make connections with what's on the page. After eight or nine months, model the reading first, so that the child gets the gist of the story, but in repeated readings take plenty of opportunity to pause, reflect, point out, and comment. Use common sense and trust your own judgment. Your dialogue should reflect the level at which you think your child is able to think about and respond to what's on the page.

In *What's Going On in There: How the Brain and Mind Develop in the First Five Years of Life*, neurobiologist Lise Eliot offers extremely high praise for reading aloud early:

> There's nothing like cuddling up together with a story to create the perfect, cozy opportunity for language-learning. Simple, bright picture books captivate babies and guarantee that they are focused on precisely the items your words are referring to. Illustrated storybooks help toddlers and young preschoolers understand long phrases and sentences. For older preschoolers and grade-schoolers, pictureless books teach that words alone can create imagery and entice them to want to read on their own. And try, if you can, to keep up your own reading, especially in front of the kids, since this sets a powerful example they will want to imitate.[7]

Great Books for Phase 0

Goodnight Moon by Margaret Wise Brown, illustrated by Clement Hurd (Harper, 1947)
A classic bedtime story loved by parents and children alike for its endearing text and musical calming effect. A little bunny says "goodnight" to all the familiar things in his room. This may be one of the first books your child learns to read from memory.

Fingerplays and Songs for the Very Young by Carolyn Croll (Random House, 2001)
This wonderful little board book gives all the classics, with easy-to-follow instructions for what to do while chanting or singing the rhymes. Actions involve baby's hands, feet, and toes.

The Helen Oxenbury series, including books such as *Clap Hands*, *Say Goodnight*, and *Tickle, Tickle* (Little Simon, 1999)
These books feature babies in the illustrations and include both visual and physical stimulation. Babies love looking at other babies!

The Going to Bed Book by Sandra Boynton (Simon and Schuster, 1982)
A lovely board book for learning words about taking a bath, finding pajamas, brushing teeth, and saying good night.

The Berenstain Bears Old Hat, New Hat by Stan and Jan Berenstain (Random House, 1970)
A wonderful board book with two-word sentences that babies can later learn to read from memory.

Ten, Nine, Eight by Molly Bang (Greenwillow Books, 1983)
A board book for counting when baby is ready for bed.

Moo, Baa, La, La, La by Sandra Boynton (Simon and Schuster, 1995)
Every baby loves to play, "What does the _______ say?" This is a perfect little board book where dogs "bow wow," cats "meow," cows "moo," and pigs say "la, la, la." A great choice for teaching sounds and later for reading syllables. Perfect interest level and word choice for early reading. This book is pure fun!

But Not the Hippopotamus by Sandra Boynton (Simon and Schuster, 1982)
A great board book for teaching rhymes. All kinds of things happen in this book where the "hog and the frog hurry out for a jog."

Pat the Bunny by Dorothy Kunhardt (Random House, 1940)
A wonderful interactive touch and feel-good book that encourages babies to do all the fun things babies love to do: pat the bunny, look in the mirror, wave bye-bye, clap with delight, and gesture that bunny and baby are "Soooo big!"

Mice Squeak, We Speak by Arnold Shapiro, illustrated by Tomie dePaola (G. P. Putnam's Sons, 1997)
What a clever book for baby who is learning to talk! All of baby's favorite animals are here to neigh, cluck, howl, growl, and croak—all beautifully illustrated in vivid colors. With just two words on almost every page, this is a great book to be any Phase 0 child's first reader.

Piggies by Don and Audrey Wood (Harcourt Brace, 1991)
Beautifully illustrated by Don Wood, this lovely interactive touchy and feely book is another wonderful first reader for Phase 0 with bold print and two or three words on a page.

Brown Bear, Brown Bear, What Do You See? by Bill Martin, Jr., illustrated by Eric Carle (Harcourt Brace, 1967)
A delightful easy-to-read story with repeated pattern and rhyme recommended for Phase 0–2 that many children learn to memory read independently by the time they move into Phase 2. Children delight in the animals, color words, and beautiful illustrations, and it's a great book for building a beginning reader's confidence.

Time for Bed by Mem Fox, illustrated by Jane Dyer (Harcourt Brace, 1993)
"It's time for bed" for all the little animals—and baby, too. A beautifully illustrated time-for-bed book with repeated text and lovely illustrations. Perfect for early memory reading.

A Is for Astronaut by Sian Tucker (Simon and Schuster, 1995)
The perfect lift-the-flap ABC book for learning to speak and later to read new words, with bold colors and clear illustrations that babies and toddlers will love.

The Seals on the Bus by Lenny Hort, illustrated by G. Brian Karas (Henry Holt, 2000)
Based on the song, "The Wheels on the Bus Go Round and Round," this is a great sing-along book with all kinds of great words for learning sounds as the monkeys go eeeeh, eeeeh, eeeeh; the skunks go sssss, sssss, ssss; and the vipers go hiss, hiss, hiss, along with all kinds of other surprises. Words are presented in big bold letters so baby or toddler can "read" along, pointing to the words on the page as soon as he can speak.

Where Is the Green Sheep? by Mem Fox, illustrated by Judy Horacek (Harcourt, 2004)
Another great book by Mem Fox, this one is perfect for learning to speak and later read new words. Perfect word choice and repetition for early readers.

Reading aloud offers the perfect opportunity for your baby and toddler to learn to READ as you interact with Repetition, Enthusiasm, and Activity and eventually move on to Drawing through pencil-and-paper activity. But don't stop with reading aloud, because babies and toddlers have great capacity for learning about reading simply by playing around with words. With a little help from you, they can figure out how words work.

LABELING AND READING AROUND THE ROOM

Materials

Markers; 5×8 blank word cards on sturdy cardboard; tape or clips.

Skills Learned

Concept of word; reading words as "logos" (logographically); labeling play; the concept that words are made of sounds; attention to the sounds in a word; the concept that letter-symbols represent sounds; showing directionality from left to right by "reading with your finger"; reading first sight words; connecting new print information to what's already known.

When to Start

Six to twelve months and beyond. (If you start early and establish a routine it will be easier to keep the baby interested. Waiting eighteen months or later may make it harder to get the toddler interested in this activity.)

Directions

In this activity you post and point out word labels in your child's room that you have created, and you engage in labeling play by using sight, sounds, and action in the here and now to draw attention to the words. Reading around the room is a good way to focus your child's attention on individual words, which may be pulled from words in read-alouds or from common conversation.

Parents often ask, "When do I begin labeling and reading around the room?" I recommend starting this word game around six months of age with just a few word cards, but you should use your own judgment. These facts about your baby's capabilities will help you: Research shows that five-month-olds can recognize and remember a visual stimulus for up to two weeks after seeing it.[8] Furthermore, babies may understand words five months before they speak them. These facts suggest an early start, and in the final analysis, it's never too early to start. The worst that can happen is that you will be ignored, but you won't miss the opportunity to create and capture baby's early interest in words.

The "Reading Around the Room" game has five basic steps:

1. Use words that your baby sees and hears in favorite books or hears in conversation.
2. Make labels and post them in your child's room.
3. Use the left-to-right finger-tracking procedure presented below.
4. Show the words once or twice a day.
5. Make the word viewing interactive and fun.

Begin by labeling a few familiar objects in baby's room. Labeling and reading around the room is a supplement to reading aloud to children, so you should allow your read-aloud book selections to help guide you in deciding what word cards to choose as labels. For example, if you're reading a book about red fire engines, write "red" on a number of word cards and attach them to everything that is red in your baby's room. Your child will benefit from the repetition of seeing and hearing the words both in repeated read-alouds and as labels. Color words may be written in the appropriate color.

Start with just five to ten words. Choose simple words, often with a consonant-vowel-consonant pattern, such as *bed*, *box*, *red*, *hat*, but don't be reluctant to include any words baby delights in or words that are part of baby's daily routine, such as *door*, *chair*, *truck*—or a pet or family member's name taped to a photo. Tape *fish* or *hamster* to the respective aquarium or cage. But remember, you only start with about five words. Once your baby starts to show interest in this activity, gradually add more words to the five you started with. Good words to include later on are the names of body parts, such as *eyes*, *toes*, *nose*, *ear*, *lips*, *foot*, *hand*, *finger*, or *hair* placed near the tub or diaper changing area. When you are changing a diaper you can jiggle the foot and talk about baby's foot to highlight the word *foot*. This may be the same word the baby sees and hears in a book labeling body parts. The idea is simply to provide repeated exposures to seeing and hearing a few high-frequency words so that your baby or toddler is exposed to them in an active context over and over. It's appropriate to include words that you use frequently during everyday activities such as *tub*, *soap*, and *brush*, and, of course, favorite toys: *bunny*, *bear*, *baby*, *doll*, *truck*, *duck*, or *fish*, as well as action words such as *clap*, *smile*, *arms up*. Start with just a few words that your baby will hear often and delight in, provide lots of repetition, and when baby or toddler begins to recognize a few words, gradually add new words to the activity. You may add additional words based on your child's responses.

Write the words on 5×8 cards. Post them on objects as labels or keep a few word cards, such as those for body parts, handy for use during daily routines such as bathing or changing diapers. For example, if you have been reading *Fingerplays and Songs for the Very Young* by Carolyn Croll and highlighting the words *finger*, *hand*, and *toe*, you may extend the read-aloud exposure to these words with word cards for *finger*, *hand*, and *toe* in the bath area.

Create the appropriate mindset. Remember, this is a game, not a lesson. You are simply engaging in word play, labeling play, and having fun with sounds. The session may be as brief as thirty seconds three times a day. Think of it as a ninety-second-a-day word game that may be extended if you and your baby are enjoying it. Keep in mind that your baby's brain loves repetition. As you move about the room pointing to words, incorporate movement such as bouncing or spinning as you encounter a word to be practiced, simply to make it active. Feel free to giggle and have fun. Make sure your baby hears the word, sees the word, and tracks eye movement each time you play the game, while you incorporate repetition and enthusiasm. You will also begin to draw attention to the sounds in words. By repeating the word as stretched-out sounds, you are practicing phonemes. This activity will not hurt your baby and many parents report their babies can read some of the words within six months after they begin playing the labeling game with a few word cards.

Word-Reading Routine

Put the word in some meaningful and fun context and make the word encounter interactive. Make sure the word is close enough for your baby to see. Point under the first letter and start reading, moving your finger from left to right while saying, "This says ______! You can read ______! Make sure you have your child's attention so that her eye tracks your finger as it moves from left to right each time you say the word.

Next, stretch out the sounds in a word and point to the letters in sequence: *red*—/r/-/ĕ/-/d/—*red*. You are using the age-old ABC method of teaching reading, but remember to say the *sounds*, not the letter names, and to treat the activity as a game, not a lesson.

Here's an example: With the card for *bed*, follow the routine using the motherese style of speech:

> Here's baby's *bed*! (Maybe gently shaking the bed to get baby's attention.) Let's *read* the word *bed*! Pointing to the word say, "This says *bed*," while tracking your reading of the word from left to right, with your pointer finger gliding under the word. Then, using the *sound* of the letter instead of the *name* of the letter, glide the finger under the three sounds of *bed* as you pronounce it in stretched-out sounds: /b/-/ĕ/-/d/—*bed*.

ACTIVITIES FOR PHASE 0 WRITING (DRAWING AND ART)

Phase 0 activities are geared toward strengthening your baby's muscles and conditioning them to draw and write. It's important to understand which art activities are appropriate during this developmental phase.

Conditioning your baby's muscles starts at birth and later includes classic play activity, such as the following:

- Interactions with blocks, puzzles, and book handling
- Using alphabet blocks and magnetic letters to talk about sounds and letter names
- Using puzzles to match labels and words

Art Activities

Materials

Various kinds of baby-safe markers, crayons, and pens; assortments of paper; stickers; glitter; glue; finger paints, paints, and brushes; chalk; craft materials; clay or Play-Doh for toddlers. The possibilities are endless.

Skills Learned

Intelligence; creativity; symbolic representation; fine motor skills for writing; social interaction; self-confidence; expression of feelings.

When to Start

Art begins at birth. As soon as baby can grasp, you can introduce activities that will develop the muscles and coordination involved in later drawing and writing. When your baby reaches about one year of age you can help her hold a crayon and make a mark. She will love the cause and effect. Smearing food is a precursor to finger painting. Making foot or hand imprints in sand at the beach or in clay is a precursor to sculpting, which, like reading, is a representational form of communication. Independent pencil-and-paper activity may begin soon after twelve months of age.

Expressions of creativity should be encouraged as soon as your baby can explore the visual images on a page. Getting muscles ready to draw and write begins with early grasping. By two years of age, give your child a crayon and paper and you'll have a masterpiece for the refrigerator door.

Your baby's brain is wired up for symbolic representation and she thinks symbolically when she plays with a doll or soft toy, waves "bye-bye," head-shakes "no," makes marks and tells you what they mean, or scribbles and asks, "What did I write?" In the beginning, babies should be encouraged to scribble for the sheer joy of scribbling. Eventually, this intensely creative thinking activity leads not only to art, but also to letters that symbolize sounds, and later to representations of words and writing.

How soon does representational drawing begin? Researchers who gave crayons and paper to babies between one and two years of age, and asked them to draw "Mommy," found that the scribbles and markings for the head were at the top, the markings for the feet were at the bottom, and the markings for the tummy were in the middle.[9] Babies learn to trust in themselves and in what they are doing in art activity, which builds self-confidence.

Early scribbling gives babies control over cause and effect. Self-confident pen-and-paper children whose abstractions on paper represent whatever they want them to become self-confident writers and readers. Pencil-and-paper kids become risk-takers who aren't afraid to make mistakes, which is necessary for natural language development and later for the child's natural developmental first attempts at spelling and writing. Early drawing builds the stamina and interest to be self-motivated and self-directed and the ability to work hard, engaging in a task for sustained time, which are important foundations for reading and later academic pursuits.

Directions

There is no right or wrong way to begin art or pencil-and-paper activity as long as the activity is safe, interesting, and fun. Follow these tips for budding artists and writers:

Tips for Getting Started in Art and Writing Projects

Help your baby develop hand and finger muscles (by giving him toys to hold and shake, such as rattles or soft toys that can be squeezed, especially ones that squeak).

Draw attention to illustrations in books.

Talk about colors and shapes.

Guide babies in making marks with markers.
Model drawing.
Draw something together.
Draw while you tell your child a story.
Connect literacy and labeling to play activity.
Make pretend grocery lists, signs, and card messages.
Take turns using the crayon.
Experiment with tearing and crumpling paper.
Remember that smeared food is a precursor to drawing.
Think of your baby's joy or fascination with smearing food as a cue to introduce art.
Draw lines in sand at the beach or in a sandbox, in snow, or in the fog on the shower door.
Finger paint.
Encourage play with magnetic letters and shapes.
Experiment with clay.
Give interesting drawing and writing tools for holiday gifts.
Give your child interesting pads of paper.
Use dry-erase boards.
Use magnetic boards, magic slates, and magnetic letters, which are great for the refrigerator.
Involve toddlers in e-mails and text messages to correspond to family and friends.
Have your toddler tell about his drawing.
Always praise and never criticize attempts at art.
Make books for your baby with photos of faces, body parts, and familiar items.
Sign and date your child's artwork and writing.
Celebrate and display art and early writing.
Give your child's signed artwork as gifts.

Name Writing

Your child will open the door to print awareness, letter knowledge, and phonemic awareness once she moves from pretending to write to writing her name. Learning to write one's own name is one of the most important early literacy milestones and is correlated to many later literacy accomplishments. Children have a natural proclivity to wanting to do it. Being able to write one's own name is a huge confidence booster.

Materials

Pencils, pens, markers, paper, pads. Use writing materials that are safe, comfortable, and motivating for your child.

Skills Learned

Symbolic representation, letter names and formation, the concept of what a word is, left-to-right directionality of print, many of the foundational aspects of reading words.

When to Start

After your child starts to pretend to write, often around two or three years of age.

Directions

Many children who scribble and draw early learn to write their own names roughly between two and three years of age or soon thereafter. There seems to be a wide range for name writing, perhaps because it depends on pencil-and-paper experience. If your child is pretending to write, it may be time to try helping her write her name.

Begin by teaching your child how to hold the pencil, as illustrated in Figure 4.2. Don't worry about placement of the name on the page—paper position will come later. If your child has developed a clear preference for one hand or the other, it's recommended that you teach him or her to use that hand in writing. To find out whether your child is left or right handed, place a hand puppet on the table and observe which hand he or she puts the puppet on, which is usually the dominant hand. You may also note hand preference for actions such as hammering nails, throwing a ball, or placing caps on objects. Be flexible after demonstrations of proper handgrip and allow your child to explore his or her own preference.

The basic techniques for learning to write one's name are tracing and copying. Invite your child to try tracing his name. Write his name with a yellow highlighter and place your hand on top of his to show proper letter strokes and left-to-right directionality. Offer lots of praise. Repeat the process frequently and encourage both name writing and name tracing. Make a big deal about signing artwork and labeling things in the home with your child's name. Hand strength, dominance, and precision may develop gradually, so be patient.

Figure 4.2: Pencil Position and Paper Position

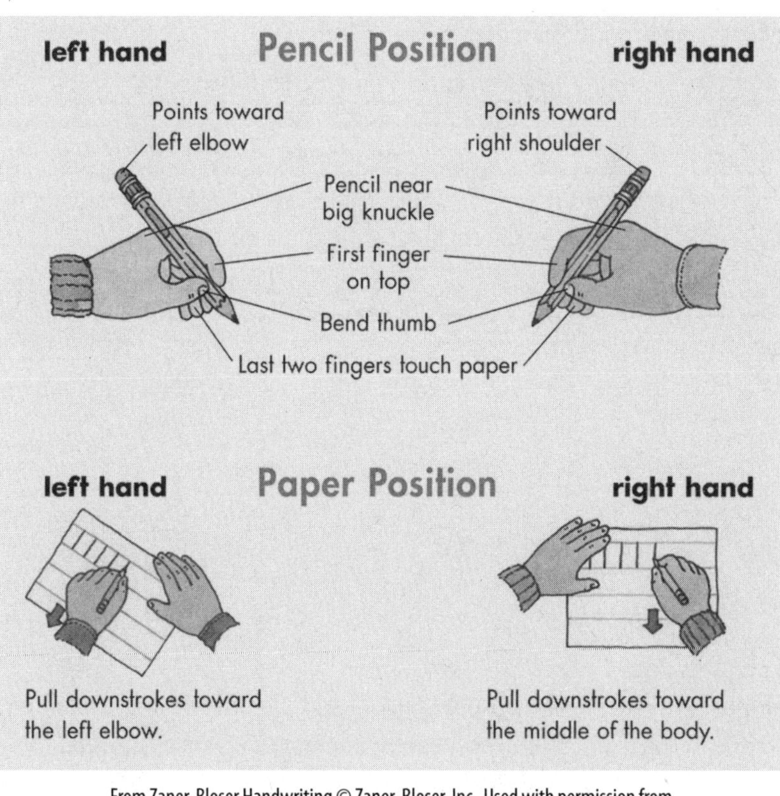

Figure 4.3: Manuscript Alphabet

Zaner-Bloser Manuscript Alphabet

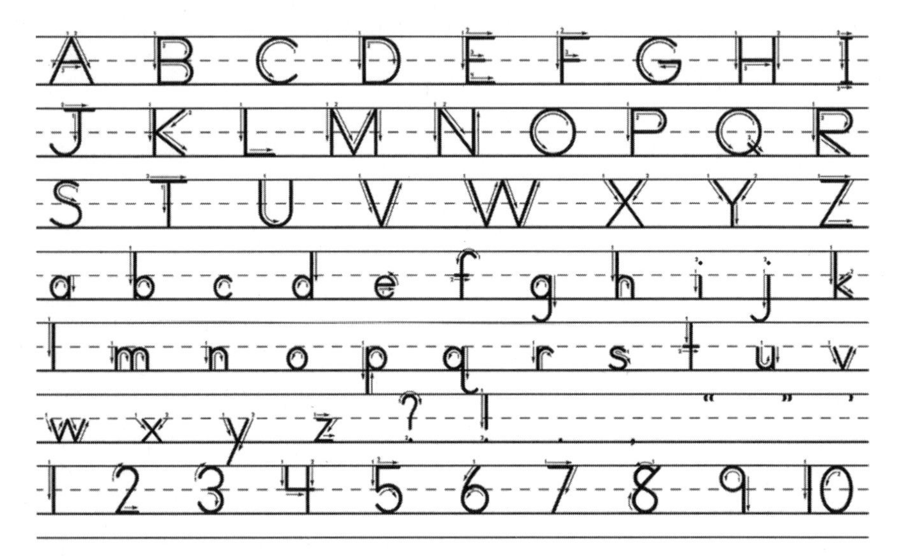

Figure 4.3 shows the proper stroke sequence to use as a model when you work with your child on letter formation. For example, for the letter "b," trace the vertical bar from top to bottom and then make the circle. Continue to encourage both tracing and copying to lead your child to write his or her name independently. Children are generally not expected to develop perfect manuscript letter formation until the

end of first grade, so even though you model correct letter strokes, be very tolerant of imperfect letter formation from preschoolers. Practice name writing in short, frequent sessions, making sure to always make the lesson upbeat and fun. Letter recognition should begin long before your child enters school. After your child becomes thoroughly familiar with the letters in his or her name, confident reading and writing will follow far more easily.

Book Making

Make easy-to-read homemade books with photos, labels, and phrases that you want your baby to recognize and remember. Use heavy cardboard and sturdy materials that will allow for rereading homemade books and handling them over and over again. Remember that babies are innately interested in faces and in exploring themselves and things within their reach. Photos of baby's family, baby's world, or baby's activities make great first homemade books that baby will "read" by memory with repetition—sometimes soon after he begins speaking.

Here are some models to get you started. Notice that I'm asking you to start out with easy one-word labels. Your baby will delight in memory reading these easy books soon after he begins to speak. The models below incorporate rhythm and rhyme to make them more appealing and fun. Make a title page and a page for each photo with one word or phrase on a page:

Who Is This? (Title page)

Baby (Page 1—photo of your baby)

Mom (Page 2—photo of baby's mom, and so on, with photos for each page listed below)

Dad
(sister)
(brother)
Grandma
Grandpa
(pet's name)

Look at Me! What Is This? (Title page)

Eyes (Page 1—close-up photo of baby's eyes)

Nose (Page 2—close-up photo of baby touching his nose, and so on, with photos for each page listed below)

Ears
Toes
Fingers
Feet
Belly Button
Tickle, tickle, tickle.

All About Baby (Title page, with photos of your baby for each page listed below)

Baby sleeps.
Baby eats.
Baby smiles.
Baby cries.
Baby moves feet and toes.
Baby grows, and grows, and grows!
Three months!
Six months!
One year! Wow!

I Can (Title page, with photos of your baby for each page listed below)

I can smile.
I can clap.
I can coo.
I can nap.
I can reach.
I can sing.
I can do most anything!

ACTIVITIES FOR PHASE 0 SOUNDS, SPEECH DEVELOPMENT, AND PRE-SPELLING

Activities for sound and speech development as well as pre-spelling activities have been embedded in all the activities that have been introduced thus far in this chapter. All read-aloud books, especially caption books, rhyming books, predictable pattern books, and easy alphabet books, provide excellent resources for developing all language skills. Every time you read them your child will be taking in information about the sounds in words, rhyming sounds, and syllable sounds as well as learning new words. There is a wide range of attention spans in children, even when they are the same age. Your child's attention span might be a few seconds, or it might be forty-five minutes. It can change depending on how tired or alert she might be, how interesting the activity is to her, and other circumstances. Don't force an activity beyond the point where your child is engaged.

Remember to talk to your baby, read aloud often, and incorporate sounds into everything that you do. When specifically focusing attention on letters, start out with the sounds of the letters rather than letter names. It's easier for Phase 0 children to grasp that the letter "M," for example, is the sound /m/ than to learn that it has the letter name "em." Teach the sound first, and then teach the concept that the letter has a name. Once babies and toddlers begin to recognize some letters and the basic sounds that they make, it's easy to follow through and learn the names of the letters. Eventually your child will master the sounds, names, and forms of all of the letters.

Record your baby's progress in the "Literacy Milestones Diary" at the end of this chapter and in your journal of "Special Memories and Keepsakes," which can be found in the Appendix. Once your child is able to spell her name, it's time to move to the next chapter, Phase 1.

Tips for Teaching Sounds

- Read rhymes, chants, and songs because of their repetitious and musical qualities.
- Include actions during read-alouds, such as tickling baby's toes and stomach.

- Give your toddler a high-five for rhyming words.
- Fluctuate the pitch of your voice to make read-alouds fun.
- Teach your baby the rhymes and chants that you learned as a baby or toddler.
- Use fingerplays (rhymes, poems, or songs with simple actions or finger movements that relate to the content), hand motions, and songs.
- Use repetition so that your baby will expect the actions that go with the rhyme.
- Repeat what your baby says as if his verbal response is language.
- Talk to your baby about what you are doing.
- Use different expressions, tones, and volumes when you speak to your baby.
- Adjust your actions to the level of development of your baby.
- Choose a position so that your face, your body movements, and the book page can be seen by your baby.
- Read often so that your baby or toddler commits rhymes to memory.
- Read in motherese.
- Combine rhymes and songs with movement.
- Clap out syllables in words.
- Use sound effects for animals, vehicles, and actions.
- Let your baby's interest and moods help you gauge when to end the activity.
- Make sure you're having fun!

PHASE 0 LITERACY MILESTONES DIARY[10]

Learning to read is a major step in child development. The milestones checklist below gives you a map of the approximate age and order when important reading, drawing, writing, speaking, and spelling milestones might be expected. Every child develops on his or her own time schedule—so be patient! You may supplement this easy checklist with your own notes and observations. Record favorite books and memorable vignettes marking your child's literacy development. A "Special Memories and Keepsakes" template provided in the Appendix will aid you in sharpening your focus.

This easy guide for checking off milestones can be a delightful record of your child's progress and make your child's literacy development more transparent. You may not have recognized that many of the items you check below are marking posts for literacy development.

Watch Me Grow in Reading

Enjoy seeing evidence of your child's literacy development while reading aloud. Watching your baby or toddler's responses during read-alouds is one of the best ways to monitor development. For example, you will note that higher intellectual functioning, enhanced memory, more expressions of emotion, and general awareness surge around eight months of age. Another breakthrough comes once your child begins to use about fifty words—often around eighteen months to two years of age, with a surge in word learning. Around this time young children have the capacity to learn as many as two new words an hour. This word surge is enhanced enormously by reading aloud.[11]

My Firsts: Reading

BIRTH TO AROUND SIX MONTHS

- ☐ I respond physically to speech during read-alouds (grasping, sucking, body movements).
- ☐ I smile when you smile during read-alouds.
- ☐ I turn toward your voice during read-alouds.
- ☐ I respond to fingerplays (rhymes, poems, or songs with simple actions or finger movements that relate to the content) with happy reactions and alertness.
- ☐ I look back and forth from the book to your face.
- ☐ I have baby-talk "conversations" with you.

AROUND SIX MONTHS TO TWELVE MONTHS

- ☐ I increase in vocalization and speech development during read-alouds.
- ☐ I respond to particular books with joy, surprise, laughter, and curiosity.

- [ ] I respond to illustrations.
- [ ] I attempt to turn pages.
- [ ] I anticipate what's coming next and express emotions appropriate for the text.

AROUND TWELVE MONTHS TO EIGHTEEN MONTHS

- [ ] I continue to grow in intellect and memory as evidenced in read-aloud responses.
- [ ] I continue to grow in emotional and social awareness as evidenced in read-aloud responses.
- [ ] I advance in language, labeling, and responses to illustrations.
- [ ] I can hold a book right-side-up.
- [ ] I understand where to start and how to turn pages in order.

AROUND EIGHTEEN MONTHS TO TWO YEARS

- [ ] I ask and answer simple questions while reading.
- [ ] I pretend to read on my own.
- [ ] I point out and show understanding of familiar illustrations in favorite books.
- [ ] I can crawl or walk to the book box and select my own books.

AROUND TWO YEARS TO THREE YEARS AND BEYOND

- [ ] I can talk about past events and about what I know and expand upon it.
- [ ] I can answer who, what, when, where, how, and why questions.
- [ ] I can anticipate what's coming next in a story and talk about it.
- [ ] I can retell stories and create my own narratives.
- [ ] I can pretend to read with more than one action, such as mimicking, memorizing a few words, turning pages, and naming objects and illustrations.
- [ ] I enjoy listening to more elaborate stories.

Watch Me Grow in Drawing and Writing

Within three or four months your baby can begin paying attention to color, art, and illustrations. When choosing books and drawing your baby's attention to illustrations, keep in mind that babies are attracted to bold patterns and primary colors. Babies can recognize faces immediately after birth and have an innate preference for looking at faces—even in illustrations. Five-month-olds can remember a visual stimulus two weeks after seeing it. Below you will note precursors to drawing and writing related to visual and fine-motor development.

My Firsts: Drawing and Writing

BIRTH TO SIX MONTHS

- ☐ I attempt to grasp the book.
- ☐ I attempt to turn pages.
- ☐ I attempt to pick up a book.
- ☐ I attend to cause-and-effect book features such as flaps with hidden pictures or buttons for sound.
- ☐ I respond to touch-and-feel books.

AROUND SIX MONTHS TO TWELVE MONTHS

- ☐ I am more responsive to illustrations.
- ☐ I demonstrate motor development, grasping pages, and crawling or rolling to pick up a book.
- ☐ I can select a favorite book.
- ☐ I'm very interested in cause-and-effect features in books, such as flaps with hidden pictures or buttons for sound.

AROUND TWELVE MONTHS TO EIGHTEEN MONTHS

- ☐ I make sweeping and writing motions, creating marks and images in high-chair spills or with finger paints.
- ☐ I can grasp baby-safe writing and coloring tools.
- ☐ I show interest in making marks.
- ☐ I express a desire to draw or write.
- ☐ I like to try drawing or writing with the help of a caregiver.

- [ ] I can tell you about object names in my drawings (after speaking begins).
- [ ] I make some marks that represent writing.

AROUND EIGHTEEN MONTHS TO TWO YEARS

- [ ] I enjoy drawing and coloring activities.
- [ ] I use various drawing and writing tools (markers, crayons, fat pencils, paint brushes, finger paints, chalk).
- [ ] I use marks to record messages.
- [ ] I can draw a picture and pretend to write about it.

AROUND TWO YEARS TO THREE YEARS AND BEYOND

- [ ] I scribble or use wavy writing or loopy writing to express messages.
- [ ] I can think up things to draw or write about on my own.
- [ ] I enjoy more complex illustrations in books.
- [ ] I can plan to write specific content before making marks, such as planning to make a grocery list.
- [ ] I show interest in letters and know that they represent language.

Watch Me Grow in Sounds and Spelling

Learning how sounds and letters work together is a major part of learning to read quickly and well. Part of the neural circuitry for mapping letters to speech sounds begins in Phase 0 with your baby's speech development. Likewise, your child's pretend writing with scribbling and her wavy and loopy writing are symbolic representations that precede spelling. These forms of early writing surface dramatically during Phase 0. As you follow the checklist below, remember that there are wide age variations in normal development.

My Firsts: Sounds and Spelling

BIRTH TO SIX MONTHS

- [ ] I make my first coo's, ooh's, and aah's.
- [ ] I laugh and smile with you during read-alouds.
- [ ] I can have a "conversation" with you during read-alouds.

AROUND SIX MONTHS TO TWELVE MONTHS

- [ ] I can recognize spoken words.
- [ ] I can link symbols with sounds, objects, people, actions, and concepts.
- [ ] I can "get the book," wave bye-bye, and recognize a brother, sister, or family member's name.

AROUND TWELVE MONTHS TO EIGHTEEN MONTHS

- [ ] I can babble sounds such as "ma," ba," "na," "da," and "ga."
- [ ] I can use at least four consonants.
- [ ] I can use single words to express ideas, such as "baba" (bottle), meaning "I want some milk."

AROUND EIGHTEEN MONTHS TO TWO YEARS

- [ ] I can put two words together to make short sentences, such as "baby book" or "algone milk."
- [ ] I can make comments about characters in favorite books, such as "fox bad!"
- [ ] I learn words quickly from illustrations.
- [ ] I understand 50 to 150 words and use 10 to 50 or more words.

AROUND TWO YEARS TO THREE YEARS AND BEYOND

- [ ] I have a surge in word learning—as many as two hundred a month.
- [ ] I move beyond two-word utterances and demonstrate an explosion in grammar skills by stringing more and more words together in meaningful speech.
- [ ] I can talk about past events and about what I know and expand upon it.
- [ ] I can respond to simple phonological games, such as recognizing rhyming words and clapping syllables.
- [ ] I can scribble and make letter-like features or letter-like forms.
- [ ] I can attempt to write my name.

Note: When your child can write her name independently, she has moved to Phase 1.

5

TEACHING READING IN PHASE 1

It's Time for the ABC's!

YOUR TODDLER HAS now learned how to write her name. In Phase 1, she will learn how to read a few words. She will use random letters to write messages, and she will attempt to imitate the reading of easy books. This is also a time for learning all about the alphabet.

Look at the sample of Phase 1 writing in Figure 5.1. You will not be able to read this sample because, as with all Phase 1 writing, the letters do not match the sounds; the letters are just random. This is the phase of writing development that is most like babbling in spoken language development. When a parent looks at this kind of babble of random letters, it's impossible to know exactly what the child was attempting to communicate. Just as your child begins speech by babbling the sounds that are the building blocks of spoken language, she will begin to explore early writing with letters—the building blocks of the printed word.

Phase 1 is the perfect time to intensify your focus on the alphabet with your child—moving beyond alphabetic symbols as sounds to letter names as well as the sounds they represent. Continue to read aloud, but now with more attention to how words and letters work. Keep your child engaged, challenged, and proud of his early writing explorations.

Figure 5.1: Sample of Phase 1 Writing

Inspired by your enthusiasm, your child may share what a particular piece of Phase 1 writing means. Write what your child says at the bottom of the page, using your child's own words, so that she can "read back" the word or phrase from memory. "My goodness," you will exclaim. "You can read adult writing!" Your little one is gaining confidence and taking her first steps toward reading.

Phase 1 is the first time you really begin focusing on your child as a writer. Here's what you should expect:

- The journey begins with your child learning to write her first name—a huge breakthrough.
- Letters are used to represent a message.
- Your child's first "spellings" will be with random letters.
- No letter-sound correspondence is evident.

- Your child may not start with left-to-right directionality.
- Letters may float on the page—top to bottom or sideways.
- Spacing may not occur between words.
- Your child is just beginning to learn letter names and letter formation.
- Many letters may still be unknown.
- Full alphabet knowledge will take time.
- A few letters may be repeated in letter strings.
- There may be a preference for uppercase letters.
- Uppercase and lowercase letters are mixed in most of your child's writing.

In Phase 1, your child's naive and relatively unsophisticated strategies for writing may parallel her early attempts to read words. Since she doesn't yet know that letters represent sounds, she's not "sounding out" words; rather, she's probably relying on pictures or guessing. She may not be able to match a word that you have read aloud with the correct word unless you point to it. She's "reading" a word like *McDonald's* as a visual logo by cueing on the golden arches—not the letters.

All of this being said, your little Phase 1 genius will shock you with what she *can* do: She can memorize and read back names, signs, labels, short nursery rhymes, poems, verses, and songs with repetition. She can use her memory to read words back to you.

Phase 1 is a great time for memorizing favorite caption books, easy pattern books, pop-up books, board books, and concept books. Your child will have favorite subjects and favorite books, but remember, her favorites may not be yours. If she delights in what seems to you to be a silly, unliterary little book with a finger puppet, then that's what the two of you should be reading. When you can say, "This is a book she *really* enjoys," you have made the right choice for Phase 1.

Phase 1 is when your child:

- Writes with letters but without letter/sound knowledge
- Uses arbitrary cues for word-reading
- Invents spellings with random letters

GET SET FOR PHASE 1 BY GATHERING MATERIALS AND PREVIEWING ACTIVITIES

Books

Add the following books to your collection of favorites from Phase 0:

Wordless picture books
Nursery rhyme books
Books you can chant
Books you can sing
Pattern books (easy-to-read books with predictable, repeated patterns of text)
Board books (sturdy cardboard books that withstand baby handling)
Soft cloth books
Story books
Information books

Materials for Writing and Book Making

A variety of papers, baby-safe pencils, markers, and crayons
Glue, tape, scissors, stapler, construction paper, paste, safety scissors

Materials for Letter Learning, Word Games, and Sound Play

Blocks, letter tiles, magnetic letters, magnetic boards, 3×5-inch index cards for labels
Specialty books for rhyming and word play
Picture cards

Overview of Activities and Techniques for Phase 1

This list will help you anticipate the activities and techniques ahead for teaching your child in Phase 1.

Activities and Techniques for Reading

Reading aloud (continues from Phase 0)
Labeling and reading around the room (continues from Phase 0)

Activities and Techniques for Drawing and Writing

How to position the paper
Art activities
Book making (continues and builds on books started in Phase 0)

Activities and Techniques for Sounds and Pre-spelling

Using rhymes and predictable pattern books (continues from Phase 0)
Blocks and letter tiles (continues from Phase 0 with more emphasis on letter names and letter formation)

ACTIVITIES FOR PHASE 1 READING

Continue the two major reading activities from Phase 0: reading aloud and labeling and reading around the room. Continue to read from your child's favorite books, and notice how her repertoire is growing: She can read more and more books from memory. Engage your child in reading aloud as a knowledge-building experience. Now is the time to focus on the alphabet and how a word is built. Extend the labeling and reading around the room activity to include not only letter sounds but also *letter names.*

Reading Aloud

If you started read-alouds in Phase 0, you are already familiar with the procedure. If you are reading aloud for the first time, go to Chapter 4 to review the basic techniques. Remember, a daily read-aloud routine involving both father and mother, or other primary caregiver, will build your child's language skills and intelligence, and, more importantly, create a bond of comfort and a love of reading. As in Phase 0, feelings come first when reading aloud in Phase 1. The major difference now is that you are going to be pausing more frequently to draw attention to words, letters, and how words work.

Characteristics of Level A Texts for Phase 1

A good match for Phase 1 has two to five words on each page, very uniform structure, and strong picture clues. Examples of materials that may be read from memory by the child in Phase 1 after repeated rereadings include rhymes such as "Jack Be Nimble," poems such as "Roses are Red," and very easy book selections such as *The Pancake* by Roderick Hunt, an example of a Level A book. At first your child will know what words to say by looking at the pictures. Eventually, with repetition from repeated readings, your child will learn to recognize some of the words automatically.

To summarize, good selections for Phase 1 have the following characteristics:

Heavy support from illustrations
Consistent placement of print
Familiar ideas and concepts
Repetition of 1–2 phrases or very short sentence patterns ("I am Sam. Sam I am.")
Repetition with very few word changes
Language similar to your child's speech
Use of labels and phrases[1]

Tips for Reading Aloud at Phase 1

- Read the whole story first and talk about the meaning.
- Model the expression, fluency, feelings, and emotions that you want your child to eventually invoke when reading the material from memory.
- Model and talk about print concepts, such as how to hold the book and turn the pages, where to start on a page, and how directionality of print works.
- Add appropriate sound effects or movement such as animal noises or flapping like a bird's wings to make it fun.
- Talk about words and about the letters in targeted words to reinforce the alphabet knowledge your child already has and extend

her alphabet knowledge. ("This word begins with the same letter as your name!")

- Talk about how the letters match to targeted sounds in words.
- Experience all aspects of the book to extend the activity beyond reading aloud and listening.
- Have a lot of conversation during book-sharing experiences—don't simply read it aloud but use these experiences for knowledge-building.
- Tell about things on the page, explain things, ask questions, think aloud.
- Point to words and track the words in phrases from left to right as you read them.

(Note: If your Phase 1 child seems advanced and is really having an easy time tracking words and memorizing easy text, go to Chapter 6 for information on how to respond during reading aloud at the next level, Phase 2.)

Materials

Easy Level A books and old favorites. (See below for recommendations.)

Skills Learned

Comprehension and concept building; fluency, sight-word recognition, and vocabulary; attention to words and letter knowledge.

When to Start

At birth continuing throughout Phase 1 and beyond.

Directions

In Phase 1, you will read and reread your child's favorite books, making sure the selected books have lots of repetition for easy memorization. Try new books as well to continue introducing fun stories and new vocabulary. Continue the daily read-aloud routine involving Mom and/or Dad or another primary caregiver, and remember that feelings come first.

Rules for Reading Aloud in Phase 1

Keep the reading level simple—caption books with labels and phrases are especially good for Phase 1, as are nursery rhymes.

Enhance the reading-aloud experience by talking about and clarifying your child's understanding of the book being shared.

Use elaborations, make connections. Talk about what's happening in the story.

Use affirmations, and don't make corrections. Be patient and offer lots of praise.

Don't set rigid goals for how long it will take your child to memory read. As long as you both are enjoying the repeated reading of a favorite book, you're making progress. If your child loves long read-aloud sessions, ride the wave. If your child seems reluctant or does not seem interested, try to find a book on a topic he's passionate about. Books with humor often turn the tide with children who have difficulty sitting even for a short session.

Keep the sessions short, light, and fun.

Reread the same selection as often as you can.

If your child isn't responding well with a book, choose another one.

Keep the reading interactive by inviting the child to turn the pages.

Point to the words as you read them, moving at a natural pace.

Read with exaggerated expression so that your child can easily mimic your fluent reading.

Pay attention to the level of text. Begin with Level A books with one-word labels or up to three to five words on a page. As your child moves into Phase 2 you will move up to Level C selections, which often have one or two sentences per page. It is certainly appropriate to read more complex stories to your child as read-alouds as long as she is engaged and enjoying it and wanting to hear more. But the books she will first memorize will likely be the easier-leveled texts.

Great Books for Phase 1

Goodnight Moon by Margaret Wise Brown, illustrated by Clement Hurd (Harper, 1947)

A classic bedtime story loved by parents and children alike for its endearing text and musical calming effect. If you started reading this book in Phase 0 and it became a favorite, your child may read it by memory in Phase 1.

Wiggle Waggle by Jonathan London, illustrated by Michael Rex (Harcourt Brace, 1999)

Use this book to gauge the perfect text size, amount of print on a page, and word choice for Phase 1 readers. Horses clippity-clop; elephants clomp, clomp; and kangaroos boing, boing through the book, which can be wonderfully interactive as your Phase 1 reader imitates how each animal walks. This book is pure fun for a beginning reader.

The Hidden Alphabet by Laura Vaccaro Seeger,
illustrated by Laura Vaccaro Seeger (Roaring Book Press, 2003)

Don't miss this beautiful lift-the-flap, multimedia alphabet book that is like a visit to a favorite art museum. It's a deep-level conceptual book that also offers up wonderful new words for vocabulary building, but just on the Phase 1 child's interest and ability level. One word on a page makes it perfect for sight-word recognition. Truly an amazing book on many levels. This is the type of book that teaches your child to read without anyone realizing they are having a reading lesson. *The Hidden Alphabet* is a hidden treasure!

The Napping House by Audrey Wood, illustrated by Don Wood (Harcourt Brace Jovanovich, 1984)

Deftly illustrated and appealing with four words on a page, making it perfect for developing Phase 1 readers. This is a gentle story that sets the mood for waking up in the morning. You'll read the pages with several lines and your Phase 1 reader will take over on pages that he can read.

Fingerplays and Songs for the Very Young by Carolyn Croll (Random House, 2001)

Listed here because rhymes that were enjoyed and memorized in Phase 0 can often be memory read in Phase 1.

Brown Bear, Brown Bear, What Do You See? by Bill Martin, Jr.,
with wonderful illustrations by Eric Carle (Harcourt Brace, 1967)

A great Phase 1 book! This is a delightful, easy-to-read story with repeated pattern and rhyme recommended for Phases 0–2 that many children learn to memory read independently by the time they move into Phase 2. Children delight in the animals, color words, and beautiful illustrations, and it's a great book for building a beginning reader's confidence.

Chicka Chicka Boom Boom by Bill Martin, Jr., and John Archambault, illustrated by Lois Ehlert (Simon and Schuster, 1989)
Phase 1 is the time to start learning the letters. If you haven't already started this book, start it in Phase 1, along with lots of other easy alphabet books to help you teach letter names and letter recognition. This one has a wonderful rhythm and is perfect for learning individual letter names. You'll have fun seeing if your Phase 1 learner can pick out the letters piled up under the coconut tree!

Green Eggs and Ham by Dr. Seuss (Random House, 1960)
An enormously popular book that is perfect to begin in Phase 1. Your child can learn to read the title and the easiest pages or selected phrases such as "I am Sam," "Sam I am," "Do you like green eggs and ham?," "Thank you! Thank you, Sam-I-am!" The book in its entirety is end-of-first-grade level, but it's an appropriate challenge to begin with this book in Phase 1 because your child will love rereading it hundreds of times over the months or years ahead until the whole book can be read from memory. The words and word patterns in this book are appropriately repeated and perfect for beginners.

Finger-Point Reading

Finger-point reading is an important technique to use during Phase 1 through the beginning of Phase 3. This technique will teach your child how to read smoothly, and, most importantly, will help your child gain an understanding of what a word actually is.

Materials

Easy Level A books and favorites to facilitate fluent reading.

Skills Learned

Fluency, expression, and the flow of reading; the concept of what a word is; linking what the child says to the print on the page.

Directions

When reading with your child, have your child point to each word as you read in a normal voice. Your pace should be natural. Readers at Phases 1 and 2 are still learning how to match voice to print. For example, when they hear the phrase "Onceuponatime," they may think of it as one word as opposed to four: once—upon—a—time. At Phase 1, having your child point to each word in a line of text as the word is pronounced helps him match the voice with the print as he maintains a conversational flow of speech. Reading with your child should always be relaxed and enjoyable; just make finger-point reading a part of the usual routine.

During the initial memorizing, allow your child to "ride" your index finger with his own index finger as you read, pointing to each word as you read it. Pause from time to time to allow your child to chime in with other words or phrases. Use the prompt, "Read it with your finger." Have the Phase 1 reader point to each word as he says it from memory, running the finger smoothly under the words to match the voice. After several repetitions, you may want to prompt the child to try reading the page by saying, "Can you read it with your finger?" Accept your child's response. Your child will let you know when he feels confident. Avoid slow, halted, word-by-word reading when rereading a piece aloud to him. Finger-point reading helps children *feel* the flow of fluent reading.

It will take time for your child to master all of the complexities of reading so that it flows smoothly and sounds like normal speech. If your Phase 1 reader is trying to figure out text that is being read for the first time, *expect* him to read slowly, often focusing on individual words. There is a heavy load of new information in texts that have not yet been memorized for Phase 1 children—new words, new letters, new vocabulary, new concepts—so do not expect him to be able to read new text automatically. You will still need to be using repetition, reading a book numerous times aloud before he will be able to "read" it on his own. Remember, he is still most likely reading from memory, not sounding out the words.

Labeling and Reading Around the Room

Labeling and reading around the room, which started in Phase 0, continues in Phase 1. To review the procedure, go to Chapter 4.

In Phase 1 you will follow the same basic steps:

1. Make sight-word labels.
2. Post them around the room.
3. Use the left-to-right finger-tracking presentation.
4. Practice the words often.
5. Make the viewing interactive and fun.

You can substantially increase the number of words your child is learning in Phase 1 as compared to Phase 0. Another major change in Phase 1 is that you expand upon the left-to-right tracking procedure, not only stretching out the sounds in a word as you point to the letters in sequence (*bed*—/b/-/ĕ /-/d/—*bed*), but also presenting the word on occasion with the letter names (*bed*—b-e-d—*bed*, with bee-ee-dee instead of the sounds buh-eh-du). Thus, reading around the room becomes an important Phase 1 activity for teaching both letter sounds and letter names and how they map onto a word. Revisit word labels your child already learned to read by sight in Phase 0, and nudge the child to build upon what he already knows by adding the letter-name spelling. This is a great activity to help Phase 1 children move into Phase 2.

Here's an example of the word-presentation routine for Phase 1:

Say: "Let's read it by its sounds: *hat*, /h/-/ ă /-/t/, *hat*."
"Can you spell *hat*? Let's try it: *hat*, H-A-T, *hat*."
(Explain that H makes the /h/ sound, A makes the / ă / sound, and T makes the /t/ sound. At Phase 1, you are focusing on both letters and sounds.)

ACTIVITIES FOR PHASE 1 WRITING

How to Position the Paper

If you haven't done so already, Phase 1 is a good time to show your child how to hold the pencil and how to position the paper for writing. Refer to Figure 4.2 in Chapter 4 for how to hold the pencil and position the paper. You may also refer to Figure 4.3 for modeling correct letter strokes.

Kid Writing

Writing and reading aren't segregated skills; they use much of the same brain functioning. As you have learned, many children in fact learn to read by writing because writing is concrete and slows the process down. Kid writing is one of the most powerful teaching techniques that you can use at home. Make this a mainstay of literacy activity at home for Phases 1 and 2 and the beginning of Phase 3.

Kid writing in Phase 1 is an extension of the kid writing children begin in Phase 0, when you start by encouraging scribbling. Now your Phase 1 child is writing with random letters. Set appropriate expectations by studying the sample of Phase 1 writing in Figures 5.1 and 5.2, each demonstrating messages written with random letters. You cannot read writing like this on your own so you will have to ask your child to tell you what it says. Help your child frame her writing in simple, age-appropriate Phase 1 productions by encouraging labels and phrases.

Your Phase 1 writer is beginning to show some control of letters, but she doesn't yet know how the system works. That's fine for this stage. Below you will learn how to encourage your child so that she can progress.

Materials

A variety of pencils, pens, crayons, markers, and types of paper.

Skills Learned

Integration of all reading and writing skills, fostering a slow analysis of print from left to right; scanning letters in a word from left to right;

moving from ideas in the imagination to spoken words to printed messages that can be read; connecting reading and writing.

Directions

Follow these steps for kid writing:

1. Have your child draw a picture.
2. Ask your child to tell you about the picture. Invite him to write about it.
3. If your child doesn't know where to start, frame and scaffold the story. Here's how. First, "frame" the story by selecting one key phrase (three to six words) that your child used to describe his picture. Then draw a blank space, or "scaffold," for every word. See Figure 5.2 as an example.

At four years of age Leslie drew the picture in Figure 5.2. She described her drawing by telling an elaborate story about being at her grandmother's house in the country, surrounded by "a flock of butterflies" (her exact words).

Leslie's story might be framed as follows:

PARENT: That's a great idea for a story. Let's write, "A flock of butterflies." (The parent repeats "A" as he/she draws the first line; "flock" as he/she draws the second line; "of" as he/she draws the third line; and "butterflies" as he or she draws the third line, resulting in the scaffold of four blank lines with the length of each line roughly matching the length of the word. It will look like the lines below.)

__ ________ ____ ______________.

PARENT: Here's where you write it. Read these lines.
CHILD: A flock of butterflies. (Parent encourages child to point to the corresponding line for each word.)
PARENT: Now write each of the words on a line.
Child writes in random letters: EAII VELLOBNLI EDNMP RMNE.

Don't fret if your child initially makes too many or too few letters for a line—just go with the flow. Remember, you are enjoying literacy and giving her opportunities to test hypotheses about how it works—not teaching a formal lesson. If she is writing too many letters, just think of it as extra letter practice. But don't worry if some of the letters are formed incorrectly, either. Just praise the child's effort. Getting your child to think about the letters and try them out is more important than focusing on correct letter formation at this phase. If she's sticking to the letters in her name and only using a few different letters, you might gently nudge: "Want to try some new letters?" But don't push. New letters will come in time as she builds confidence.

4. Offer praise and have the child read back the "kid writing" several times to help him remember what he wrote:

CHILD: A flock of butterflies. A flock of butterflies.
PARENT: Great! Read the kid writing again.
CHILD: A flock of butterflies. A flock of butterflies.

5. Encourage your child to write at least one story each week. The drawing and story writing don't have to occur in the same session.
6. Make a big deal about kid writing, offering lots of praise and encouragement. Display kid writing in your child's room. Keep all samples to monitor growth.

Adult Underwriting

Parents can use a powerful technique called "adult underwriting" for connecting Phase 1 writing with reading. In this procedure, the parent provides a conventional manuscript copy of what the child wrote in the same line order and word order that the child used, but written underneath the child's entire piece as opposed to under each of the child's misspelled words. Adult underwriting is easier to read back than a sample where the parent has written the correct word under the child's misspelled word because the latter would require the eyes to move unnaturally up and down in a line of print. Adult underwriting allows for natural reading eye movement, which consists of scanning a line of print from left to right, moving in small, imperceptible steps called "saccades." Adult underwriting allows the child to read back what she wrote from conventional script as opposed to kid writing.

Having children read back their own writing from adult underwriting is as powerful as reading and rereading easy books because the adult underwriting is meaningful print that came from your child's own thinking. It's something he knows about and is interested in because he wrote it himself. Usually children are highly motivated to read back adult underwriting. Note that reading back adult underwriting is easier for your child than reading back his or her own invented spellings because the adult underwriting provides more cues.

Materials

Samples of your child's drawing with kid writing.

Skills Learned

Integration of all reading skills; the reading and writing connection.

Directions

1. Begin the adult-underwriting process soon after your child completes a piece of kid writing, while the child's message is still fresh in her mind.
2. At the bottom of the page, write in conventional English the exact phrase (e.g., "a flock of butterflies") that your child wrote in "kid writing." Do not simply write the correct spelling under your child's misspelled word as doing so destroys the integrity of the child's piece and may upset the child. Always be sure to praise your child's "kid writing" and explain that he isn't supposed to write like an adult yet.
3. Have your child read his story, using the conventional, adult underwriting. Praise the child: "Wow, you can read the adult writing!"
4. Have your child read and reread the story over and over until it's memorized. Don't rush the process. Reread the same stories day after day and week after week. Make sure the child is having fun and moving

at his own pace. The goal is to collect a variety of your child's writings so that they can be read back from conventional writing in the months and weeks ahead, relying upon repetition to build automatic word recognition and fluency. In Figure 5.2, note how the adult underwriting, written in conventional English by the parent below the child's piece, provides a conventional model for the child to read back.

Figure 5.2: Sample of Phase 1 Writing with Adult Underwriting

Book Making

If you haven't already started making easy-to-read homemade books with photos, labels, and phrases, start them now. Look at the book-making suggestions in Chapter 4 if you are starting for the first time. If you made books for your child during babyhood, she will enjoy rereading them over and over again in Phase 1.

Use sturdy materials that will allow for rereading. Photos of activities such as a trips or holiday events make great Phase 1 books. Ask your child to tell you what's happening in each picture, and frame the child's response in a short phrase or sentence that will be easy for her to remember. Always use your child's own words so that she can read the text back from memory.

Here are some models for Phase 1. Notice that these models move a little beyond the very easy one-word labels that were used in Phase 0. The goal is to challenge the Phase 1 reader just a bit more. Make a title page and a page for each photo or illustration. Homemade books don't have to be perfect!

Make a riddle book about family members with each page illustrated by the child:

Who Is This? (Title page)
She has black hair. (Page 1)
She has brown eyes. (Page 2, and so on below)
She loves to sing.
Her favorite food is ice cream.
She can dance!
She likes to cook.
She makes great spaghetti!
Mom!

Remember the *Look at Me! What Is This?* book you made for your child in Phase 0? It had photos and each of the following words on a separate page: *eyes*, *nose*, *ears*, *toes*, *fingers*, *feet*, and so forth. Reread the book and use it as a model to nudge your child forward by making a new book with the same words in short sentences:

Look What I Can Do! (Title page)
I shut my eyes and . . . (Page 1—close-up photo of toddler's closed eyes)
I touch my nose. (Page 2—close-up photo of toddler touching nose with eyes shut)
I cover my ears! (Page 3—photo of toddler covering ears with hands)
I wiggle my fingers. (Page 4—photo of toddler wiggling fingers)
I wiggle my toes. (Page 5—photo of toddler wiggling toes)
I kick my feet! (Page 6—photo of child kicking feet in tub or pool)
I stand on my head. (Page 7—photo of child standing on her head with help from an adult)
Eyes, nose, ears, fingers, toes, feet—
All UPSIDE DOWN! (Page 8—just the words)

The book doesn't have to say exactly what is suggested here. Get your child to help you decide what to say for each item. The book can be silly and unliterary but your child will remember how to read it back, will love reading it over and over, and will feel like a reader. This project is a great confidence builder. Phase 1 readers like to create books about pets, special events, family members, or really anything that they like to think about.

ACTIVITIES FOR PHASE 1 SPELLING AND PHONICS

It's very important to continue rhyming and syllable-clapping activities during Phase 1 and into Phase 2. You will have a new spelling and phonics activity as well: initiating talk about a few letter-sound correspondences.

Goals for Phase 1 spelling and phonics:

- Extending the concept of what a word is
- Clapping out syllables in words
- Shouting out or otherwise designating rhyming words in poems and nursery rhymes
- Isolating beginning sounds and letters in target words
- Calling attention to letter recognition, letter naming, and letter formation
- Beginning to recognize basic letter-sound associations

Activities for Teaching Letters

Materials

Magnetic letters, puzzles, puppets and soft toys, and blocks; sort-and-match letter cards and word-making games; alphabet books, books with predictable patterns with letter themes, rhyming and poetry books with letter themes, books with photographs that have alphabet themes, informational books about science and nature with alphabet themes, and picture dictionaries; an alphabet chart; labels around the house; your child's name displayed on art and in various contexts ("Max's toy box"); newspapers and magazines for letter hunts; rubber alphabet stamps.

Skills Learned

Letter recognition, letter names, letter formation; sounds in words; the concept that a word has parts such as a beginning and an ending; alphabetical order

Directions

Add to your collection of favorite alphabet books in Phase 1, and, as you read aloud, model elongating and enunciating the beginning sounds for targeted letters:

Explore alphabet books that rhyme.
Use alphabet books with labels and names.
Choose alphabet books with themes (cars, flowers, dinosaurs, monsters).

Here are some of my favorite alphabet books. Some of these are for older children but the art or content make them appropriate for all ages. Start early and talk about the letters and illustrations. The more advanced selections will become favorites that children keep for years and respond to at higher levels of sophistication as they become older:

Alligators All Around by Maurice Sendak (HarperCollins, 1962)
Ashanti to Zulu: African Traditions by Margaret Musgrove, illustrated by Leo and Diane Dillon (Dial Books, 1976)
Eating the Alphabet: Fruits and Vegetables from A-Z by Lois Ehlert (Harcourt Brace Jovanovich, 1989)
The Dinosaur Alphabet Book by Jerry Pallotta, illustrated by Ralph Maisiello (Charlesbridge, 1990)
The Z Was Zapped by Chris Van Allsburg (Houghton Mifflin, 1987)

When you teach alphabet knowledge, letter sounds, letter names, and letter formation, start with your child's first name. Research has shown that there is a definite own-first-name advantage.[2] Talk about letters and sounds in a variety of contexts and through multiple tasks. Learning the letter names can be a little complex for your child, so be patient and give him plenty of time to explore and learn the letters without pressure or formal instruction.

It may not have occurred to you that some letter names are much harder than others to learn. When the name of the letter has the sound as a part of its name, such as *b*, *a*, and *p*, it's typically easier to learn than letter names that do not have this correspondence, such as *h*, *w*, and *y*. To make things more confusing, sometimes the sound of the letter is in the first part of the letter name, such as with *a*, *d*, and *p*, but sometimes the sound comes at the end of the letter name, as in *f*, *m*, and *s*. The first set is generally easier to learn. Frequently occurring letters such as *r*, *t*, and *n* are generally easier to learn than letters children don't see in print as often, such as *x*, *j*, and *z*. Some sounds of letters are harder to say than others, coming later in sound acquisition. For example, the sounds that go with the letters *l*, *r*, *v*, *z*, *sh*, *ch*, *j*, and *zh*, and the two sounds of *th* in *then* (voiced) and *thin* (unvoiced), are often acquired by children after age four. There's quite a science to learning letters, but don't let that worry you.[3] Just have fun exploring and talking about how letters work with your child. You have plenty of time, and there is no need to rush.

There are countless ways to engage your child with learning the letters of the alphabet. Below you will learn about a few more activities besides just reading and exploring alphabet books together.

My Name Game

Write your child's name on an index card. Have your child cut the letters of his first name apart. Then have your child scramble the letters of the name and reorder and name the letters while spelling it. Play beat the clock to see how many seconds it takes to put the letters in the correct order. Give points for every letter name your child can name correctly. Give extra points when your child can tell you what sound it makes.

Alphabet Order

Teach your child the traditional alphabet song to the tune of "Twinkle, Twinkle Little Star" or some version that you like. Take advantage of the alphabet order by singing, chanting, and playing games that emphasize both the names and sounds in the order of the alphabet. Display an alphabet strip in your child's room and point to the letters as you sing the song "in slow motion."

Here are some other ideas:

- Introduce alphabet puzzles.
- Practice letter writing on erasable drawing boards or paper. Have your child circle the letter she likes best.
- Once your child starts writing with letters, it's good for him to be able to see a letter model up close. If he has a writing table in his room, make an alphabet strip about the size of a ruler and list both uppercase and lowercase letters.
- Play "Stomp the Letter" by writing letters on the sidewalk in chalk and having your child jump on targeted letters. Do the same activity when the sound of the letter is called.
- Use computer and board-based games for learning the letters.
- Play "I Spy" with letter names and sounds. Give your child a spy glass with the target letter taped on the lens. Have your child search for the letter in the home, in books, or in newspapers or magazines. Cut the letters out of old magazines or ads and glue them on a chart with pictures that begin with that letter.
- Find all the words on a page starting with a particular letter (for example, all words starting with *b*) during a read aloud.
- Find items in the room that begin with a particular letter (for example, for *b*, you could find *book*, *bag*, *box*, *ball*, *bat*, *broom*).
- Draw a scene in which everything in the picture begins with a certain letter, or make up a " silly sentence" with words beginning with a certain letter.
- Cut and paste a chart with words and pictures of things that begin with a certain letter.
- Use prepackaged refrigerated dough to have the child form letters and then bake and eat them.
- Use glue and construction paper and something that starts with a given letter to make that letter on the paper: For example, glue

down beads in the shape of B/b. (After cutting her son's hair, one creative parent I know used the clippings for H/h.)

- Make sandpaper letters or trace letters in the sand during sandbox play.

PHASE 1 LITERACY MILESTONES DIARY[4]

Keep track of your child's accomplishments. As your child completes each milestone, check off the appropriate box. This easy guide for checking off milestones can be a delightful record of your child's progress and make your child's literacy development more transparent.

Items that don't receive checks will help you decide which activities need more focus. You may supplement this easy checklist with your own notes and observations, recording favorite books and memorable vignettes marking your child's literacy development. A "Special Memories and Keepsakes" template organized by phases is provided in the Appendix to aid you in sharpening your focus.

Watch Me Grow in Reading

Monitor your child's reading development by keeping a list of the easy Level A books and favorite books that she has memorized as well as noting sight-word collections.

My Firsts

- ☐ I am beginning to recognize some words on sight.
- ☐ I am beginning to make the voice to print match.
- ☐ I am beginning to memorize Level A books.
- ☐ I increase the number of words I read back from memory.
- ☐ I increase the number of books I read back from memory.
- ☐ I can read back adult underwriting of my writing.
- ☐ I can read from memory or give the correct word after repeated rereading.
- ☐ I enjoy listening to more elaborate stories.
- ☐ I can talk about past events, about what I know, and expand upon it.

- [ ] I can answer who, what, when, where, how, and why questions.
- [ ] I can anticipate what's coming next in a story.
- [ ] I can retell stories and create my own narratives.
- [ ] I can talk about my own interests, feelings, emotions, and attitudes during story reading.
- [ ] I can talk about what happened and predict what will happen before going to the next page or section.
- [ ] I can retell stories telling what happened "first, then, next, and last," when prompted.
- [ ] I understand more and more print concepts, such as cover, title, first page, reading left page then right page, what "spelling" means, what a "word" is, what "title" means, what "author" means. (Circle the ones you observe.)

Watch Me Grow in Drawing and Writing

Phase 1 represents a turning point as a writer—the first real writing with letters. Take special care to collect samples of drawing and writing that show development of letter use as your child's writing moves away from previous pretend writing attempts when no actual letters were used. Collect a few samples that are especially memorable as keepsakes.

My Firsts

- [ ] I can think up things to draw or write about on my own.
- [ ] I write using letters.
- [ ] I can plan to write specific content before putting down letters in lists or signs.
- [ ] I'm really getting interested in letters and how they represent language.
- [ ] I can write my name and am learning to write a few other words.
- [ ] I am learning to hold the pen or pencil correctly.
- [ ] I'm learning to position paper properly for writing.
- [ ] I use the alphabet but am not yet making sound associations.
- [ ] I enjoy attempting to make lists, labels, signs, letters, stories, and e-mails.

Watch Me Grow in Sounds and Spelling

My Firsts

- ☐ I can clap out syllables.
- ☐ I can recognize rhymes.
- ☐ I can tell you all of the letters in my name.
- ☐ I can sing the alphabet song and point to the letters.
- ☐ I recognize letters:
    - A few
    - Some
    - Many
- ☐ I can tell you what sounds letters make:
    - A few
    - Some
    - Many
- ☐ I can tell you the names of letters:
    - A few
    - Some
    - Many
- ☐ I invent spellings with random letters.
- ☐ I generally prefer uppercase letters.
- ☐ I intersperse upper- and lowercase letters.

Note: Your child has moved to the next phase, Phase 2, when he begins to start words with the correct letter-sound match, instead of using the random letter strategy. He is probably also beginning to build a little repertoire of words he can spell correctly.

6

TEACHING READING IN PHASE 2

Mapping Letters to Sounds—It's EZ for U to Read!

YOUR TODDLER CONTINUES building letter knowledge and begins matching beginning and prominent letters to sounds in Phase 2. He starts labeling drawings or writing messages with a few letter-sound matches. You can sometimes read them. He reads some easy books from memory.

The first time you can parse the letters of your child's writing is a major milestone in your child's development. This likely happens in Phase 2. It may be a sign that expresses strong emotions—RUDF (Are you deaf?) taped on the bedroom door showing frustration after not being heard; a label for a drawing of a favorite nursery-rhyme character, HMT DPD (Humpty Dumpty); a title for a picture of the family motor boat, MY MR BT; or any one of countless possibilities, all pointing to magnificent creativity in a young mind bursting into literacy. Phase 2 is a time to celebrate your child's emerging creativity as a writer. Reading is advancing by leaps and bounds, too, but you may not see it as concretely. Be a good listener in Phase 2; your child's ability to talk about what he's reading or writing will tell you how much he is advancing. You may see him solidifying his understanding of how to make his voice match the words on a page.

Out with his family at the mall, Phase 2 Connor shocked everyone when he read the name that was written on his cup: "Hey, this word says ICEE!" he exclaimed. The letter I says / ī / and the C-E-E spells 'see'! I-C-E-E spells *icy*!" Connor had made a reading/writing connection because the spelling on the cup looked a lot like the spelling that he was doing himself as a Phase 2 writer. Confident reading unfolds naturally, informally, and with great delight in Phase 2.

Look at the four samples of Phase 2 "kid writing" in Figure 6.1. Notice that each child wrote by representing some, but not all, of the sounds in a word. Now look below the kid writing and see the conventional version of the same piece that a parent has provided: adult underwriting. Adult underwriting, which is one of the most powerful teaching techniques for Phases 1, 2, and 3, is reviewed again in this chapter, now with illustrations for children who are in Phase 2.

Now you are ready to review what is happening to your Phase 2 reader, writer, and speller. Get ready to choose just the right activities to move him or her forward. What makes your job easy is that much of what you were doing in Phase 1, such as reading aloud and adult underwriting, continues into Phase 2—only with higher expectations. It's easy to monitor growth by tuning into your child's growing sophistication—more stories read from memory, more letters and sounds learned, and a growing accuracy in writing. Notice the sparkle in your child's eye as she makes new discoveries as a reader, writer, and speller day after day. Phase 2 is the first time *you can read your child's writing* so it's a giant leap for the parent, too. Here's what you should expect.

Phase 2 is exciting for both children and parents because everyday life explodes with examples of literacy learning. This is when children begin reading lots of easy little books from memory and writing their first legible messages. Your child will begin to learn how sounds match with letters and will be able to talk about sophisticated concepts during read-alouds and book sharing. Knowledge about letters and sounds grows in leaps and bounds. Imagine the thrill of a parent being able to read the first written message from a child such as C MOM! I KN RT (See Mom! I can write).

Figure 6.1: Four Samples of Phase 2 Writing with Adult Underwriting

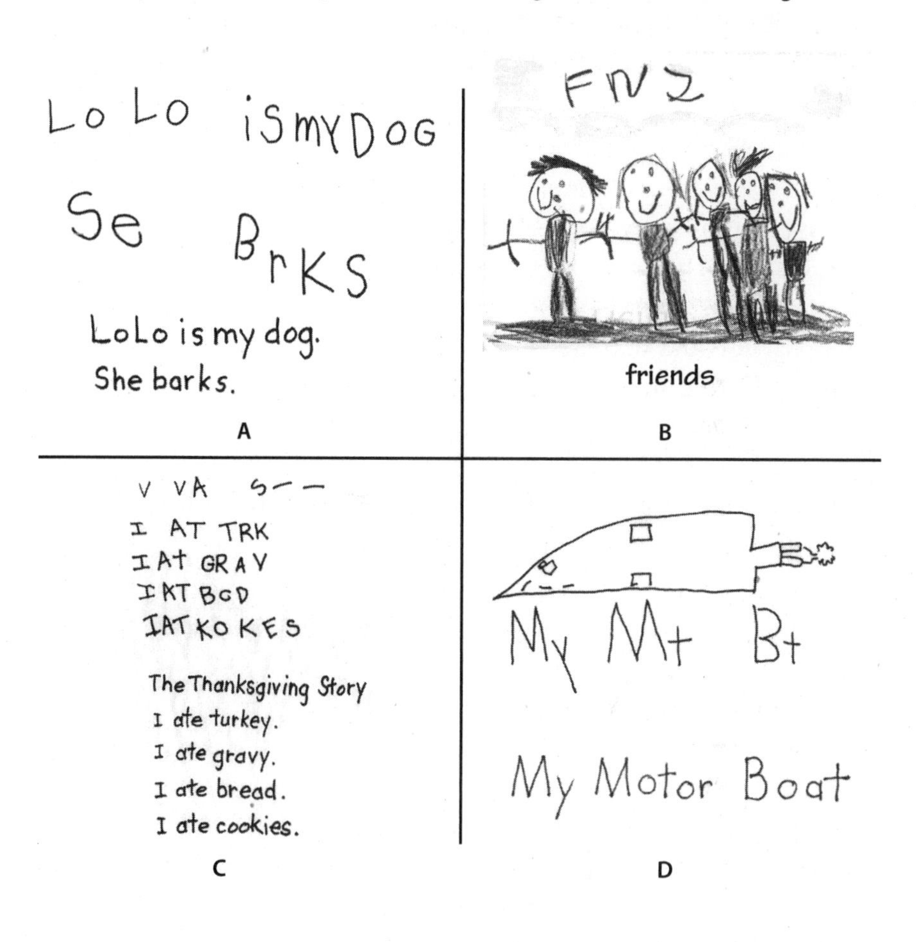

Phase 2 is when your child:

- Reads and writes using partial letter-sound matches, such as FNZ for *friends*
- Cues mainly on beginning letters for reading new words
- Invents spellings such as BT for *boat*, leaving out some sounds
- Reads a greater number of books from memory
- Learns to read more words automatically from memory

GET SET FOR PHASE 2 BY GATHERING MATERIALS AND PREVIEWING ACTIVITIES

Books

Continue with your favorite books from Phase 1, but add slightly more advanced selections of these categories to the collection:

Rhyming and pattern books
Information books
Story books
Alphabet books (extended from Phase 1)

Materials for Writing and Book Making

A variety of papers, pencils, markers, and crayons
Glue, tape, scissors, stapler, construction paper

Materials for Word Games

Letter tiles, magnetic letters, magnetic boards
3×5-inch index cards, hole puncher, ring clip

Overview of Activities and Techniques for Phase 2

This list will help you to anticipate the activities and techniques ahead for teaching your child over the next few months.

Activities and Techniques for Reading

Side-by-side reading
"Reading For-, With-, and By-Your-Child"
Finger-point reading
Read-alouds and story retellings
Ring clip for sight-word practice
"Write, Clap, and Chant for Learning New Words"

Activities and Techniques for Writing

Kid writing
Adult underwriting

Activities and Techniques for Sounds and Spelling

Hand spelling
Making words with letter tiles
Spelling words correctly from memory

ACTIVITIES FOR PHASE 2 READING

During Phase 2, it's important to move beyond simply reading aloud. Help your child move forward by using four easy teaching techniques: "Reading For-, With-, and By-Your-Child"; finger-point reading; ring-clip sight-word collections; and "Write, Clap, and Chant for Learning New Words."

Reading For-, With-, and By-Your-Child

Materials

Easy Level A to Level C books and old favorites. (See below for recommendations.)

Skills Learned

Comprehension; fluency and sight-word recognition; vocabulary.

Directions

1. Read *for your child* to model the process.
2. Read *with your child* until the material is memorized.
3. Encourage the reading *by your child* when she can handle it independently.

Reading for your child is the first step. Model the same actions you want your child to demonstrate when he or she eventually reads alone. Modeling demonstrates expression, fluency, feelings, and print concepts such as page turning and directionality.

Allow your child to choose which books he wants to read, making sure that the books are easy enough for him to memorize. Be patient. Don't set rigid goals for how long it might take for your child to memory read a selection without your help. As long as you both are enjoying the repeated reading of a favorite book, you're making progress. Keep the sessions short, light, and fun, but over the long term there will be scores of repetitions so the book can be learned. Selections may be reread over a period of weeks or even months and sometimes years! Revisit the rules for reading aloud in Chapter 5 for additional tips and more information on read-aloud sessions.

Reread the same selection as often as you can. Offer lots of praise. Children generally love to read favorite selections over and over again. If your child isn't responding well with a book or it seems too hard, choose another one. Keep the reading interactive by inviting the child to turn the pages. Talk about what's happening in the story. Point to the words as you read them, moving at a natural pace. Read with exaggerated expression so that your child can easily mimic your fluent reading.

Paying attention to the level of text is key to For-, With-, and By-Your-Child reading success. Begin with Level A easy books with three to five words on a page. Eventually you will move up to Level C selections, which often have one or two sentences per page.

Characteristics of Level A to Level C Texts for Phase 2

A good match for Phase 2 has one to three lines of type on each page, very uniform structure, and strong picture clues. Level C books, such as *Run, Run!* by JoAnn Vandine, are perfect for Phase 2 readers. Level C books have short sentences on each page. By contrast, an easier Level A book would have two or three words on a page. Adjust the level to what your child responds to positively. At first your child will know what words to say by looking at the pictures. Eventually, repetition during repeated readings will enable your child to learn to recognize some of the words automatically.

To summarize, appropriate text levels for "Reading For-, With-and By-Your-Child" for Phase 2 readers have these characteristics:

Heavy support from illustrations
Consistent placement of print
Familiar ideas and concepts
Repetition of one or two phrases or sentence patterns
Two to three words on a page for Level A
Up to short sentences on a page for Levels B and C
Repetition with very few word changes
Language similar to your child's speech[1]

Reading with your child is a time to explore all aspects of the book. You are not just reading aloud to your child, you are showing him or her how to experience the book by clarifying, connecting, validating, and extending her understanding of it. Reading with your child includes conversations about the reading. If your child doesn't understand a word in the story or something that's occurring, give information by telling, or clarify by explaining. Show your child how to think during a story by saying your thoughts out loud. Guide your child's thinking by asking questions, not to test or assess, but to lead to understanding.

Reading by your child first occurs when your child begins supplying a few words or phrases during the shared, repeated reading of an easy text. The goal is that eventually, she will memory read the book independently. Reading by the child builds confidence and enhances reading skills even when much of processing during Phase 2 relies upon memory and picture cues. Importantly, your child gets in the flow and *feels* like a real reader. Once a child memorizes a book, he will delight in reading it over and over and in displaying the reading skill to others. Every time he rereads an easy book, he's reinforcing important neural connections.

Great Books for Phase 2

Go Away, Big Green Monster! by Ed Emberly (Little, Brown, 1992)
An ingenious cutout book that moves to the perfect word choice and challenge for Phase 2 readers while chasing away nighttime monsters. With beautiful colors, this book is a perfect choice for encouraging a child to make predictions regarding what's going to happen next. It provides for another wonderful reading lesson without the feel of a teaching tool. It's just a fun book to share.

The Deep Blue Sea by Audrey Wood, illustrated by Bruce Wood (Scholastic, 2005)
A concept book and book of colors, this is the perfect selection for giving Phase 2 readers confidence as they get in the flow of reading. Repeated sentence stems and color words build on a repeated pattern. Before she knows it your child is reading eight lines of text on the page.

Is This Maisy's House? by Lucy Cousins (Candlewick Press, 2004)
Your Phase 2 reader will love reading about Maisy and have an easy time doing it. This wonderful story about Maisy the mouse in a lift-the-flap surprise book format will delight any Phase 2 reader. Great for sight-word recognition in a "find the hidden picture" format. "Does Maisy live here?" Your child will read and read and read until she finds out!

Green Eggs and Ham by Dr. Seuss (Random House, 1960)
An enormously popular book that is perfect to begin as a read-aloud. It illustrates how books can be enjoyed on different levels over several phases. In Phase 2, your child can build on learning to read the title and the easiest pages or selected phrases, such as "I am Sam," "Sam I am," "Do you like green eggs and ham?," "Thank you! Thank you, Sam-I-am!" If you started this book in Phase 1, definitely continue reading it in Phase 2. The book in its entirety is end-of-first-grade level, but it's an appropriate challenge continuing into Phase 2 because your child will love rereading it hundreds of times over the months or years ahead until the whole book can be read from memory. The words and word patterns in this book are appropriately repeated and perfect for beginners.

Goodnight Moon by Margaret Wise Brown, illustrated by Clement Hurd (Harper, 1947)
This classic bedtime story was recommended in Chapters 4 and 5, and it is still well worth recommending for Phase 2. Even if you started this one in babyhood, it's great to keep bringing it out. This is the first book that some Phase 2 children learn to read from memory. I keep repeating it in the lists of favorites to remind you of the power of repetition for teaching beginning reading.

Brown Bear, Brown Bear, What Do You See? by Bill Martin, Jr., with wonderful illustrations by Eric Carle (Harcourt Brace, 1967)
A great Phase 2 book! This is a delightful, easy-to-read story with repeated pattern and rhyme recommended for Phases 0–2 that many children learn

to memory read independently by the time they move into Phase 2. Children delight in the animals, color words, and beautiful illustrations, and it's a great book for building a beginning reader's confidence. Pull it out from time to time and check to see if your child can read the color words. Write the color words on word cards, and have your Phase 2 reader match the card to the appropriate word in the book. Play a game to see how many of the color words your child can read from the word cards without seeing the color cues on the pages of the text.

Run! Run! by JoAnn Vandine, illustrated by Kevin O'Malley (Mondo Press, 1995)

Making connections to other texts or stories is an important comprehension skill even for Phase 2 readers. Here's a wonderful little book connecting all your child's favorite story characters—the three pigs, Jack and the beanstalk, Red Riding Hood, and others, and your child can actually read it! A perfect example of a Phase 2 easy Level C book that your child can learn to read from memory while connecting to other texts.

Chicka Chicka Boom Boom by Bill Martin, Jr., and John Archambault, illustrated by Lois Ehlert (Simon and Schuster, 1989)

Continue this wonderful alphabet book into Phase 2, along with lots of other easy alphabet books, to help you teach letter names and letter recognition. This book was recommended for teaching letter names in Phase 1. If it becomes a favorite, continue enjoying it in Phase 2.

Wonderful Worms by Linda Glaser, illustrated by Loretta Krupinski (Millbrook Press, 1994)

A great information book, especially for boys in Phase 2.

The Very Hungry Caterpillar by Eric Carle (Philomel, 1969)

A classic pattern book with simple Phase 2 text that shows the process of metamorphosis as a caterpillar eats its way through the days of the week and lots of delicious fruits and vegetables. Just the perfect amount of word repetition for Phase 2.

Where the Wild Things Are by Maurice Sendak (Harper and Row, 1963).

A great storybook for reading aloud and stretching your child's imagination. Have your Phase 2 reader point to and read targeted phrases on the page, such as "King of the Wild Things!" Since the book is only ten sentences long, it's a perfect challenge for Phase 2 readers. Toddlers who love to dress up will relate to Max in his wolf costume misbehaving and being sent to his room, and they'll love his adventures with "wild things" before all is resolved in a happy ending. This is truly a picture-book masterpiece of children's literature.

The Cat and the Hat by Dr. Seuss (Random House, 1957)
Beginning on page one with, "The sun did not shine. It was too wet to play. So we sat in the house all that cold, cold, wet day," your Phase 2 reader is introduced to important CVC (consonant-vowel-consonant) short-vowel pattern words such as *cat*, *hat*, *sun*, *wet*, *sat*, and *that*, which makes this a great selection for beginning in Phase 2 and moving your child into Phase 3 and beyond. This is a wonderful book for developing Phase 3 reading skills, which often begin as a read-alouds in Phase 2.

The Z was Zapped by C. Van Allsburg (Houghton Mifflin, 1967)
Great for concepts and word building: "A was in an avalanche. B was badly bitten. C was cut to ribbons." Three to five words on a page promotes Phase 2 reading. The repeated stem "_____ was _____ . . ." is great for Phase 2 repetition.

Finger-Point Reading

Finger-point reading was introduced in Phase 1 and continues in Phase 2. Finger-point reading teaches the concept of what a word is and helps your child learn how to read smoothly with expression, avoiding word-by-word reading (see Chapter 5). It's important to continue finger-point reading in Phase 2 because research shows that most Phase 2 readers are still mastering the voice-to-print match. Using the finger generally is dropped by the beginning of Phase 3, or whenever your child can reread a book with fluency and expression, making the voice-to-print match without the support of finger pointing. Finger-point reading works like using training wheels for teaching your child to ride a bike; you'll know when your child is ready to go without it.

PHASE 2 TEACHER TALK: COMPREHENSION, FLUENCY, SOUND AWARENESS, PHONICS, AND VOCABULARY

When teaching children how to read in school, teachers focus on five research-based elements: comprehension, fluency, sound awareness, phonics, and vocabulary. It's important for you to understand this "teacher talk" so that you can later communicate with your child's teachers and appreciate what's happening during your child's formal reading instruction. Below are suggestions as to how to introduce your child to comprehension, fluency, sound awareness, phonics, and vocabulary at home.

Comprehension. Observe and ask questions to make sure your child is paying attention to the meaning of the text. Ask him to tell you what happened in the story. Ask your child *where* the story happened, *who* the main character is, *what* happens in the story, and *when* events occur. After read-alouds and storytelling, practice retelling the story and talking about it, asking and answering interesting questions. Even in retelling very simple stories your child will demonstrate understanding or lack of understanding of setting, character development, events, and plot development. Remember to include modeling, telling, explaining, and thinking aloud in your conversations during read-alouds and retellings.

Fluency. Fluency practice focuses attention on reading rate, phrasing, and expression. You want your child to mimic your fluency and expression, so don't hesitate to exaggerate a little to get your child to notice how reading should sound. Demonstrate falling intonation at the end of a sentence and rising intonation at the end of a question. Selecting repetitive texts and reading the same book over and over will help your child develop fluency. Once your child has memorized a book, practice it until fluency is achieved. Your fluency goal is to have your child read a story with appropriate speed, phrasing, expression, and attention to punctuation such as periods, question marks, and exclamation points.

Sound awareness and phonics. As a Phase 2 reader, your child is using letters to cue reading by matching letters to sounds for the first time. She is no longer relying on pictures or reading a word as a logo, such as cueing on the golden arches to read *McDonald's*. But a defining feature of Phase 2 is that for both reading and writing, letter-sound matches in a word are partial or incomplete.

A Phase 2 reader often focuses attention on only the first or last letters of words. Many words stored in your child's memory at this stage are likely to be neural traces or pictures of the word in the mind that are rudimentary. Research shows that the Phase 2 reader's brain may have formed a neural connection making it possible for him to retrieve a word such as *hot* by associating the word with its beginning and ending letters, but not all of the letters. For example, when you read *hot* the word-form area or "letterbox" in your brain registers or sees *hot*; in contrast, your Phase 2 child who reads *hot* is only processing *hxx* or *hxt* (the *x* in these examples simply indicate a place holder for unprocessed letters). This rudimentary Phase 2 letter/sound matching system may allow your child to cue on *hot* and differentiate *hot* versus *sun*, but he will have difficulty reading *hot* versus *hat* or *hut* at this stage because he's not really taking in information from or processing the middle part of the word. Mastering *hot* versus *hat* or *hut* happens in Phase 3.

At Phase 2 your child is just beginning to see the pattern of regularity in English print, but it's an incomplete picture. The good news is that she is relying more and more on the alphabet to read. Don't be surprised that your child's attention to the middle of the word is limited, because the middle of the word is often constituted of vowel patterns or vowel chunks that are more complex than the single letter-sound correspondences that your Phase 2 reader is noticing. Remember, letters are processed individually rather than in chunks at Phase 2.

Beyond that, your child may not know all of the letters of the alphabet, or may know some letters but not their sounds. Research shows that your Phase 2 reader probably can't read unknown words such as *bat*, *hat*, and *fat* by making an analogy to a known word such as *cat* even though the words are in the same "word family." Word families are rhyming words that share common parts, such as *at* in *cat*, *bat*, *hat*, and *fat*. Usually Phase 2 readers can only use the known word to read a new word in the same family when the word family is listed so that she can see them together.

Vocabulary. There is a direct correspondence between the number of words your child can read automatically and the level of text she can read and comprehend. In the early phases, word recognition is the most important contributing factor to reading comprehension. There are a number of studies revealing that early word recognition predicts reading comprehension almost exclusively, so it's very important at Phase 2 that you teach your young reader to recognize many more words automatically. Increasing the words your child recognizes automatically improves comprehension.

Ring Clips for Sight-Word Practice and "Look What I Can Read!" Celebrations

Materials

Ring clip, 3×5-inch index cards, hole puncher.

Skills Learned

Automatic sight-word recognition; extension and reinforcement of both reading and writing vocabularies. Collections of known words can be used for teaching new letters and sounds and for linking new words to words your child already knows.

Directions

1. Write the words your child can read on an index card.
2. Collect these words on a ring clip.
3. Practice them over and over.

Have your child use a ring clip for collecting "Words I Can Read." Put each word on an index card and punch a hole in the top left-hand corner. Make a game out of practicing the words and have "Look What I Can Read!" celebrations. Your child will enjoy showing how many words he can read to others and this builds confidence. If you want your child to be a reader, he has to *feel* like a reader! Keep a list of the words your child can read automatically and replace words that may have gotten torn from the ring clip or lost. Choose other books that give your child exposure to the same high-frequency words that he is currently learning. For example, read several cat books, pig books, or books on the same theme to provide repetition of familiar words.

The words your child stores in his memory depends upon which words he has been exposed to. Every time your child reads a word, constellations of neurons fire off in the brain forming a matrix, linking the word to meaning, sound, and eventually to correct spelling. Repetition is important because it allows your child to develop automatic recognition. The ring clip not only provides a record of which words your child already knows, but also motivation to learn new words. Store up to twenty words on the ring clip. As children move into Phase 3 and develop larger sight-word vocabularies, word cards can be stored in boxes, indexed alphabetically, and used for word games. Practicing a newly learned word is important, because if they don't use it, they may lose it!

Choose one or two high-frequency words from the books you are reading or from your child's writing to try to add to her repertoire each week. High-frequency words are words that your child can use when writing, such as *go*, *pig*, *love*, *Mom*, *Dad*, *by*, *from*, and *love*. For very young children, adding one word per week would result in a growth of fifty words in just one year, which would be an extraordinary achievement for a preschooler or kindergartner.

Write, Clap, and Chant for Learning New Words

Materials

3×5-inch index cards, marker.

Skills Learned

Sight-word recognition; correct spelling.

Directions

To use the Write, Clap, and Chant technique to practice a new word, follow these steps:

Step 1: Write the word to be learned (such as *go*) on a card together. With your child holding the pen or marker and your hand over hers,

Figure 6.2: Sample Word Card

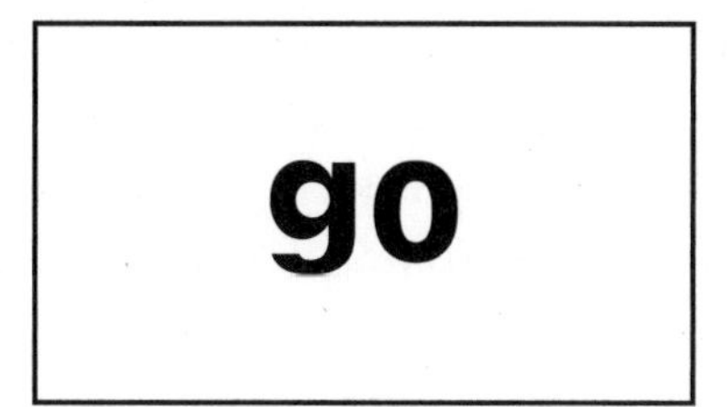

Go, g-o, go!

demonstrate the correct sequence of strokes for forming each letter in the word, as shown in Figure 4.3. You can say, "The *g* starts here and goes this way," but do this incidentally and informally. Your focus with this activity is teaching the sight word and letter sequence, not letter formation or sounds.

Step 2: Pronounce the word and clap and chant the spelling with your child, repeating the chant several times. Have your child touch the letters *g* and *o* as you say the chant: "Go, g-o, go!" (see Figure 6.2).

Step 3: Create a game-like atmosphere (as opposed to treating this activity as a lesson) and play the "word game" during free moments several times every day. Remember, your child's brain *loves* repetition! Write the same word in soap during a bath, in the snow, in the sand, in finger paints—whenever an opportunity presents itself.

ACTIVITIES FOR PHASE 2 WRITING

Here again are two really great techniques for teaching writing at home in Phases 1 through 3: kid writing and adult underwriting. Kid writing and adult underwriting allow children to read back a story that they wrote from their imagination in conventional English before they can spell conventionally. Remember, reading words correctly is easier than spelling words correctly, so reading back the adult underwriting is easier than reading back the kid writing and comes before writing in conventional spelling.

Kid Writing

Materials

A variety of pencils, pens, crayons, markers, and paper.

Skills Learned

Integration of all reading and writing skills, fostering a slow analysis of print from left to right; ability to scan letters in a word from left to right; ability to move from ideas in the imagination to spoken words to printed messages that can be read; ability to make connections between reading and writing.

Directions

Kid writing in Phase 2 is an extension of the kid writing that children begin in Phases 0 and 1. Set appropriate expectations by studying the samples of Phase 2 writing in Figure 6.1. Each demonstrates incomplete letter-sound associations in words. Can you read them?You will be helping your child frame her writing in simple age-appropriate Phase 2 productions like the labels, phrases, or simple line stories or sentence stories illustrated in these samples.

Phase 2 writers make the connection that letters may represent some of the sounds in words. Prominent sounds, such as the beginning and ending sounds in a word, are more often represented than medial sounds, or the sounds in the middle of a word, which often are made up of complex vowel patterns. Your child demonstrates understanding of directionality of print at Phase 2, and some correct spellings may appear in the message. Invented spellings are abbreviated, and sometimes a few letter-sound matches are mixed in with random letters. As in Phase 1, follow these steps:

1. Have your child draw a picture.
2. Ask your child to tell you about the picture and invite her to write about it.
3. If your child doesn't know where to start, frame and scaffold the story. Using *your child's own words*, frame the story by retelling it in a few

lines or phrases that will make it easy for your child to write the basic message. Use a marker to make lines to draw a scaffold to hold the words.

Here's an example. A child's elaborate verbal story about Thanksgiving dinner might be framed as follows:

PARENT: That's a great idea for a story. Let's write, "I ate turkey." (The parent repeats "I," while drawing the first line; "ate," while drawing the second line; and "turkey," while drawing the third line, resulting in the scaffold of three blank lines, with the length of each line roughly matching the length of the word. It will look like the lines below.)

___ _____ ___________.

PARENT: Here's where you write it. Read these lines.
CHILD: I ate turkey. (Parent encourages child to point to the corresponding line for each word.)
PARENT: Now write each of the words on a line.
(Child writes *I AT TRK*. The child's writing will be slow and analytic. She may enunciate some of the sounds in the word as she writes a letter to represent the sound. Expect that sometimes she may only get the beginning letter. Praise the child's effort and don't worry if some of the letters are incorrect. Remember, she's still in the "babbling" stages of beginning writing.

This procedure might result in a one- or two-word story such as FNZ for "friends," or SE BRKS for "she barks," or in a more elaborate story for a more experienced Phase 2 writer, such as the following. In this story, the title "V V S" stands for "The Thanksgiving Story." Note that the choice of V for TH is perceptually accurate. The /v/ sound sounds a lot like the /th/ sound. These two sounds are formed in the mouth in much the same way:

VVS

I AT TRK	(for "I ate turkey.")
I AT GRAV	(for "I ate gravy.")
I AT BRD	(for "I ate bread.")
I AT KOKES	(for "I ate cookies.")

4. Offer praise and have the child read back the "kid writing" several times to help her remember what she wrote.

5. Encourage your child to write at least one story each week. The drawing and story writing don't have to occur in the same session.

6. Make a big deal about kid writing, offering lots of praise and encouragement. Display kid writing in your child's room. Keep all samples to monitor growth.

Adult Underwriting

As in Phase 1, parents should use adult underwriting in Phase 2 to connect writing and reading. If you are trying adult underwriting for the first time, review the description of the procedure in Chapter 5.

Materials

Samples of your child's drawing with kid writing.

Skills Learned

Integration of all reading skills; making the reading and writing connection.

Directions

1. Begin the adult underwriting process soon after your child completes a piece of kid writing while the child's message is still in his mind.

2. At the bottom of the page, write your child's exact phrase in conventional English, always praising your child's kid writing and explaining that he isn't supposed to write like an adult yet.

3. Have the child read his story back from the conventional, adult underwriting model. Praise the child: "Wow, you can read the adult writing!"

4. Have the child read and reread the story until it's memorized. Remember, the goal is to collect a variety of your child's writings that can be read back from conventional writing in the months and weeks ahead. Through the repetition your child will build automatic word recognition and fluency.

In the Phase 2 samples shown in Figure 6.1, note how the adult underwriting, added to the pieces below by the parent, provides a conventional model of the child's writing for the child to read back. Compared to Phase 1 writing, the writing in Phase 2 is generally greater in volume and more sophisticated.

ACTIVITIES FOR PHASE 2 SPELLING AND PHONICS

Phase 2 readers and writers continue to develop their awareness of sounds in words as well as the concept of what a word is. Recognizing rhyming words and clapping the syllables in words carries on into Phase 2. Once your child grasps the concept of what a word is, he can frame the word for analysis, that is to say, recognize that a word can have a beginning and an ending. Eventually, your child will realize that words have a middle as well, and that the middle might give away some cues, too.

Goals for Phase 2 include the following:

- Extending the concept of what a word is
- Clapping out syllables in words
- Shouting out or otherwise designating rhyming words in poems and nursery rhymes
- Isolating beginning sounds in target words
- Extending letter recognition, letter naming, and letter formation
- Recognizing basic letter-sound associations

Hand Spelling to Help Your Child Recognize Beginning Sounds

Hand spelling is a way of drawing attention to the first letters and first sounds in a word. This activity will help children who are having difficulty hearing or isolating a word's beginning sound. It helps your child focus on hearing the beginning sound of words that sound alike. The technique uses a tangible object—the hand—and physical movement to make it easier for your child to grasp the concept of the beginning sound. Begin by teaching the procedure with a set of words that is easy to rhyme, such as *rat*, *cat*, *fat*, *sat*, and *bat*.

Materials

A poem or alphabet book; photos or illustrations of items that begin with a particular sound.

Skills Learned

Letter-sound correspondence, spelling, phonics.

Directions

1. Select a word. In this example, we'll say the targeted word is *rat*.
2. Pronounce the target word with your hand in a fist.
3. Lift your thumb and pronounce the beginning /r/ sound.
4. Say the rest of the word, *at*, with your hand extended in the handshake position.
5. Say the word again, returning to the fist position.
6. Once your child gets the hang of hand spelling, practice with other *–at* words that begin with different sounds, such as /k/ for *cat*, /f/ for *fat*, /s/ for *sat*, and /h/ for *hat*.

You'll find hand spelling symbols in Figure 6.3. Use picture cards, books with hidden pictures, or alphabet books to practice hand spelling the sound you are targeting for practice. After your child learns to hand spell the first sound in words such as *cat*, *fat*, *sat*, and *hat*, move to hand spelling the beginning sound of words that start with the same sound but do not rhyme, such as the /h/ sound in words beginning with *h*: /h/-/-ouse/, *house*; /h/-/-ill/, *hill*; /h/-/-ive/, *hive*; /h/-/-ole/, *hole*; and /h/-/-ut/, *hut*.

Making Words: Using Letter Tiles or Magnetic Letters

Teachers often use letter tiles or magnetic letters for phonics instruction. Making words with letter tiles, homemade letter cards, or magnetic letters is a great activity for Phase 2 learners at home as long as it's de-

Figure 6.3: Hand Spelling Symbols

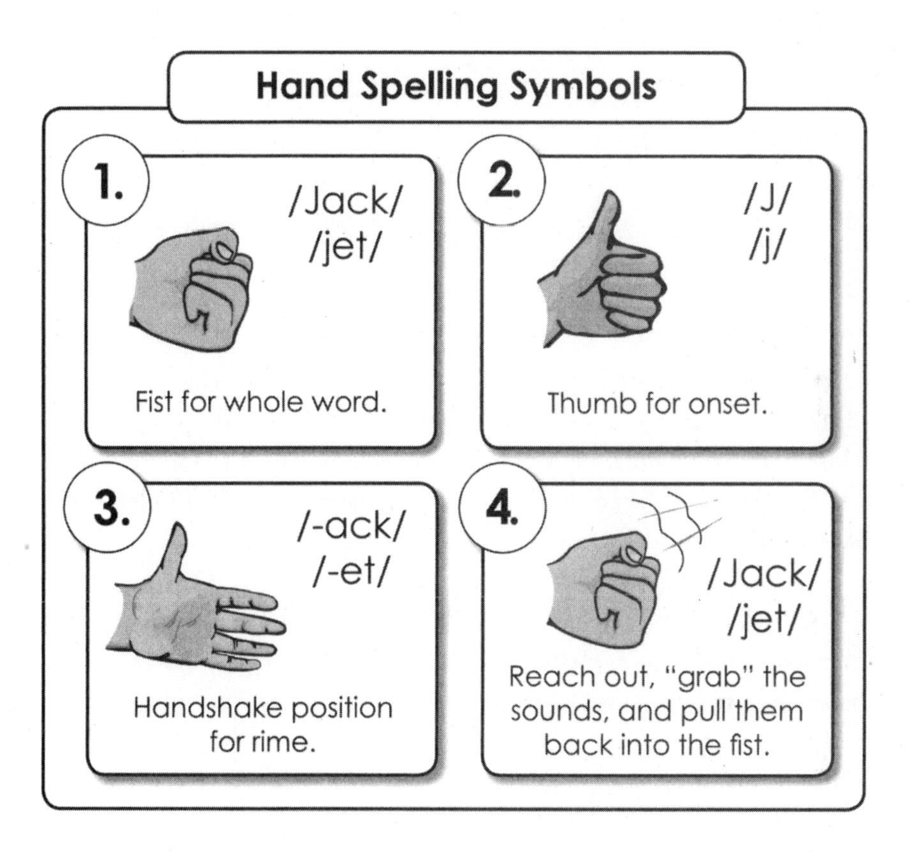

livered in a game-like context as opposed to formal structured lessons. The idea is to make it fun. You might also try building in a competitive element if competition fits your child's disposition.

Many children will be motivated by "Let's see how many words we can make with these letters!" Offer lots of praise, or perhaps even a little prize, as an incentive and just to add to the fun. Sometimes it's not what you do but how you do it that makes the difference between a "lesson" and a "game." Don't overdo the activity. Keep in mind that the collaboration is what makes it fun.

Materials

Magnetic or plastic letters, homemade letter cards, or letter tiles; magnetic board.

Skills Learned

Sight-word recognition; concept of what a word is; constructing and reconstructing known words; left-to-right letter sequence in words; pulling words apart and putting them back together; matching letters to sounds; phonics; spelling.

Directions

1. Sit at the left side of your child with the letter tiles placed between you. Start by saying: "Let's play a game with these letters. It's called 'Making Words.' The object of the game is to make words with letters. It's a brain teaser game! I can make some words, you can make some words, and we'll see how many we can make together."

2. Begin by using high-frequency two-letter words. Choose letters o, g, n, and s for making *go*, *no*, and *so*. Choose letters e, m, w, b, and h for making *me*, *we*, *be*, and *he*. Start with known words, then move to the unknown. For example, it's good to start with letters your child already knows. It's also good to start with *words* your child already knows from his or her ring clip. Remember that it's easier for your child to read a word than it is for him to spell a word correctly. He may recognize a word by sight but not know how to choose the correct letters to make it by moving from left to right. Making words helps children discover how words work and learn how to spell them. Once kids know how the game works, it can be used with three-letter patterns and for learning new words.

3. Model first: "These two letters make *go*—g and o." (Place the letters from left to right to form the word *go*.) "Watch me run my finger under the word as I say it. GO. (Say the word slowly, emphasizing each sound.) Now you try. Say it slowly and move your finger under it to show how the letters make the sounds."

4. Pass your child the g and the o in order. Say "now you try it. Make *go*."

5. Now—if your child is enjoying the activity—pass n and o in order and model how to make *no*.

6. If your child gets the concept, move to making new words by changing the letters. For example, use three o's and g, s, and n. Use the prompt "Change the g in *go* to make *so*." "Change the s in *so* to make *no*." Eventually you can introduce "sticky letters that stick together" like *sh*, making substitutions with two-letter words like *he* to make *she*. Figure 6.4 gives letters for high-frequency two-letter words.

Figure 6.4: Letters for High-Frequency Two-Letter Words

Letters	Words
o, g, s, n	go, so, no
e, m, b, h, sh	me, be, he she

7. Play the game informally, using letters and words your child knows and is using in reading and writing. Keep score. "How many words can you make today?"

8. Move to making words with three-letter combinations, such as using a, d, h, b, and s to make *dad*, *had*, *mad*, *sad*, *bad* and the consonants m, t, n, and s to make *mat*, *man*, *Nat*, *tan*, *sat*, *Sam*, *at*, and the like.

Making Words by Blending Sounds

Note: Materials and Skills Learned are the same as those in "Making Words," above.

Directions

1. Move from focusing on a few known words with two- and three-letter sequencing and sounds to challenging your beginning reader by

making many words by blending sounds. When the *sounds* of four or five consonants and a short vowel have been learned, you and your child can place letter cards or letter tiles together in sequence to form and sound out many new words. For example, place the tiles p, t, and o in the t-o-p sequence to make *top*. Then say: "These letters make *top*."

2. Point to each letter, elongating each sound as you blend the sounds into a recognizable word: tttoooppppp, top.

3. Have your child move his finger under each letter as he repeats the sounds with you and then says the word.

4. Have your child repeat the sounds and the word in unison with you. Then say the stretched-out sounds faster and faster until your child recognizes how the sounds blend into a word.

5. Once your child is able to blend and read the word *top*, change the order of the letters so that your child can blend and read *pot*. Later, replace the o with a to make *tap*, replace the t with h to make *hop*, and so forth.

6. Have your child keep a list of the words he has learned.

7. When your child grasps this activity, he has likely moved into Phase 3.

The phonics chart in Figure 6.5 will give you a global view of the kind of letter-sound knowledge your child is learning, starting in Phase 2 and continuing into Phase 3.

Figure 6.5: Phonics Chart I: Key Sound-Symbol Relationships

These sound-symbol relationships are typically learned first:			
a as in bat	**l-/l/amp**	**v-/v/an**	**m-/m/oon**
o as in hot	**e as in bed**	**t-/t/op**	**h-/h/at**
u-e as in use	**s-/s/un**	**u as in cup**	**p-/p/ot**
I as in sit	**c as in cap**	**w as in wet**	**f-f/ish**
b-/b/all	**j-/j/et**	**a-e as in cake**	**n-/n/est**
i-e as in like	**d-/d/og**	**k-/k/ite**	**y as in yoke**
r-/r/ing	**o-e as in home**	**z-/z/oo**	**g as in goat**

Tips for Observing Your Phase 2 Reader

Grow in Confidence with Sounds and Spelling

You can observe your Phase 2 reader grow in confidence in phonemic awareness and in operating with sounds and spelling by checking to see if he can do activities with matching, sound isolation, sound substitution, or blending. Only some of these tasks are typically mastered in Phase 2. Others will extend into Phase 3.

Try *some* of the following tasks with familiar words:

Matching: "Which words begin with the same sound?"
Sound Isolation: "What sound do you hear at the beginning of Jack?"
Sound Substitution: "What word would you have if you changed the /j/ sound in Jack to the /b/ sound?"
Blending: "What word would you have if you put these sounds together: /j/ plus /-ack/?"

If your child is successful with some of these tasks, he or she is making the move into Phase 3!

PHASE 2 LITERACY MILESTONES DIARY[2]

Keep track of your child's accomplishments. As your child completes each milestone, check off the appropriate box. This easy guide for checking off milestones can be a delightful record of your child's progress and make your child's literacy development more transparent.

Items that don't receive checks will help you decide which activities need more focus. You may supplement this easy checklist with your own notes and observations, recording favorite books and memorable vignettes marking your child's literacy development. A "Special Memories and Keepsakes" template organized by phases is provided in the Appendix to aid you in sharpening your focus.

Watch Me Grow in Reading

Monitor your child's reading development by keeping a list of the easy Level A–C books and favorite books she has memorized as well as noting sight-word development. Note that some of the questions in this section were presented at earlier phases but are rechecked here to indicate accomplishment with higher levels of text.

My Firsts

- ☐ I am beginning to memorize Level B and Level C books.
- ☐ I increase the number of books I read back from memory.
- ☐ I can read back adult underwriting of my writing.
- ☐ I continue to enjoy books and respond to a broader range through read-alouds.
- ☐ I can recognize thirty or more sight words from memory.
- ☐ I make the voice-to-print match when reading.
- ☐ I can read back books from memory with fluency.
- ☐ I can retell stories in my own words.
- ☐ I demonstrate text understanding in conversations during and following shared reading.
- ☐ I enjoy listening to more elaborate stories.
- ☐ I can talk about past events, about what I know, and expand upon it.
- ☐ I can answer who, what, when, where, how, and why questions.
- ☐ I can anticipate what's coming next in a story.
- ☐ I can retell stories and create my own narratives.
- ☐ I can talk about my own interests, feelings, emotions, and attitudes during story reading.
- ☐ I can talk about what happened and predict what will happen before going to the next page or section.
- ☐ I can retell stories, telling what happened "first, then, next, and last" when prompted.

Watch Me Grow in Drawing and Writing

Your Phase 2 writer has advanced so that you can often read some of his writing. Take special care to collect samples of drawing and writing that show development similar to the samples presented in this chapter. Collect a few samples that are especially memorable as keepsakes.

My Firsts

- ☐ I am increasing the length of my written productions.
- ☐ I am matching more letters to sounds in my writing.
- ☐ I know how to hold a pencil.
- ☐ I know how to orient print to the page.
- ☐ I know how to position the paper.
- ☐ I can name most letters.
- ☐ I can form most letters.
- ☐ I sometimes intersperse uppercase and lowercase letters.
- ☐ I continue to enjoy writing.

Watch Me Grow in Sounds and Spelling

My Firsts

- ☐ I can clap out syllables.
- ☐ I can recognize rhymes.
- ☐ I recognize and name the letters:
    - Many letters
    - All of them
- ☐ I can match many letters with a sound.
- ☐ I invent spellings that have partial letter-sound matches.

Note: Your child is ready to move to Phase 3 when she begins to represent virtually all of the sounds in a word when she writes. She is not yet writing in chunks of phonics patterns, so many of the spellings look unusual, but you can read ALMOZT EVRE WRD YOR KED RITS. Once you notice this pattern, it's time to move on to the next chapter.

7

TEACHING READING IN PHASE 3

Spelling with a Letter for Each Sound—"The Cat Sat on the Mat" + Phonics = Reading Up a Storm!

YOUR BEGINNER REDS (reads), RITS (writes), and SPELS (spells), using one letter for each sound. She grows in phonics knowledge and can spell new words by thinking about words she already knows: If *cat* is C-A-T, then *mat* is M-A-T. She can read many easy books from memory and recognizes scores of words on sight.

Phase 3 is a time for celebrations and for building confidence. Your child is on the cusp of being an independent reader. It's an incredibly exciting phase for a parent or caregiver because there is an explosion of literacy accomplishment that is apparent and easily recognized by both you and your child. By Phase 3, children often can name and form all the letters of the alphabet and know a lot of single letter-sound matches. Your child doesn't simply guess a word by looking at the first or last letter anymore, but rather reads more accurately by attending to each letter in the word. You'll notice how your child's repertoire of books increases in volume and in sophistication because of this newfound, efficient strategy.

Making word analogies for spelling also typically begins in Phase 3. For the first time, your child can figure out how to read a word she's never seen by making a mental comparison to the letters in a word she already knows. If she knows *cat*, she uses this knowledge to figure out how to read *bat*, *sat*, *rat*, *pat*, and *chat*. This new strategy enables her to increase the number of words she can read exponentially. Along with the big boost in sight-word recognition comes an increase in the level and sophistication of the texts your child can read.

Phase 3 readers move from reading Level C easy books with very simple text, such as "Run, Jack, run! The giant wants to eat you!" to reading Level H books with far more complex text, such as "In the great green room there was a telephone and a red balloon and a picture of the cow jumping over the moon," from Margaret Wise Brown's *Goodnight Moon*. It seems that everything about reading is ratcheting upward in Phase 3. The most important advancement is that your child begins to *feel* like a reader. There is a new self-reliance and confidence. She's eager and proud to show off her accomplishments.

Your child will be using the same strategy that she uses to read when writing: She will be matching every sound with a specific letter. Phase 3 is when it's really apparent that it's harder for your child to spell a word correctly than to read it correctly. She may read a word such as *boat* easily after repetition, but if she's writing about a *boat* she may spell it BOT. This is perfectly normal and to be expected. All children should be able to read more words than they can spell because spelling the word correctly is harder. Look at the two samples of Phase 3 kid writing in Figure 7.1. The samples are easy to read because they are spelled phonetically—with one sound per letter.

Unfortunately, English spelling doesn't always work phonetically, so Phase 3 is characterized by many creative and unusual spellings. You need not worry—these spellings will not linger into adulthood once spelling is taught formally in school. Just as babies babble before they speak like adults, writers invent spellings before they spell like adults. These invented spellings are powerful indications of your child's growing knowledge as a reader. They play a crucial role in his early development by helping him move more quickly toward automatic reading, when attention to exact spellings will no longer be the driving force behind the reading process.

Figure 7.1: Two Samples of Phase 3 Writing

The Three LITL PIGZ

One day a MUTHR pig sent her three LITL PIGZ
OT INOT the WOD'S. The FRST LITL pig MAT
a man with a BUNDL UV CTOR (straw). The pig
SED to the man. GEV (give) me CTOR (straw) to BILD
My HOS (house).

HALUWEN (Halloween)

I like HALUWEN BECUZ it is fun!
I WET (went) CR ER CRET N (Trick-or-treating).
I DRASD (dressed) IS (as) SPIDR Man (Spider-man).

Phase 3 writing is exhilarating and often quite amusing for parents to read. There is a great deal more sophistication, and you'll likely hear your child's "writer's voice" for the first time, flowering with wonderful individuality and creativity. Her thoughts on paper may surprise you! Her story writing is more highly crafted and will likely move from the stories of a few lines or sentences that she has been producing to more elaborate structures with a beginning, middle, and ending, or with events recounted in a first, then, next, last sequence.

Let's review the milestones of a Phase 3 reader, writer, and speller and then choose just the right activities to help your individual child move forward. Remember, you can always go back to the activities from previous phases, now with higher expectations.

Phase 3 is when your child:

- Reads and writes using complete letter-sound matches
- Attends to full letter-sound matches for word reading instead of just looking at beginning and ending letters

- Distinguishes among similarly spelled words, such as *hot*, *hit*, and *hut*, which were easily confused at the previous phase
- Begins to read new words by analogy by seeing relationships in word families, such as *mat*, *cat*, *sat*, and *fat*
- Invents spellings with one letter for each sound in the word, such as BOT for *boat*
- Increases the number of words spelled correctly from memory
- Stabilizes the concept of how words work, but may not yet chunk letters into phonics patterns
- Increases the number of easy books read from memory
- Learns to read many more words automatically from memory, moving into the range of about one hundred words recognized on sight

GET SET FOR PHASE 3 BY GATHERING MATERIALS AND PREVIEWING ACTIVITIES

Books

Continue with your favorite books from Phase 2, but add to the collection and increase the level of difficulty:

Rhyming and pattern books
Information books
Story books

Materials for Writing and Book Making

A variety of papers, pencils, markers, and crayons
Glue, tape, scissors, stapler, construction paper

Materials for Word Games

Letter tiles, magnetic letters, magnetic boards
3×5-inch index cards, hole puncher, ring clip

Overview of Activities and Techniques for Phase 3

This list will help you to anticipate the activities and techniques ahead for teaching your child over the next weeks and months in Phase 3.

Activities and Techniques for Reading

"Reading For-, With-, and By-Your-Child"
Finger-point reading
Read-alouds and story retellings
Ring clip for sight-word practice
"Write, Clap, and Chant for Learning New Words"

Activities and Techniques for Writing

Kid writing
Adult underwriting

Activities and Techniques for Sound and Spelling

Finger spelling
Making words with letter tiles
Spelling words correctly from memory

ACTIVITIES FOR PHASE 3 READING

During Phase 3 your child will continue the "Reading For-, With-, and By-Your-Child" technique, using higher levels of text than in Phase 2, but you will phase out finger-point reading. You will continue read-alouds and storytelling, ring-clip sight-word collections, and a variation of the "Write, Clap, and Chant for Learning New Words" activity, which now advances to teaching polysyllabic words.

Word recognition is the most important contributing factor to comprehension in Phase 3, so working on recognizing words is an important way of *improving* your child's reading comprehension. In addition to targeting high-frequency words such as *your*, *when*, *things*, *school*, *people*, and *because*, which are among the one hundred most frequent words in English, you want to focus attention on a few polysyllabic words—

especially ones with syllables that you think your child may recognize as familiar patterns. For example, this is a good time to show your child how words like *interesting* can be read as in-ter-est-ing rather than i-n-t-e-r-e-s-t-i-n-g. Learning how to read a few "big words" is a great confidence builder for your child.

Reading For-, With-, and By-Your-Child

Materials

Easy Levels C through Level G books and old favorites. (See below for recommendations.)

Skills Learned

Comprehension, fluency, sight-word recognition, vocabulary.

Directions

You are probably already familiar with how to use the "Reading For-, With-, and By-Your-Child" activity from having used it in Phase 2. If you are beginning it for the first time, go to Chapter 6 to review the procedure.

Remember, selections may be reread over a period of weeks or even months. Reread the same selection as often as you can. Offer lots of praise. Children generally love to read favorite selections over and over. If your child isn't responding well with a book or it seems too hard, choose another one. Keep the reading interactive by having conversations about what you are reading. Occasionally talk about a specific word—what it means or how to sound it out. Read with exaggerated expression so that your child can easily mimic your fluent reading.

Perhaps the greatest change in "Reading For-, With-, and By-Your-Child" in Phase 3 is the wider range and increasing difficulty of the text that Phase 3 readers can handle. It's a time for more and more books and for advancing step by step. As you select books for repeated reading in Phase 3, notice that each reading gives your child lots of practice with more and more words. Books in the mid-range levels for Phase 3 have many more words than the much easier Phase 1 and Phase 2 selections.

For example, *The Foot Book* by Dr. Seuss, which is Level E, has a total of 122 words. Your child will love reading it over and over because of the rhyme and the fun of it. But additionally, she will be reinforcing the neural pathways for each of the 122 words in the book every time she reads it.

The great beginning reading educator Marie Clay explained it this way: "Every time a child reads a sentence . . . every single word in the sentence profits by being used . . . moving further towards fluency and automatic responding."[1] That's exactly why repeated readings are so important in Phase 3: They capitalize on the repetition your child's brain needs to move toward automatic reading.

Sometimes you may need to work on fluency in Phase 3 during "Reading For-, With-, and By-Your-Child." You may want to challenge your child to work through one small section at a time to make it perfect—then put the whole thing together. Try to think of lots of ways to share the book to keep it interesting. Chant line by line or page by page, echoing each other, or read one page and then have your child read the next. Share, laugh, joke about the stumbles, and then try it again. Keep it interesting by being enthusiastic and varying the ways you interact with the book.

Ultimately, you want your Phase 3 child to practice reading the same books until he sounds like a skilled reader. By memorizing the book, he gains confidence—and he loves reading it. He learns to recognize the words accurately and rapidly without conscience effort. He learns to adjust phrasing and expression so that it sounds like natural speech—not slow, halting, word-by-word reading. When the reading of a book becomes easy, your Phase 3 child will be thrilled to read it. The "reading lights" in his brain will light up all of his reading circuits. Every word in the story will be firing off neural traces in the brain.

Characteristics of Level D to Level G Texts for Phase 3

Levels D through G move your child into much more elaborate stories than those you read aloud in Phases 1 and 2, with repetition of three or more sentence patterns and more varied language, often interspersed with repeated phrases or refrains. You'll find a blend of conversational and written language structures, and the content may range from familiar experiences to fantastic happenings. Illustrations provide moderate support. To summarize, appropriate text levels for "Reading For-, With- and By-Your-Child" for Phase 3 readers have these characteristics:

Repetition of three or more sentence patterns
Varied sentence patterns
Written language structures, such as "Once upon a time . . ."
Varied subject matter and genres, including fantasy, informational texts, and stories about familiar experiences
Illustrations providing moderate support, but not carrying the story[2]

A good match for the end of Phase 3 is a book such as *Zoo Looking* by Mem Fox.[3] The delightful story about Flora and her dad's fun-filled day at the zoo has repeated phrases such as "She looked at the ______ and the _______ looked back" for each of the enchanting zoo animals she encounters. The book highlights the *–ack* word family, with *–ack* words on almost every page: *back*, *black*, *crack*, *smack*, *whack*, and *snack*. This word-family feature is highly desirable in Phase 3 because you are moving your child to Phase 4, the chunking phase, and *–ack* is a high-frequency chunk. There are dozens of high-frequency words based on the *-ack* pattern. In all, 129 English words end in *–ack*!

In addition to the *–ack* pattern, *Zoo-Looking* has close to 150 words, along with wonderful challenges for a Phase 3 reader such as *giraffe*, *panther*, *penguin*, *ostrich*, and *koala*. The bear *gobbled* up its snack and the camel had *humps* on its back.

This expansion of vocabulary both conceptually and in reading difficulty is characteristic of Phase 3 texts. Phase 3 texts are varied in genre and style. They don't have to have patterns or highlight chunks. An example that is quite different from *Zoo-Looking*, but is also a great Phase 3 selection, would be a Level K text such as *Dinosaurs* by Michael Collins. This book has just a few sentences on each page, but appropriate text complexity, such as "Long, long ago, before there were people, dinosaurs lived on Earth. The word dinosaur means 'terrible lizard.'" It also includes labels that will challenge and delight any budding Phase 3 dinosaur aficionado: austrosaurus, muttaburrasaurus, allosaurus. Clapping out the syllables and reading these labels will help your child move into Phase 4. Remember to engage in modeling, telling, explaining, thinking aloud, and asking questions during your shared readings and to highlight new words and concepts.

Repetition—repeated reading of favorite books and memory reading—continue to be important strategies for reading at home. During Phase 3, your child is not only drawing upon her knowledge of phonics much more than in Phase 2, but also drawing upon her knowledge of grammatical structures and meaning. In fact, phonics, sentence structure, and meaning are equally important to your child in Phase 3 for figuring out unknown words. Phase 3 readers bring grammar, meaning, and phonics into play simultaneously as they read. This vignette described below models a typical discussion about words during side-by-side reading.

Figuring Out Unknown Words in Phase 3

Kevin, a Phase 3 reader, is reading a Level C book with me. This is a book he has read over and over again. As he's reading, he miscues on the word *curtain* in the sentence, "My little cat can climb up the curtain." Instead of reading *curtain*, he says *window*. I let him read to the end of the little book without correcting him. Interrupting would break his flow and the fun he's having showing me how well he can read. I praise him at the end of the story, but I ask him to go back to the "My little cat can climb up the curtain" page to see if he will notice and correct his mistake. Rather than tell him he's wrong, I want to see if he can self-correct. (If he didn't self-correct when I took him back to this page, I would point to *curtain* and help him figure out the word.) Here's our conversation surrounding this incident, beginning when he finished reading the book:

GENTRY: Wow, Kevin, you are a great reader! You did a great job with this book. Let's look at something. I want to go back to one page. See if you can read this page for me again.

KEVIN: My little cat can climb up the window—no wait. My cat can climb up the curtain.

GENTRY: How did you know to change that last word?
KEVIN: Because cats can't climb up windows! They may scratch them! (Kevin's using a meaning cue to help him read correctly and make the change so that the text makes sense to him.)
GENTRY: Yes, that's great thinking! It makes better sense to say *curtain*.
KEVIN: And it starts with a *C*. Windows starts with a *W*! (Kevin is also using phonics to correct his miscue, demonstrating the complex and sophisticated level at which Phase 3 readers are thinking as they read!)
GENTRY: Wow, Kevin! You know a lot about how to figure out unknown words! That's the sign of a good reader!

Great Books for Phase 3

Green Eggs and Ham by Dr. Seuss (Random House, 1960)

An enormously popular book that is perfect to begin in either Phase 1 or Phase 2, when your child can learn to read the title and the easiest pages or selected phrases such as "I am Sam," "Sam I am," "Do you like green eggs and ham?" or "Thank you! Thank you, Sam-I-am!" If you started this book in Phase 1, definitely continue reading it in Phase 2. If you started soon enough, this book can be read independently in Phase 3. The book in its entirety is end-of-first-grade level.

Zoo-Looking by Mem Fox, illustrated by Candace Whitman (Mondo, 1996)

This is a perfect Phase 3 book about a young child's trip to the zoo with her father. The repeated pattern and introduction of the *–ack* word family make it a valuable tool for teaching a child to read as well as a wonderful excursion for the child's mind. *Zoo-Looking* is beautifully illustrated in torn-paper collage.

Goodnight Moon by Margaret Wise Brown, illustrated by Clement Hurd (Harper, 1947)

This wonderful bedtime story is another classic that often is mastered by Phase 3 readers.

Here Are My Hands by Bill Martin, Jr., and John Archambault, illustrated by Ted Rand (Henry Holt, 1985)

This book, with sentences such as, "Here are my hands for catching and throwing," moves into the level of text appropriate for Phase 3 and yet maintains pattern and rhyming sets—nose blowing, hands throwing—which are great for developing reading skills in Phase 3. *Chewing*, *blushing*, *washing*, and *brushing* all introduce *–ing* words in repeated patterns—a perfect Phase 3 advance. This book begs your child to try the actions on the pages and treats the reader to a multicultural experience through the illustrations.

Tough Boris by Mem Fox, illustrated by Kathryn Brown (Harcourt Brace, 1994)
A great book for tough boys, who learn that even pirates have hearts. This story includes great vocabulary words for beginning Phase 3 readers, with just the right amount of repetition and challenge. Your mean, greedy, fearless pirate will love this one.

From Head to Toe by Eric Carle (HarperCollins, 1997)
Imitating all the animals, beginning with the beguiling gorilla on the cover, this beginning Phase 3–level text makes reading interactive and fun. Thump your chest, arch your back, bend your knees—perfect word choices for Phase 3.

Chicken Butt! by Erica S. Perl, illustrated by Henry Cole (Henry N. Arams, 2009)
When thinking about variety in your child's reading material, don't forget humor. Boys especially will love *Chicken Butt!* and read it over and over and laugh out loud. A little boy faces off with his dad in this comic masterpiece. A good example of Phase 3 reading levels.

Whoever You Are by Mem Fox, illustrated by Leslie Staub (Harcourt Brace, 1997)
There are lots of possibilities for getting your Phase 3 reader to engage in deeper levels of thinking. This multicultural masterpiece introduces her to children all over the world who are just like her in so many ways. The subtle repeated patterns make it easy reading for Phase 3 with a global appeal.

Where the Wild Things Are by Maurice Sendak (Harper and Row, 1963)
A great storybook for reading aloud and stretching your child's imagination. Have your Phase 2 reader point to and read targeted phrases on the page, such as "King of the Wild Things!" Since the book is only ten sentences long, it's a perfect challenge for Phase 2 readers and is often read cover to cover in Phase 3. Toddlers who love to dress up will relate to Max in his wolf costume misbehaving and being sent to his room, and they'll love his adventures with the "wild things" before all is resolved in a happy ending. This is truly a picture-book masterpiece of children's literature.

The Cat and the Hat by Dr. Seuss (Random House, 1957)

Beginning on page one with "The sun did not shine. It was too wet to play. So we sat in the house all that cold, cold, wet day," your Phase 2 and Phase 3 reader is practicing CVC (consonant-vowel-consonant) short-vowel-pattern words such as *cat*, *hat*, *sun*, *wet*, *sat*, and *that*. This pattern is hugely important in Phases 2 and 3, making this title a great selection throughout both of these phases. It is a wonderful book for developing Phase 3 reading skills.

The Z was Zapped by C. Van Allsburg (Houghton Mifflin, 1967)

Alphabet books can be enjoyed at a more sophisticated level in Phase 3. For example, now that your child is paying attention to all the letters in words, this is a great book for exploring more challenging words such as *avalanche* in the first entry: "A was in an avalanche." Clap out the syllables in *avalanche*. Show your Phase 3 reader how *avalanche* is built in chunks: av-a-lanche. Talk about what *avalanche* means. If your child thinks this is a cool word, he might like to draw a picture and write a story about an avalanche. How many *A* words can he think of that were buried in the avalanche? Perhaps an *ape*, *alligator*, *automobile*, *apple*, and the like. Be creative and have fun with it.

Finger-Point Reading

Finger-point reading is generally dropped in Phase 3 unless your child is having difficulty with fluency. If this is the case, review the finger-point reading instructions in Chapter 5. If your child is able to make the voice-to-print match easily and her reading is smooth, with good expression, after practicing a piece, gradually nudge her to read without pointing to the words. Say, "You are such a good reader I bet you can read this without pointing to the words. Let's try it. . . . See what a great reader you are!"

When moving away from finger-point reading, your child may fall back into the habit of using the finger to track eye movement. Gently put your hand over your child's hand and move the hand away from the page. You generally don't even have to say anything—moving the hand gently away from the page will remind your child that she's reading like a grown-up reader. Practice reading easy books that your child has memorized without the finger-point technique, then move to reading the harder selections without finger pointing.

PHASE 3 TEACHER TALK: COMPREHENSION, FLUENCY, SOUND AWARENESS, PHONICS, AND VOCABULARY

In the preceding chapter, we discussed five aspects of reading supported by research and championed by the National Reading Panel—comprehension, fluency, sound awareness, phonics, and vocabulary. These five concepts often serve as talking points for teachers when they discuss reading improvement. If you are considering these talking points for the first time, it might be a good idea for you to review the discussion on this subject in Chapter 6 before considering how your child will advance on all these fronts in Phase 3.

Comprehension. During read-alouds, continue to observe and ask questions to make sure your child is paying attention to the meaning of the text. The change to expect in Phase 3 is that the text levels are more advanced, moving up to Level G (for example, *Zoo-Looking* listed above). Ask your child to tell you what happened in the story. Ask him *where* the story happened, *who* the main character was, *what* happened in the story, and *when* events occurred. After read-alouds and storytelling, practice retelling the story and answering interesting questions. Talk about setting, character development, events, and plot development. Remember to include modeling, telling, explaining, and thinking aloud in your conversations during read-alouds and retellings.

Fluency. Fluency practice in Phase 3 focuses attention on reading rate, phrasing, expression, and moving from the known to the unknown. You want your child to mimic your fluency and expression, so when you model reading, don't hesitate to exaggerate a little to get your child to notice how the reading should sound. Demonstrate falling intonation at the end of a sentence and rising intonation at the end of a question. Select higher levels of text comparable to *Zoo-Looking* and the other "Great Books for Phase 3" listed above, and practice a few favorite pattern books until fluency is achieved.

Repetition in the story and reliance on memory frees your child's brain to begin focusing on word patterns and other text elements that he did not notice previously. For example, once he can read a selection with fluency aided by memory from repeated readings, his attention is free to notice that the word *curtain* starts with a *c* and use that letter cue to decide what the word is. He might be thinking that he shouldn't call the word *window* even though he sees a window in the illustration, because *window* starts with *w*. This level of ongoing analysis and complex thinking develops naturally during Phase 3. For the first time he focuses on new "items" that he or she might not have noticed before.

Children who read a text over and over again can move from the known to the unknown. Since they do not have to concentrate on what they already know, new learning can more easily occur in the familiar text. Your goal is to have your child read a familiar text like *Zoo-Looking* by Mem Fox with appropriate speed, phrasing, expression, and attention to punctuation, in a sense putting all of the complex elements of the reading process together so that they work in concert.

Sound awareness and phonics. In Phase 3, your child begins to pay attention to all of the letters in words for the first time. Often the middle part of the word is harder for Phase 3 spellers, because the middle of the word may consist of a phonics pattern, or a spelling chunk of several letters that work together to map to a sound. The letter "o" makes different sounds in *not* and *note*, for example, because of the way the chunks of letters work. Phase 3 is when your child first starts to master many of these patterns.

Phase 3 readers often try to decode new words letter by letter, but they are not yet working with chunks much. That is a characteristic of Phase 4. During Phase 3 your child forms complex association matrices in the brain, storing full letter-sound representations for many words. Phase 3 readers begin analogizing to figure out *mat*, *sat*, and *pat* from their recognition of its association to a word they already know, such as *cat*. At Phase 3 your child gets full control of the alphabet and greatly increases her knowledge of letter-sound regularity while increasing the number of words she recognizes automatically.

Vocabulary. As already noted, there is a direct correspondence between the number of words your child can read automatically and the level of text he or she can read and comprehend in the beginning phases of reading, including Phase 3. In the early phases, word recognition is the most important contributing factor to reading comprehension. There are a number of studies that reveal that early word recognition predicts reading comprehension almost exclusively, so it's very important at Phase 3 that you continue to teach your Phase 3 reader to recognize words automatically. Increasing the words he recognizes automatically improves comprehension, so your goal is to increase his vocabulary by as many words as possible. Choose from the activities below to help your Phase 3 reader increase automatic word recognition.

Read-Alouds and Story Retellings

Choose books that may be too hard for your child to read independently, but appropriate for listening, intellectual development, and enjoyment. The range of options is limitless! Reading aloud and having "book talks" with your child is an important way to develop comprehension. Have your child make connections to his experience, to other books you have read together, and to his knowledge of the world. Model how good readers think by "thinking aloud" as you talk about a book. For example, model how you think as a reader by saying, "This story brings back memories of . . . [something in your own life]." Show your child that by connecting to his own experience he can understand the story better. In addition, make text-to-text connections, such as "________ [the text you are reading] reminds me of ________ [another text you have read together]." Reading books aloud that are beyond your child's reading level helps to build background knowledge and strengthen comprehension by connecting what he already knows to new reading.

Ring Clips for Sight-Word Practice and "Look What I Can Read!" Celebrations

Materials

Ring clip, 3×5-inch index cards, marker.

Skills Learned

Sight-word recognition; correct spelling.

Directions

If your Phase 3 reader still has a sight-word recognition vocabulary of thirty or fewer words, review the ring-clip word practice activity described in Chapter 6. Once your child can read thirty or more words—which typically happens as your child moves into Phase 3—store the word cards in a "word bank" arranged alphabetically (recipe boxes work perfectly). Use the word cards to play games, such as sorting words according to patterns. Your child can consult the word bank when writing to find the correct spelling of words she's not sure how to spell. Treat the word-bank activity as a game, not as a lesson.

Write, Clap, and Chant for Learning New Words

Materials

3×5-inch index cards, marker.

Skills Learned

Sight-word recognition; correct spelling.

Directions

Phase 3 readers can add words to their word banks by writing, clapping the letters, and chanting them until they are recognized automatically. In addition to using this method for high-frequency words, such as those practiced with "Write, Clap, and Chant" in Phase 2 (see Chapter 6), your child may enjoy employing the strategy to practice theme words or challenge words until she can recognize them automatically. For example, with a book such as *Zoo-Looking*, described above, your child might enjoy adding "animal words" such as *giraffe*, *panther*, *penguin*, *ostrich*, and *koala* to her personal word bank. Giving children choices raises their confidence and makes the activity more fun, so allow your child to choose the animal word. Practice these words until she can read them automatically. Remember, this is still a game, so discontinue the activity if it is not successful. You are simply upping the ante by adding more advanced words to your child's automatic-recognition repertoire.

To use the Write, Clap, and Chant technique to practice a new word, follow these steps:

Step 1: Ask your child to choose a word from a favorite read-aloud book, such as *ostrich* from *Zoo-Looking*. Write the word on a card with your child's help. When modeling the reading, divide long words into syllables: "Os, o-s—trich, t-r-i-c-h—ostrich!" Treat this as a challenge and have your child choose just a few favorite challenge words to memorize. If the word seems too difficult, put this activity on the back burner or choose easier words. Try one challenge word per week.

Step 2: Pronounce the word and clap and chant the spelling of each syllable with your child, repeating the chant several times. Have your child touch the letters as you say the chant.

Step 3: Play the "word game" during free moments several times every day. Remember, your child's brain *loves* repetition!

You'll find more activities for learning new words in the spelling and phonics section below.

ACTIVITIES FOR PHASE 3 WRITING

Kid writing and adult underwriting continue at the beginning of Phase 3 but should be phased out as soon as your child starts to spell words phonetically, although not necessarily correctly. Remember, reading words correctly is easier than spelling words correctly, so reading back the adult underwriting is easier and comes before writing in conventional spelling. Early writers aren't supposed to spell like adults, so be very tolerant of invented spelling. Allow the invented spelling to help you decide which high-frequency words might be good words for your child to learn to spell correctly. Don't feel compelled to correct every misspelled word, or you will stifle your child's joy in writing. The more she writes, the more she will learn about literacy, so celebrate her accomplishments. Perfect spelling comes later.

Kid Writing

Materials

A variety of pencils, pens, crayons, markers, and paper.

Skills Learned

Integration of all reading and writing skills; ability to produce a variety of short compositions, ranging from simple descriptions and stories to longer, more elaborate compositions; ability to write in various genres; informal development of skills in spelling, punctuation, and other writing conventions; ability to move from ideas in the imagination to presentation of the information in print; ability to make connections between reading and writing.

Directions

Kid writing in Phase 3 is an extension of the kid writing done in the earlier phases. Set appropriate expectations by studying the samples of Phase 3 writing in Figure 7.2, each demonstrating use of some correct spelling, with a letter for each sound in words with invented spellings. Generally, Phase 3 writers advance in sophistication from writing stories with three to six lines, to more advanced stories consisting of a few sentences, and finally to more elaborate stories with a beginning, middle, and ending, or perhaps a first, then, next, last sequence.

You can encourage Phase 3 writers to write more elaborate stories by giving them three or four sheets of paper and plenty of time to plan and carry out a piece of writing on a topic they have chosen. In the first, then, next, last sequence, have the child draw what happened *first* on the first page; what happened *then*, or second, on the second page; what happened *next* on the third page; and what happened *last* on the fourth page. Each of the drawings will serve as a plan for an elaborate story. In one of the samples below, a Phase 3 writer worked for several weeks to make a wonderful homemade book following an elaborate plan. Figure 7.2 shows a range of typical Phase 3 writing.

Figure 7.2: A Range of Phase 3 Writing Samples

Phase 3 with Adult Underwriting

TUTH FARE

WON NIT I WAZ in MI
bed and the TUTH FARE CAM.

Tooth Fairy

One night I was in my
bed and the tooth fairy came.

Phase 3 Sample with First-Then-Next-Last Sequence

Adult Underwriting is not needed with this piece.

Chiquita's Bath

Chiquita likes to
SLEP WETH me. One day
My mom DECIDET to
give Chiquita a bath. I HOD Chiquita. (hold)
Mom had to get a TAVEOL. (towel)
She DUSET like (doesn't)
for me to TECK (take)
her a bath. I LIT (let)
her go and
she WET UNDR the CUVRS. (went under the covers)

ACTIVITIES FOR PHASE 3 SPELLING AND PHONICS

Phase 3 readers and writers make great gains in phonics knowledge and spelling. Phonemic awareness and manipulation of sounds in words are important sound work in Phase 3. The tasks listed below generally begin in Phase 2 and are completely mastered in Phase 3. These tasks are presented below from easiest to hardest. Use this list when you talk to your child about how words work and bring attention to the sound features in words:

Matching: "Which words begin with the same sound?"
Sound Isolation: "What sound do you hear at the beginning of *Jack*?" (Answer: /j/.)
Sound Substitution: "What word would you have if you changed the /j/ sound in *Jack* to the /b/ sound?" (Answer: *back*.)
Blending: "What word would you have if you put these sounds together: /j/ plus /–ack/?" (Answer: *Jack*)

It's particularly important that Phase 3 readers learn the spellings for high-frequency short vowel words with the Consonant-Vowel-Consonant (CVC) pattern in words such as *cap*, *pet*, *hit*, *hot*, and *cup*. As illustrated in the spelling samples in Figures 7.1 and 7.2, CVC short vowel words are often misspelled at the beginning of Phase 3. When Phase 3 writers sound these words out, they often match the short vowel sound to a letter name for *a*, *e*, *i*, *o*, and *u*, which results in using *a* for the short e sound, *e* for the short i sound, *i* for the short o sound, and *o* for the short u sound.

Here are some of the examples from Figure 7.2. All of these are typical early Phase 3 short vowel spellings: MAT for *met*, WET for *went*, DRAS for *dress*, SEX for *six*, FEM for *film*, ET for *it*, EF for *if*, BALT for *belt*, WETH for *with*, LIT for *let*, and KED for *kid*. This simply illustrates that these very important short vowel patterns have to be taught. Keep in mind that the Phase 3 children who wrote these words could *read* them all correctly, but spelling them correctly is harder. Short vowel patterns should be mastered by the end of Phase 3 as your child moves into Phase 4. This can happen informally if you simply make short vowel patterns part of your focus during Phase 3 and choose some of the activities below to help keep your focus on short vowels and the CVC pattern, or word families such as *–at*, *–et*, *–it*, *–ot*, and *–up*.

By the end of Phase 3, your child will:

- Demonstrate the ability to manipulate the sounds in words
- Recognize basic letter-sound associations and some word-family patterns
- Know the short vowel spellings of a number of high-frequency CVC words (*cap*, *pet*, *hot*)
- Know how to spell more words correctly

Finger Spelling

Finger spelling is a way of drawing attention to each sound or phoneme in a word to help children who are having difficulty hearing or isolating a word's constituent sounds. It is designed to help your child learn how to match a letter for each sound in a word. The technique is exactly like hand spelling, described in Chapter 6, except that in this case the focus is on each sound in the word. Finger spelling uses a tangible object—the thumb and fingers—and the physical movement of raising a finger for each sound to make it easier for your child to grasp the concept of how many sounds make up a particular word. For example, *rat* has three sounds: /r/, /ă/, /t/. *Ape* has two sounds: /ā/, /p/. *Night* has three sounds: /n/, /ī/, /t/. Begin by teaching the procedure with a set of words that is easy, such as words with two sounds instead of words with three sounds.

Materials

A poem, picture chart, picture cards, or word cards for focusing on words with two sounds, words with three sounds, short vowel CVC words, or any one-syllable word to be spelled.

Skills Learned

Letter-sound correspondence, spelling, phonics.

Directions

1. Pronounce the target word with your hand in a fist: "rat."
2. Lift your thumb and pronounce the beginning /r/ sound.
3. Lift your index finger and pronounce the /ă/ sound.
4. Lift your third finger and pronounce the /t/ sound.
5. Reach out and "grab all the sounds" as you say "rat" again, returning the hand into the fist position to represent pulling all the sounds back into the word.
6. Once your child gets the hang of finger spelling, practice with two-sound words and three-sound words.

Practice Words with Two Sounds

do	to	is	shoe	be	hi	see	toe	zoo
key	it	me						

Practice Words with Three Sounds

cat	can	nap	sun	cup	bed	zap	pan	bat
cab	bug	net	man	top	mom	top	jeep	book
feet	hop	hope	rat	rope	tan			

Fun with Word Families

One of the most powerful activities for raising confident readers in Phase 3 springs from activities and games with word families—an extension of working with rhyming words. It involves choosing high-frequency spelling patterns that are easy for your child to learn. This technique is extremely useful for adding many new words to the repertoire that he can read automatically and eventually spell correctly. This leads to chunking in Phase 4. Once your child learns a few patterns and understands how word families work, the number of words he can recognize by sight and the number of words he can spell correctly skyrockets.

Word families are based on elements of sounds in words that are easier for your child to perceive than the individual sounds or phonemes in a word. These units of sounds are referred to as *onsets* and *rimes*. The onset is the part of sound represented by the consonant or consonant-cluster spelling pattern that comes before a vowel in a one-syllable word, such as the /r/ or *r* in *rat*. The rime is the chunk represented by the spelling pattern that begins with the vowel and completes the word, such as the /ăt/ or *–at* in *rat*. You already worked with onsets and rimes if you did the hand spelling activity in Phase 2 (see Chapter 6). In Phase 3, your child is ready to use onsets and rimes for *reading* new words and eventually for *spelling* them correctly. It's easy to show your child how the sound units in onsets and rimes can be recognized and used in common spelling patterns.

WORD	ONSET	RIME
big	b	–ig
pig	p	–ig
dig	d	–ig
sprig	spr	–ig
back	b	–ack
track	tr	–ack
whack	wh	–ack

Blending onsets and rimes enables Phase 3 readers to put these two units of sound together to make a new word. Thirty-seven rimes will enable your child to recognize about 500 words by the end of Phase 4. But Phase 3 is the time to begin working with this easy-to-grasp concept. Begin by tapping into what your child already knows. Choose a word family from which your child already recognizes several words. Then play games or create word-card or writing activities to see how many more words he can learn.

Great Word Families for Building New Words

–ack	–an	–aw	–ice	–in	–ir	–ore
–ain	–ank	–ay	–ick	–ine	–ock	–uck
–ake	–ap	–eat	–ide	–ing	–oke	–ug
–ale	–ash	–ell	–ight	–ink	–op	–ump
–all	–at	–est	–ill	–ip	–or	–unk
–ame	–ate[4]					

Materials

3×5-inch index cards for making word-family cards; or a commercial set of word-family cards; spinners, dice, materials for games and for making game boards.

Skills Learned

Sight-word recognition; ability to make word analogies; ability to construct and reconstruct known words, to pull words apart and put them back together, to match letters to sounds, and to recognize onsets and rimes (see definitions above); phonics; spelling.

Directions

1. Start with words your child already knows.
2. Have your child hand spell the word (see Chapter 6 and Figure 6.3) and call attention to the rime or chunk.
3. Blend the onset into the rime: "/n/ + /ĕt/, *net*."
4. Choose other onsets and have your child make the new word: For example, hand spell and say: "n-et, *net*. What would you have if we put the /j/ sound before –et?" (Answer: /j/ /ĕt/, *jet*.) "The /p/ sound?" (Answer: /p/ /ĕt/, *pet*.) And so forth: Continue with other initial consonants.
5. Treat units such as *str*, *ch*, and *–ight* as one sound unit rather than sounding them out letter by letter.

6. Teach new words this way:

N, E, and T spells *net*.
Watch me spell *net*.
/n/ /ĕt/
(Name the two parts.)
N spells the /n/ sound.
ET spells the /ĕt/ sound.

7. Practice reading word-family words.

net, get, let, bet, set, jet

8. Have your child practice writing and spelling words with the same pattern.

9. Teach double and triple onsets, such as *st*, *str*, *ch*.

10. Create sets of word-family cards for games and speed practice. Board games, speed-sorting games, games with spinners, dice games, and classic card games can be adapted to give your child practice with word-family cards.

Sample Game: Jack and Jill

- Read the rhyme "Jack and Jill."
- Make a set of word cards for the *–ack* family and the *–ill* family.
  –ack: Jack, back, crack, hack, lack, pack, knack, rack, sack, tack black, shack, smack, snack, stack, track, whack, quack
  –ill: Jill, bill, Bill, dill, fill, gill, hill, kill, mill, pill, rill, sill, till, will, chill, drill, frill, grill, quill, shill, spill, still, swill, trill
- Make a board game with a starting and ending point and a word card from the list above for each space.
- For one turn, the player spins and moves forward the number of spaces shown by the spinner. The player reads the word. If incorrect, she moves back a space. Every time the child gets a word correct, the child moves forward, but in addition, the adult player *loses* the same number of spaces on the spinner, or a given number of spaces, such as two, if you prefer.
- Players alternate turns.

Vary the game to fit the circumstances. For example, you can make the game easier by including just a few of the easier words. You can add harder words and patterns as your child is ready. Choose the words from a favorite read-aloud story. For example, variations of this game could be played after reading *Zoo-Looking* by Mem Fox with the following *–ack* word-family words from the story: *back*, *black*, *crack*, *smack*, *whack*, and *snack*.

Making Words: Using Letter Tiles or Magnetic Letters

Continue using the Phase 2 "Making Words" activity in Phase 3 (see Chapter 6). The major change in Phase 3 is that you can play the making words game with new patterns and harder words. Practice word families in Phase 3 using patterns such as those listed in "Great Word Families for Building New Words" above.

Making Words by Blending Sounds

Note: Materials and Skills Learned are the same as for "Making Words" in Chapter 6.

In Phase 2, you started making words by blending sounds, using the sounds of four or five consonants and a short vowel. Continue making words by blending sounds in Phase 3, following the steps in Chapter 6, but expand your child's repertoire, taking advantage of his new understanding of consonants and vowels. In Phase 3 your child will delight in adding many more words and patterns to the game.

The phonics charts in Figure 7.3 will give you a global view of the kind of letter-sound knowledge your child is learning, generally starting in Phase 2 and continuing in Phase 3.

Phase 3 has provided a growth spurt in reading level as well as in comprehension, sight words, fluency, and phonics knowledge. The qualitative change that is perhaps easiest to see, however, is your child's move from spelling with a letter for each sound to spelling INN chunks of FONNICKS PATTURNS, along with lots of WURDS SPELDED COWECKLY. Chunking indicates the move to Phase 4 and readiness for the next chapter.

Figure 7.3: Phonics Charts: Key Letter-Sound Associations

A: Phonics Chart I: Key Sound-Symbol Relationships

These sound-symbol relationships are typically learned first:			
a as in bat	l-/l/amp	v-/v/an	m-/m/oon
o as in hot	e as in bed	t-/t/op	h-/h/at
u-e as in use	s-/s/un	u as in cup	p-/p/ot
I as in sit	c as in cap	w as in wet	f-f/ish
b-/b/all	j-/j/et	a-e as in cake	n-/n/est
i-e as in like	d-/d/og	k-/k/ite	y as in yoke
r-/r/ing	o-e as in home	z-/z/oo	g as in goat

B: Phonics Chart II: Digraphs

Once the key letter-sound associations in Chart 1 are mostly mastered, focus on the following:		
ch as in chip	ou as in cloud	kn as in not
ea as in meat	oy as in boy	oa as in boat
ee as in need	ph as in phone	oi as in boil
er as in her	qu as in quick	ai as in maid
ay as in day	sh as in ship	ar as in car
igh as in high	th as in thank	au as in haul
ew as in new	ir as in girl	aw as in paw

PHASE 3 LITERACY MILESTONES DIARY[5]

Keep track of your child's accomplishments. As your child completes each milestone, check off the appropriate box. This easy guide for checking off milestones can be a delightful record of your child's progress and make your child's literacy development more transparent.

Items that don't receive checks will help you decide which activities need more focus. You may supplement this easy checklist with your own notes and observations, recording favorite books and memorable vignettes marking your child's literacy development. A "Special Memories and Keepsakes" template organized by phases is provided in the Appendix to aid you in sharpening your focus.

Watch Me Grow in Reading

Monitor your child's reading development by keeping a list of the Level C–G books and more advanced favorite books she is reading. You should begin to see a move to greater reading independence.

My Firsts

- ☐ I can read back Level C through G books that have been read to me over and over.
- ☐ I increase the number of books I read after practice.
- ☐ I no longer require adult underwriting; you can easily read my writing, and quite a few words are spelled correctly.
- ☐ I make the voice-to-print match when reading.
- ☐ I continue to enjoy books and respond to a broader range of them through read-alouds.
- ☐ I can recognize one hundred or more sight words from memory.
- ☐ I can read back books from memory with fluency.
- ☐ I can retell stories in my own words, moving to more sophisticated levels.
- ☐ I demonstrate text understanding in conversations during and following shared reading as we move to more sophisticated levels.
- ☐ I enjoy listening to more elaborate stories.

Watch Me Grow in Drawing and Writing

Your Phase 3 writer has advanced so that you can read her writing and parse her Phase 3 invented spelling by decoding a letter for each sound. In addition, she probably already uses quite a few correctly spelled words. Take special care to collect samples of drawing and writing that show development similar to the samples presented in this chapter. Collect a few samples that are especially memorable as keepsakes.

My Firsts

- ☐ I am increasing the length of my written productions.
- ☐ I match a letter to each sound in a word when I write.
- ☐ I know how to position the paper.
- ☐ I may intersperse uppercase and lowercase letters indiscriminately, but with less abundance than at previous phases.
- ☐ I continue to enjoy writing.

Watch Me Grow in Sounds and Spelling

My Firsts

- ☐ I recognize many letter-sound correspondences.
- ☐ I spell quite a few words correctly.
- ☐ I have learned to spell some words by analogy to a known spelling in the same word family, such as knowing how to spell *chat* because I can already spell *cat*.
- ☐ I recognize and name all the letters.
- ☐ I can match virtually all of the letters with a sound.
- ☐ I invent spellings that have full letter-sound matches.
- ☐ I can hand spell onsets and rimes such as /j/ plus /-ack/ to make *Jack*.
- ☐ I can match words that begin with the same sound.
- ☐ I can isolate the sound at the beginning of a word.
- ☐ I can blend sounds together to read a word.

Note: Your child has moved to Phase 4 when she begins to invent spellings using chunks of spelling patterns and spells many words correctly.

8

TEACHING READING IN PHASE 4

From Chunking to Chapter Books— The Final Climb to Confident Reading

YOUR CHILD IN this phase reads easy chapter books, recognizes more than one hundred words on sight, and begins to spell many words correctly. She shows A-WAR-NIS of FON-ICS PAT-URNS (awareness of phonics patterns), spelling words such as EVREWHAIR (everywhere), BILLDINGS (buildings), and TIYERD (tired) in "chunks." She moves into fluid alphabetic coding ability. Mature reading kicks in as reading becomes automatic.

Take a look again at Figure I.6, the Pyramid of Beginning Reading Growth, in the Introduction. Your child is now climbing those final steps to confident reading. Phase 4 is when she reaches the top and crosses over into mature reading. It's when the lights come on. At last, your child's brain completely connects the complex circuits needed for reading. It begins to function much like the brain of an adult reader. The indicators are clear and observable.

In Phase 4, your child can read and comprehend easy chapter books, such as *Little Bear* by E. H. Minarik:

"Mother Bear,
Mother Bear,

> Where are you?" calls Little Bear.
> "Oh, dear, Mother Bear is not here,
> and today is my birthday.
> I think my friends will come,
> But I do not see a birthday cake.
> My goodness—no birthday cake.
> What can I do?"[1]

Even though this charming little chapter book with sixty-three pages has wonderful illustrations by Maurice Sendak, your child could not comprehend the elaborated episodes and events that Little Bear experiences simply by looking at the pictures. There are more sentences on a page than at previous levels, and the text plays the main role in carrying the story, with very low support from the illustrations. In Phase 4 your child also encounters more specialized and challenging vocabulary, such as the words *princess*, *China*, *Viking*, and *tomatoes* in the *Little Bear* story.

Phase 4 readers show new competence in figuring out unknown words and fully integrate sound-spelling cues, grammar cues, and cues from what makes sense while reading for meaning. A Phase 4 reader's repertoire of words recognized automatically on sight will exceed one hundred and will continue to grow rapidly. Reading, and especially rereading, will show evidence of greater fluency. Texts will offer greater opportunities for discussion and for making connections and comparisons with other stories previously read or heard read aloud. Your child is moving toward easy, fluent reading of unfamiliar and more difficult text. She's really making the climb to confident reading! Of course, that climb will continue through the grades and hopefully for all her years to come. Even lifelong readers encounter peaks and plateaus, waning interests, and new beginnings as readers. But after Phase 4, the journey is no longer a beginning—your child is really a reader.

Phase 4 writing often reveals the writer's innermost thoughts and creativity. You see the clear emergence of your child's special individuality and the flowering of a writer's voice. Other changes in Phase 4 writing are perhaps less overt when compared to the changes in previous phases, but your child's writing is growing in sophistication along many parameters. Many more words in writing are spelled correctly in Phase 4. It's reasonable to soon expect two-thirds or more of the words in this early writing to be spelled conventionally. Perhaps the most dramatic change is the newfound strategy of thinking of spellings in terms of chunks of phonics patterns.

A shift takes place in your child's thinking in Phase 4 regarding how to read and write words: It's a shift to *pattern recognition*. While there is an increase in spelling knowledge, your Phase 4 child still doesn't have enough word-specific knowledge to spell all words correctly or even to always choose the correct chunks, because English spelling is very complex. That's why you may see spellings such as YOUNIGHTED for *United* States! You should expect your child's word-specific knowledge to grow, but it will take time—English spelling is so complex that it's not until around fourth grade that writers can spell with greater than 90 percent accuracy and find most of their own misspelled words when editing.

But the important literacy achievement that you see in Phase 4 is not simply more word-specific knowledge, it's a shift in understanding. Your child has broken the complex alphabetic code of English—she now knows how the English system works. She sees new words in chunks of spelling patterns and attempts to write unknown words with this same new understanding. It's a giant step in literacy development, because it marks the crossover from beginning levels to maturity in literacy. In the brain it's the crossover from slow and analytical processing to automaticity.

Look at the two samples of Phase 4 writing in Figure 8.1. Both samples were produced by Danielle, a five-year-old as she moved into Phase 4 at the beginning of her kindergarten year. As with most Phase 4 writing, the samples are more sophisticated in content than writing in previous phases and are easy to read. A vast majority of the words are spelled correctly. The chunking strategy is evident even in most of the words that are misspelled.

Although Danielle didn't yet have the word-specific knowledge to handle hard-to-spell words such as *porridge* and *family*, she pulled from

Figure 8.1: Two Samples of Phase 4 Writing

A: Danielle—Phase 4—5 Years 7 Months

Danielle was already writing in chunks of spelling patterns early in her kindergarten year and was totally fascinated with writing as evidenced by the concentration and stamina required for her to produce this self-motivated computer-generated version of Goldilocks and the Three Bears:

GOODE LIKS and the Three Bears

OUNS upon a time there lived three bears. One day POPU Bear made PORIGE for his FANMULY. But the PORIGE was TO hot to eat. So the bears WIT for a WOCK. WEN GOODE LOKS SMEED the PORIGE she ran in to the house.

B: Danielle—Phase 4—5 years 8 Months

Danielle wrote an account of her grandpa's birthday. Eleven of the spellings are Phase 4 chunking spellings.

Today is my GRANDPAS	Today is my Grandpa's
birthday I DONT. NO	birthday. I don't know
If he is CUMING	if he is coming
BUTHOOWCASE he	because he
Is OL	is old.
My OLE family	My whole family
WIL be THEAR ISET	will be there except
Dad I FET SURPRIST	Dad. I feel surprised [about the cake].
I DONT NO WUT CID of	I don't know what kind of
CAK it is	cake it is.
My Grandma is CUMING.	My Grandma is coming.

the chunks already in her repertoire: PORIGE and FANMULY. Many words were spelled correctly and there was ample evidence of chunking: WOCK (walk), SMEED (smelled), GRANDPAS (Grandpa's), CUMING (coming), BUTHOOWCASE (because), and THEAR (there). Danielle's spelling demonstrates her growing understanding of the English language.

During this same period, Danielle was reading easy Phase 4 chapter books such as *Little Bear* and enjoying appropriate higher-level Phase 4 picture books. Figure 8.2 demonstrates what happens as children develop into mature readers. By seven years of age, Danielle was able to write short stories with near perfect spelling. Her progress is a testimony to the positive impact of invented spelling. Parents or caregivers should not worry that their child's early misspellings might somehow become ingrained. Children who write early move from their own spelling system to the standard system over time.[2]

Figure 8.2: The Valentine Girl

♥♥♥♥♥ ♥♥♥♥♥

The Valentine girl ♥♥♥♥♥♥ taught me about love. She explained to me when I give water to my cat, I'm showing love to my cat. Love is helping friends, family, and cousins. She also told me love is making my bed and HELP Connor, my brother, get dressed. She also explained to love is eating healthy foods. That is love to myself. Love is showing respect when the teacher is talking, and helping your brother with his homework.

♥

As you can see, Danielle replaced early low-level strategies with more efficient correct spelling strategies. Much of this happened informally as a result of her high level of interest and engagement and her positive experiences with reading and writing at home. Her parents had also gently and subtly addressed the issue of correct spelling. They helped her become a good speller through word games and by focusing attention on words, but at the same time they understood that expert spelling comes gradually and gets better as a child's reading knowledge grows. They were patient. They didn't push for early spelling skills through forced drills and memorization. They recognized that children benefit from formal spelling instruction once they enroll in school because English spelling is very complex.

Phase 4 is when your child:

- Shows evidence of chunking knowledge
- Stores many more words and spelling patterns in memory than before and recognizes them automatically
- Recognizes that spelling patterns such as e, ee, and ea in *be*, *bee*, and *beat* can represent the same sound
- Reads Level H through I books and moves into the grade two levels
- Moves toward independent reading without having to commit books to memory
- Increases the volume of writing
- Stabilizes the concept of how words work and integrates the use of letter-sound cues and grammar cues, paying attention to what makes sense in reading for meaning
- Invents spellings in chunks of phonics patterns
- Learns to read many more words automatically from memory, moving beyond one hundred words recognized on sight

GET SET FOR PHASE 4 BY GATHERING MATERIALS AND PREVIEWING ACTIVITIES

Books

Continue with your favorite books, but add to the collection and increase the level of difficulty:

Easy chapter books
Information books
Story books
Fantasy
Mystery
Folk tales
Various genres

Materials for Writing and Book Making

A variety of papers, pencils, markers, and crayons
Glue, tape, scissors, stapler, construction paper

Materials for Word Games

Letter tiles, magnetic letters, magnetic boards
3×5-inch index cards, hole puncher, ring clip

Overview of Activities and Techniques for Phase 4

This list will help you to anticipate the activities and techniques ahead for teaching your child over the next months in Phase 4.

Activities and Techniques for Reading

"Reading With-Your-Child"
Read-alouds and story retellings

Sight-word collections and "Look What I Can Read!" celebrations
Word games

Activities and Techniques for Writing

Kid writing

Spelling and Sound Activities

Hand spelling
Making words with letter tiles
Spelling words correctly from memory

ACTIVITIES FOR PHASE 4 READING

Reading With-Your-Child

Materials

Easy in Level H through Level J books and old favorites and beyond into grade 2 levels.

Skills Learned

Comprehension, fluency, sight-word recognition, vocabulary.

Directions

Help your child select books that are on an appropriate level, delightful, and appealing. Shift from modeling the reading of the story in the "Reading For-, With-, and By-Your-Child" activity that you did in earlier phases to simply introducing the story in Phase 4 and "Reading With-Your-Child." Your introduction should be brief and animated. It should entice your child to read the text and help him anticipate what's ahead.

When choosing a book, make sure your Phase 4 reader has enough background knowledge and understanding of specialized vocabulary to read and comprehend the story. Provide more support for more challenging texts, adjusting the level of support to whatever you think your child needs to be successful. Make connections to what your child already knows but avoid giving away too much information. Reading is a problem-solving activity driven by making hypotheses—and then reading to find out what happens next. In the search for meaning, the reader surveys the information in front of him (the cover, illustration, a blurb, or what's already been read), asks himself the question, "What do I think will happen? (or, What will I find out?), reads, and finally confirms or readjusts the hypothesis. Comprehending text isn't just about what's in the book; it also depends on what the reader brings to the text. So your child must use what he already knows in order to read and gain new information.

The length of the text, the number of words and density of sentences on a page, and the text structure should all be appropriate for your child's experience and stamina. Although your child should already know most of the words in a new book, a good match will present opportunities for new learning. If your child is having fun with a book, you know you have made a good choice.

Phase 4 is a good time to begin encouraging silent reading. When you read with your child, have him read a section silently and then talk about what he found out. Reading silently generally comes naturally with practice and is much faster than reading out loud. Encourage silent reading when your child reads independently. If your child seems to be reluctant to read silently, select easy levels of new texts to practice silently in addition to moving into the more complex Phase 4 text levels.

Characteristics of Level H to Level I Texts for Phase 4

Phase 4 reading includes a wide variety of children's literature in various genres, including chapter books and picture books with elaborate text. Expect literary language, challenging vocabulary, and character development, with varied settings and complex episodes and events. Phase 4 readers like to read favorite authors and series books. They choose books and read widely on topics or themes that interest them.

To summarize, appropriate text levels for "Reading With-Your-Child" for Phase 4 readers have these characteristics:

Varied sentence patterns, sometimes with repeated refrains
Literary language, dialogue, familiar oral language structures

Specialized vocabulary on a limited basis
Varied subject matter and genres, including fantasy, mysteries, informational texts, and stories about familiar experiences
Illustrations providing a low level of support[3]

Figuring Out Unknown Words in Phase 4

There is not a right or wrong thing to say when your child stumbles on a word. It depends on the particular circumstances—what your child already knows, what strategies she is using, the importance of the word for understanding the text, and so forth. Use your intuitive sense and your knowledge of your child as well as the word's placement and role in the text to decide how to direct your child's attention. First see if your child can figure the word out by himself by asking him to read the line again. Sometimes the running start—trying the line again—is enough to help your child figure out the unknown or missed word.

If a word is really hard or not likely to be in your child's vocabulary, one option is to simply give the word to him. If it feels right to stop and discuss the meaning of the word at this juncture, you can choose to stop reading together and discuss the word. If it feels better to keep reading, you have the option to come back to the word later if it's important in the story.

Here's an example of how to work with your child to problem-solve words. The book *Little Bear* has the word "*Viking*" in this sentence: "Then I wish that I could find a Viking boat." The illustration on the page shows a Viking ship at sea with a dragon head protruding from the bow, one large striped sail, tents and shields on deck, a row of long oars protruding from oar holes, and two Viking-like figures on board. So how would you respond if your child stumbled on *Viking*?

When a word is mispronounced or read incorrectly, you must decide what to do about it on the spot. If you choose to pause and work on problem-solving the word, there are three basic cueing systems to choose from: (1) letter-sound cues, (2) grammar or language structure cues, and (3) meaning cues. By Phase 4, your child has been using all three cueing strategies for some time, but now the sophistication of the text and occasional specialized word give your child many more opportunities to solve words.

When dealing with unknown words, choose from these options:

- Do nothing now to interrupt the flow; come back to it later if it's important.
- Probe to find out what strategy your child may be thinking of using. Say, "Let's try this word again," and if he gets it, say, "That's great. How did you figure it out?" If he misses it, demonstrate one or more of the strategies described below.
- Address the letter-sound components by breaking the word into parts or syllable chunks. Sounding out the word may provide access to its meaning.

  PARENT: Let's see if you can pronounce this word: Here's the first part, *vi–*. It's like the first part of *bi*-cycle, but with the /v/ sound. The next part is *king*. You know *king*! Try it for me.

  CHILD: Vi-king. Vi-king. Viking!
- Use the meaning of the story to get the correct word that makes sense.
- Draw attention to the illustration as support for the search for meaning. ("Can you tell what kind of boat it is from the picture?")
- Make a connection to something your child already knows. ("Remember that helmet and sword outfit you picked out for Halloween? You were a ___________.")
- Draw the child's attention to text structure. ("What kind of boat is it?" In this case, you are drawing attention to an adjective that describes the noun *boat*.)
- Try a combination of the responses above.

Remember to find a way to compliment your child even when working through a correction: "Wow, you really are good at figuring out unknown words!"

Great Books for Phase 4 and Beyond

Leo the Late Bloomer by Robert Kraus, illustrated by Jose Aruego (HarperCollins, 1971)

"Leo couldn't do anything right. He couldn't read. He couldn't write," but in this amazing story that children can read for themselves in Phase 4, the reader learns about patience. "A watched bloomer doesn't bloom"—an appropriate message for both Phase 4 readers and their parents. Leo makes it in the end and so will your little Leo as he or she moves toward confident reading.

The Very Quiet Cricket by Eric Carle (Philomel, 1970)

A beautiful multi-sensory picture book, which, along with the others in the Eric Carle series, including *The Very Hungry Caterpillar* and *The Very Busy Spider*, delights Phase 4 readers. The quiet cricket and other insects are rendered in bold, textured colors with a repetitive text perfectly leveled for Phase 4. A gentle story with a happy ending about the search for a soul mate and finding love.

NBA Action from A to Z by Brendan Hanrahan and James Preller (Scholastic, 1997)

A wonderful Phase 4 ABC book for any passionate NBA fan. For J, for example: "The slam dunk, or jam, is the most exciting play in basketball. Hugo, a mascot for the Charlotte Hornets, goes up for a monster jam." Basketball fans will pore over this book, learning many new sight words, such as *referee*, *offense*, *dribble*, and *coach*, not to mention all the words in the logos for twenty-nine teams, from the *Miami Heat* to the *Nuggets* to the *Pacers*. Who ever said you couldn't get boys to read!

The Treasure by Uri Shulevitz (Farrar, Straus, and Giroux, 1978)

Phase 4 books can be sophisticated and full of deep levels of thought and elegance. Here's a classic, richly illustrated tale of a poor man who searches far away for the treasure of his dreams, only to find it back home where he started. This book is from a wonderful storyteller who puts the whole story into words that Phase 4 readers can handle: "Sometimes one must travel far to discover what is near."

This lovely little book is based on the lofty thoughts of T. S. Eliot: "We shall not cease from exploration / And the end of all our exploring / Will be to arrive where we started / And know the place for the first time."

Lilly's Purple Plastic Purse by Kevin Henkes (Greenwillow Books, 1996)

A little aspiring teacher—or surgeon, or ambulance driver, or dancer, or hairdresser—will never forget the lessons Lilly learned. This is a great selection for girls who love purple purses and school. A perfect choice for readers in the upper Phase 4 ranges.

Amelia Bedelia by Peggy Parish (Harper and Row, 1963)

Amelia gets a list of things to do on her first day of work for Mrs. Rogers—which she takes a bit too literally. In the Amelia Bedelia series, Amelia delights young readers by creating a great ruckus with her literal interpretations of words and phrases: She makes a sponge cake with real sponges and pitches the tent *into* the woods. A humorous Level K book, appropriate for readers moving beyond Phase 4 into grade 2 levels.

Cam Jansen and the Mystery of the U.F.O. by David A. Adler, illustrated by Susanna Natti (Puffin Books, 1980)

Want to know where your little reader is going in the months and years ahead? Second-graders can read mystery chapter books such as this page-turner about the girl with the amazing photographic memory: "Aliens? Cam stood at the corner. She faced the park. 'This is where I first saw the U.F.O.'s,' Cam said. 'Sometimes, if I stand where I first saw something, it helps me remember.'" *Cam Jansen and the Mystery of the U.F.O.* is one selection from a remarkable Cam Jansen Adventure Series for readers who are taking off on their own. This book is end-of-second-grade level.

PHASE 4 TEACHER TALK: COMPREHENSION, FLUENCY, SOUND AWARENESS, PHONICS, AND VOCABULARY

The "Teacher Talk" features introduced in Chapters 6 and 7 for Phases 2 and 3 continue in Phase 4, with the major change being that there are extensions as they are applied to higher levels of text.

Comprehension. Continue to observe and ask questions to make sure your child is paying attention to the meaning of the text. As children move to the higher phases, reading generally becomes faster, and more complex processing is required. Children read and use their prior knowledge to make sense in an active search for meaning. As children move into Phase 4 and beyond, they recognize more and more words automatically and integrate all aspects of the reading process, resulting in fluency and automatic processing. In focusing attention on comprehension, you continue to address setting, character development, events, and plot development in story reading and content in informational reading. Most discussion surrounding reading with your child focuses on meaning and comprehension.

Fluency. Phase 4 is when your child most likely gets into the flow of reading and the concentration begins to seem effortless. Fluency, including reading rate, phrasing, and expression, are all expected to continue to develop, becoming more natural in Phase 4. In fact, fluency and appropriate phrasing are good indicators that your Phase 4 reader is growing into a confident reader. Expect new material to include some word-by-word reading as your child slows down for problem-solving unknown words, but if the material is read several times and the word-recognition level is above 95 percent, the reading is expected to be fluent and expressive with appropriate attention to punctuation.

If your child's reading is not fluent, continue to practice a few favorite pattern books until fluency is achieved. Phase 4 readers often benefit from working on fluency with easier text from the Phase 3 levels of difficulty, or with Phase 4 text that they like well enough to read over and over again.

Sound awareness and phonics. Phase 4 is characterized by attention to chunking. Learning many of the easier, higher-frequency chunking patterns begins with making analogies and working with word families in Phase 3. Many of these forms become automatic in Phase 4. Throughout Phase 4 and beyond, learning chunking patterns is continued, and more formal spelling lessons are introduced. Although this parenting book features activities for teaching reading informally at home, and therefore does not recommend formal spelling tests and the like, Phase 4 readers are well prepared to take on the challenge of learning to spell many words correctly. At this stage, if you choose a few words each week and challenge your child to learn to spell them, keep it fun instead of making it a chore of memorization and drills. I highly recommend spelling games and activities for extending word-specific knowledge in Phase 4.

Vocabulary. Reading vocabulary really gets interesting in Phase 4 with the introduction of many more specialized words. There are also more opportunities for children to figure out unknown words. Reading and reading aloud with discussions offer the best way for Phase 4 readers to expand their reading, writing, and listening vocabularies. The more books they read, and the more reading aloud you enjoy, the more your child's vocabulary will grow. Vocabulary development is one of the highest correlates to intelligence. Here's one parent's report on how her own mother encouraged vocabulary development in the home to foster an interest and love for words that carried into her adulthood: "I remember my mother posting a difficult word on each of our bedroom doors each week (the first week the words started with A, the second week they started with B, etc.). Then each of us (my sisters and I) were supposed to use our word in as many sentences as we could that week in normal conversation. We naturally learned each other's words as well as our own, and it was really fun to come up with ways to work them into conversation. We still joke about some of those words sometimes, decades later. (Some of them were pretty obscure!)"

Read-Alouds and Story Retellings

Just because your child is reading independently doesn't mean you need to abandon the joy of reading aloud together. Reading books aloud that are too hard for your child to read independently will foster your child's intellectual development and love for reading.

Ring Clips for Sight-Word Collections and "Look What I Can Read!" Celebrations

Materials

3×5-inch index cards, marker

Skills Learned

Sight-word recognition; correct spelling.

Directions

Since readers in Phase 4 can automatically read up to one hundred words, it's no longer practical to create word cards. It's now time to specialize! Move to practicing specialized collections. For example, Phase 4 readers who love *NBA Action from A to Z* by James Preller[4] will delight in putting all the team names from the logo page onto word cards and playing games or doing speed sorts or other activities to see how fast they can read the words. If your child is passionate about a set of words, she might like to learn to spell them correctly after learning to read them automatically on sight.

Word Games

The materials needed and skills learned are the same as for sight-word collections above. Be creative and invent word games based on familiar card games, game shows, or board games. Go Fish, Old Maid, Concentration, Hang Man, Wheel of Fortune, Read My Mind, and any board game with a spinner or dice and a starting and ending point can be adapted for practicing specialized word collections.

Sample Game: NBA Teams Word Sort

Here's a sample game to illustrate how specialty word collections can be turned into reading lessons.

Materials

3×5-inch index cards, marker

Skills Learned

Sight-word recognition; correct spelling.

Directions

The object of this game is to have your child learn to read the names of teams in the NBA automatically and to match these names to a word card that names the team's logo or mascot. For example, a "Chicago" word card will be matched with a "Bulls" word card.

1. Write each of your child's favorite teams on a word card to create a set of word cards of NBA teams (e.g., Boston, Miami, Charlotte, Chicago).
2. Write each team's logo or mascot on a separate card to create a matching set of cards with team logos (e.g., Celtics, Heat, Bobcats, Bulls).

3. Shuffle each deck.

4. Give your child the team deck and have him place them in a column. Starting at the top, have him read the names of the teams from top to bottom.

5. Give your child the shuffled logo stack and have him match the logo card to the team card by placing the logo card to the right of the team card (e.g., Boston Celtics).

6. Once you child is successful matching and reading the team names and logos, turn the activity into a speed sort by seeing how many seconds it takes to do the match.

Challenging your child to add new teams and logos will expand his automatic sight-word recognition.

Another game-like activity might be to have your Phase 4 learner develop sets of word cards for each of the two NFL conferences (American and National) and sort the word cards into teams in the four divisions (East, North, West, and South). Your young NFL aficionado might enjoy doing the research for making the word cards online by typing key words, such as "NFL teams 2010," into a computer search engine. Help your child find the listing, and he can write the team names on cards and learn to speed-sort the cards into divisions.

Any game utilizing word cards, even one as simple as the sample game described above, will reinforce recognition of the words on the cards, because multiple readings of the cards are required to play. Notice that many of the words in the example reinforce high-frequency chunks: Miami Heat, meat, treat, eat, beat; New Jersey Nets, bets, gets, sets, jets, lets, pets; Milwaukee Bucks, trucks, ducks, mucks; San Antonio Spurs, purrs, furs, and so forth. Likewise, many of the city names break into familiar high-frequency chunks: To-ron-to, Tim-ber-wolves, Sac-ra-men-to, Rap-tors.

Working with words such as these disguises the fact that you are actually teaching your child to read in chunks. If your child learns to read these words, he will greatly improve "grapho-syllabic decoding skills," a fancy way of saying he's working on seeing the chunking patterns when trying to read words with more than one syllable. Your child is delighting in an activity with team names he's passionate about, but he's also learning to read!

Choose a few teams for children just moving into Phase 4 and add new ones as long as the activity holds interest. If your child is *really* an NBA aficionado, use these words and team logos to decorate his bedroom, not only turning the room into a sports shrine, but a reading lesson! (This type of activity can be done with *anything* your child is interested in: flowers, butterflies, dinosaurs, fish, birds, cars, movie character themes, and so forth.) Once your child begins to add words to the specialized collection, you can create all kinds of activities to have him use the words over and over again until he recognizes them automatically.

Word Sorting

Word sorting helps children learn to recognize word chunks and eventually to spell words automatically. Sorting also helps them begin to recognize that certain spelling patterns are used more than others. With the NBA team theme described above, for example, you can do matching and sorting activities to create countless categories, such as teams in the same division, teams playing this weekend, teams that won, teams that lost, teams at the head of the division, and so forth. Every time your child sorts the words, it's a reading lesson. If your child likes posting these lists in his or her room, use a pocket chart or paste magnet strips on the back of each word card, and use a large cookie sheet or magnetic easel for a display board. Once your child can easily read these words, create wall charts or bring in a chalkboard for listing the team winners of the week, or whatever categories your child is interested in tracking.

Specialized word-card collections can boost reading skills quickly and easily and never seem like boring drill and practice. In the spelling activities below, there are numerous opportunities for sorting words by spelling patterns. Figure 8.3 is one of the best word sorts available for helping Phase 4 readers develop automatic sight-word recognition. Begin focusing on a particular vowel set, such as the short and long "a." Practice just a few of these vowel pairs at a time. It may take many months for your child to master all the words in the chart.

Figure 8.3: Short Versus Long Vowels, Word Sort for Phase 4

Recognizing CVC Versus CVCe Matched Pairs for Short and Long Vowel Chunks

bit, bite	cub, cube	cut, cute	can, cane
cap, cape	cod, code	con, cone	Dan, Dane
dim, dime	fad, fade	fat, fate	fin, fine
fir, fire	hat, hate	hid, hide	hop, hope
kit, kite	Jan, Jane	man, mane	mad, made
mat, mate	not, note	pal, pale	pan, pane
pin, pine	rat, rate	rid, ride	rip, ripe
rob, robe	rod, rode	Sam, same	Sid, side
sit, site	tam, tame	tap, tape	Tim, time
Tom, tome	tub, tube	van, vane	win, wine

ACTIVITIES FOR PHASE 4 WRITING

Kid writing continues in Phase 4 with increases in quality and volume.

Kid Writing

Materials

A variety of pencils, pens, crayons, markers, and paper.

Skills Learned

Integration of all reading and writing skills; ability to produce a variety of short compositions, ranging from simple descriptions and stories to longer, more elaborate compositions; ability to write in various genres; informal development of skills in spelling, punctuation, and other writing conventions; ability to move from ideas in the imagination to presentation of the information in a deliberate and organized format; ability to make connections between reading and writing.

Directions

Kid writing in Phase 4 is an extension of the kid writing done in the earlier phases. Set appropriate expectations by studying the samples presented in Figures 8.1 and 8.2, which represent the wide range of Phase 4 productions in both quality and quantity. Expect increases in volume and meaningful, independent pieces, often with a beginning, middle, and ending; a first, then, next, last sequence; or other text forms. Expect more accurate spelling, with invented spellings mostly showing evidence of a chunking strategy. Phase 4 writers choose from a wide range of topics, often using the books they are reading as springboards for topics and forms.

ACTIVITIES FOR PHASE 4 SPELLING AND PHONICS

Phase 4 readers have an expanded understanding of phonics and are more accurate spellers than Phase 3 readers. Many common spelling patterns are stored in their memory and are recognized automatically. Phase 4 readers also begin to recognize different spellings for the same vowel sound. For example, the / ā / sound can be spelled as *a*, *ay*, and *ai*, as in *bake*, *pay*, and *nail*, respectively. Common patterns are often used but confused in invented spelling during Phase 4. For example, vowel digraphs (two letters that make one sound), such as *ai*, *ea*, *ay*, *ee*, and *ow*, appear liberally in writing but often incorrectly, such as in PLAID for *played* and KEAP for *keep*.

Word sorting is a great way to help your child begin to recognize the correct patterns, and Phase 4 spellers can respond equally well to deliberate spelling study. It is also a good time to introduce contrasting high-frequency patterns such as rat/rate, hop/hope, and hat/hate. The activities described below will show you how.

By the end of Phase 4, your child should:

- Demonstrate evidence of chunking knowledge
- Respond well to spelling instruction
- Begin to master different spelling patterns for the same sound

Spelling Chunking Formations

Here's a great activity for helping your child apply what she already knows to building new words. Phase 4 readers especially like to unravel the "big words"—a true confidence builder. Starting with a known word with an identified spelling chunk, in this activity your child will see how many words she can write in a column and read them back to you.

Materials

Pen or pencil, paper.

Skills Learned

Letter-sound correspondence, spelling, phonics.

Directions

1. Start with any word that has a chunk on which you might like to focus.
2. Use the first word to create a new, longer word, such as moving from *hand* to *handle*.
3. Sticking with the basic chunk, such as –*an* in *hand*, create new words, such as *man*.
4. Make a whole column of words that share the common chunk. (If your child is having difficulty, give him clues for appropriate words, or share the pen so that you add words to the list along with your child.)
5. Have your child read back the list rapidly. Here are two examples of chunking formations:

mud	hand
Mudge	handle
fudge	man
budge	stand
bud	Amanda
buddy	woman
budget	handsome

Fun with Word Families

Materials

3×5-inch index cards for making word-family cards or a commercial set of word-family cards, spinners, dice, materials for games and for making game boards.

Skills Learned

Sight-word recognition; ability to make word analogies; ability to construct and reconstruct known words, to pull words apart and put them back together, to match letters to sounds, and to recognize onsets and rimes; phonics; spelling.

Directions

Phase 4 brings a continuation of the games and strategies that were initiated in Phase 3 for developing word families. The key in Phase 4 is to extend the activity, building new words into your child's repertoire. You'll find the complete instructions for this activity in Chapter 7. Here's the list of the thirty-seven great word family chunks, repeated here for your convenience.

Great Word Families for Building New Words

–ack	–an	–aw	–ice	–in	–ir	–ore
–ain	–ank	–ay	–ick	–ine	–ock	–uck
–ake	–ap	–eat	–ide	–ing	–oke	–ug
–ale	–ash	–ell	–ight	–ink	–op	–ump
–all	–at	–est	–ill	–ip	–or	–unk
–ame	–ate[5]					

Directions

1. Start with words that your child already knows.
2. Call attention to the chunk you are targeting.
3. Work together to generate a list and practice reading word families, such as bash, cash, hash, flash, mash, and backlash.
4. Have your child practice writing and spelling words with the same pattern. Note that in Phase 3 your child was recognizing

many chunks for the first time. In Phase 4 she's learning to spell them. Remember that reading a word is easier than spelling it correctly.

Game Suggestions:

- Make a set of word cards for any target word-family pattern.
- Make a board game with a starting and ending point and a word card for each space.
- Player spins and moves forward the number of spaces shown on the spinner.
- Player reads the word. If incorrect, she moves back a space. Make the game more competitive by making the adult's advancement harder. For example, every time the child player is correct, the adult player loses two spaces.
- Players alternate turns.
- Adapt any family game to word-card practice.

During Phase 4, your child will learn how to use chunking patterns to read many new words. Be sure to be patient and practice many patterns over an extended period of time.

Making Words: Using Letter Tiles or Magnetic Letters

Here's a popular activity for children in Phase 4 and beyond, adapted from a formal teaching activity.[6] This activity develops both vocabulary skills and spelling.

Materials

Magnetic or plastic letters, homemade letter cards, or letter tiles; magnetic board.

Skills Learned

Sight-word recognition; concept of word; ability to construct and reconstruct known words; left-to-right letter sequencing in words; ability to pull words apart and put them back together and to match letters to sounds; phonics; spelling.

Directions

1. Select a spelling chunk for your child to practice, such as *–ash*.

2. Think of challenging words that contain the pattern of the foundation word and gather as many as you can think of that are appropriate for your child to practice (see Figure 8.4).[7]

3. As the parent, give meaning clues to develop vocabulary and see if your child can guess the word, following the model in Figure 8.5.

4. Give a point for guessing the word and a point for spelling it correctly.

5. Vary the rules to fit your child's level of expertise. Play the game at a level that ensures your child's success.

6. If the pattern has different pronunciations, such as *wash* and *smash* in the *–ash* family, sort the words according to how they are pronounced.

Figure 8.4: Word Bank for *–ash*

Ash	Crash	Mash	Smash
Awash	Dash	Mishmash	Splash
Backlash	Eyelash	Mouthwash	Squash
Backslash	Eyewash	Potash	Stash
Backwash	Flash	Prewash	Succotash
Bash	Gash	Quash	Swash
Brainwash	Gnash	Rash	Trash
Brash	Goulash	Rehash	Unleash
Carwash	Hash	Rewash	Wash
Cash	Hogwash	Sash	Whiplash
Clash	Lash	Slash	Whitewash

Figure 8.5: Making Words Chart

Words	*Meaning or Other Clues*
1. mash	Do this to cream potatoes.
2. splash	Fun in the pool.
3. smash	Rhymes with *crash* and happens in a fender-bender.
4. trash	Another name for rubbish. Take it out!
5. rash	The results of poison oak.
6. whiplash	Causes a sore neck suffered after a car wreck.
7. crash	To have a wreck; rhymes with *smash*.

PHASE 4 LITERACY MILESTONES DIARY[8]

Keep track of your child's accomplishments. As your child completes each milestone, check off the appropriate box. This easy guide for checking off milestones can be a delightful record of your child's progress and make your child's literacy development more transparent.

Items that don't receive checks will help you decide which activities need more focus. You may supplement this easy checklist with your own notes and observations, recording favorite books and memorable vignettes marking your child's literacy development. A "Special Memories and Keepsakes" template organized by phases is provided in the Appendix to aid you in sharpening your focus.

Watch Me Grow in Reading

Monitor your child's reading development by keeping a list of the Level H–I books and more advanced favorite books she is reading. By the end of Phase 4 your child will be an independent reader.

My Firsts

- ☐ I can read books independently at Levels H–I and beyond into grade 2 levels.
- ☐ I expand the repertoire of easy-to-read books, working from individual collections of favorite books.
- ☐ I retell stories in my own words with more elaboration.
- ☐ I demonstrate text understanding in conversations during and following shared reading.
- ☐ I continue to enjoy books and respond to a broader range of them through read-alouds.
- ☐ I can recognize more than one hundred sight words automatically.
- ☐ I can read books in Levels H–I with fluency.
- ☐ I demonstrate text understanding in conversations during and following shared reading as we move to more sophisticated levels.
- ☐ I enjoy listening to more elaborate stories.

Watch Me Grow in Drawing and Writing

My Firsts

- ☐ I am increasing the length of my written productions.
- ☐ I spell many words conventionally when I write.
- ☐ I use chunks of acceptable phonics patterns when I invent spellings.
- ☐ I write more elaborate pieces in a variety of genres.
- ☐ I continue to enjoy writing.

Watch Me Grow in Sounds and Spelling

My Firsts

- ☐ I spell many words correctly (typical second-grade-level spelling).
- ☐ I use spelling analogies, such as BOTE (analogous to *note*) for *boat*.
- ☐ I retrieve many words and spelling patterns from memory automatically.
- ☐ I recognize that different spelling patterns can represent the same sound, as in *e*, *ee*, and *ea* for long *e* in *be*, *bee*, and *beat*.
- ☐ I can sort words according to common spelling patterns.

Note: If you are able to complete this checklist, your child is a competent, independent reader who is most likely functioning on a second-grade level or above.

9

IS EVERYTHING ON TRACK?

Awakening Literacy with Confidence

THIS BOOK began with a pledge to help you become your child's first reading teacher. By following each of the reading phases, you've created an encouraging and supportive literacy environment at home. Now how do you know if everything is on track? What if you didn't get an early start? Is it too late? What if your child is already in school and you aren't sure how things are going? Below you'll find answers to the questions you really want to ask about your child's literacy development—and recommendations for your child's path to success.

ANSWERS TO PRACTICAL QUESTIONS

What if I didn't get an early start? Is it too late?

It's not too late. This book gives you the information you need to be confident in taking charge of your child's reading future—both at home and at school—whether you are starting when your child is a baby, a toddler, or already in school. There are two steps you can take to make sure your child is on track:

1. Take action at home by choosing the right activities to move your child forward.

2. Intervene at school to make sure that your child gets the additional help he or she needs. You'll find guidelines for intervening at school later in this chapter.

What if my child seems way behind the literacy milestones described in this book?

All children grow on their own individual schedules, and there's a wide range of normal development in just about every area, whether it's learning to talk, learning to walk, or learning to read and write. Don't be alarmed if your child seems to be taking his time to meet the literacy milestones described in this book, particularly those in the Phase 0 chapter. They are not intended to make parents anxious about their child's development; rather, they are designed to help you pinpoint your child's reading phase so that you can gently lead her forward on the path to literacy.

If my child is already behind, what should we do at home?

Since all children learn to read in phases, you can follow the instructions in Chapter 3 to determine which action to take, even if your child is behind. Find your child's current phase, and go to the designated phase chapter to find activities for teaching reading at home. These activities will match your child's current abilities and will provide the exact road map for moving forward. A good instructional program should always meet your child at his current level of functioning.

How do you know if your child is behind?

The basic parameters are listed below. Rather than cloak your child's level of functioning in test results, murky jargon, and obscure numbers—"He's Level 15 and should be at Level 20"—here are a set of parameters that are easy to understand:

Entering kindergarten. Your child should be in Phase 1, which is marked by the ability to spell her name. If your child is entering kindergarten and she cannot write her name, she's behind. Your child should also be able to tell about some of her favorite books before entering kindergarten.

Middle of kindergarten. If your child is still in Phase 1 in the middle of kindergarten (or in Phase 0), he is behind. He should now be attempting to write and match some beginning letters to sounds. He should already be reading some easy books from memory—the ones with three to five words or a sentence on a page. He should be recognizing at least a few words automatically on sight. He should be able to tell you the rhyming words in a poem and clap out the syllables in a name. He should be happy in school and excited about learning to read.

End of kindergarten and beginning of first grade. At the end of kindergarten or beginning of first grade, at minimum, your child should be well into Phase 2. In addition to writing with partial letter-sound matches—DE for *daddy*, CRTS for *carrots*, HMT DPD for *Humpty Dumpty*, she should be reading books from memory with text on a page similar to "The cat sat on the mat." She should know at least thirty words on sight. She should be able to retell the gist of a story that you read aloud; answer *who*, *what*, *when*, *where*, *how*, and *why* questions; and demonstrate text understanding in conversations. She should know the letters of the alphabet, how to form them, and for most of them she should be able to give you the key sound that the letter represents. She should love being read to. She should be happy in school and excited about learning to read. Keep in mind that these are the minimal expectations. Many children are far beyond the minimal expectations outlined here. In fact, most children whose parents have engaged in literacy activities at home exceed these minimal expectations.

Middle of first grade. The minimal expectation in the middle of first grade is that your child is near the end of Phase 3. He SPELS WRDS with a LETR FOR ECH SOND, but many words are spelled correctly, including most short vowel sounds in words such as *mat*, *pet*, *sit*, *hot*, and *cut*. He has a large repertoire of easy books that he can reread with fluency and comprehension. He writes stories several lines or sentences long with a beginning, middle, and ending.

End of first grade and beginning of second grade. Your child is in or beyond Phase 4 and either functioning or nearly functioning independently as a reader. She can pick up new material and read it on her own. She can read it fairly fluently after a couple of practices. She is using the chunking strategy for spelling and for figuring out unknown words. Her writing is more elaborate and increasing in volume. She reads well over one hundred words automatically on sight and is able to read easy chapter books.

When should I contact the school to troubleshoot?

If you suspect that your child is struggling, don't wait to contact the school. You must be vigilant for your child's educational attainment. Find out what's happening in school. Too many schools wait for children to fall behind on test scores before offering special services. While this practice is changing, it's up to you to know what's happening at school. Set up a conference with your child's kindergarten or first-grade teacher and make sure your child is on their radar screen. Find out which level books your child is reading and if he is making progress. If your child is behind, you must insist that he get additional support from his teacher in class or through intervention from a special reading teacher.

If the school does not seem to be addressing your child's specific needs, take whatever action is necessary to get your child the help she needs. Make an appointment to discuss your child's situation with her teacher, the school reading specialist, and the principal. There is no need to be adversarial at this point; assume that they want the best for your child as well, and that by working together you can develop a plan to address your child's needs.

But remember that you are your child's best advocate. It's up to you to make sure that things are going well at school and to ensure that your child gets the best services the school can provide. If, after you have raised these issues, the school does not want to provide the appropriate services, don't give up. At that point you will want to become familiar with the Individuals with Disabilities Education Act (IDEA) of 2004 and proceed under those regulations. If you can afford it, you could also hire a qualified reading specialist or reading tutor. This book will help your child's reading tutor instruct your child with appropriate activities.

How do I know whether the level at which my child reads is appropriate for his grade in school?

Curricula and standards vary widely by regions and even within states and districts. Beyond that, individual schools use several different systems to indicate where children are reading in a curriculum of formal instruction, which can be very confusing to parents. Ask your child's teacher about your child's reading progress. She should be able to tell you how your child was reading at the beginning of the year and how he is reading currently by referring to specific skills and levels. Ask about how the reading instructional program is organized and about whether the teacher has small reading groups. If so, find out how your child's group is progressing in relation to the other groups in the class. Be sure to find out what leveling system is used for reading in your child's school and his current level in that scheme. The chart in Figure 9.1 will match your child's current text level in school with typical grade-level expectations.[1] Ask your child's teacher how your child's level compares with local and state expectations.

What about television and computers?

In today's world, children are experiencing information in new ways. They are interpreting videos and using sounds and images to put together a world of ideas. Your child, however, will not learn to read if you simply plop him down in front of a TV set. The American Academy of Pediatrics recommends against television viewing for children under age two. But the fact that 61 percent of children under age one watch TV, and the average two- to four-year-old in America watches television four hours a day, suggests that parents aren't listening. Here's the official policy statement from the American Academy of Pediatrics:

> Pediatricians should urge parents to avoid television viewing for children under the age of 2 years. Although certain television programs may be promoted to this age group, research on early brain development shows that babies and toddlers have a critical need for direct interactions with parents and other significant caregivers (e.g., child care providers) for healthy brain growth and the development of appropriate social, emotional, and cognitive skills. Therefore, exposing such young children to television programs should be discouraged.[2]

Figure 9.1: Expected Reading Levels for Kindergarten Through Grade 2

Grade Level	*Reading Rocovery*	*Guided Reading* *Fountas & Pinnell*	*DRA*	*Traditional Basal Equivalent*
Kindergarten	A,B	A	A	Readiness
	1		1	
	2	B	2	
	3	C	3	Preprimer 1
Grade 1	4	C	4	
	5			
	6	D	6	Preprimer 2
	7			
	8	E	8	Preprimer 3
	9			
	10	F	10	Primer
	11			
	12	G	12	
	13			
	14	H	14	Grade 1
	15			
	16	I	16	
Grade 2			18	
	17		20	Grade 2
	18	J, K	24	
	20	L, M	28	

Nevertheless, literacy technology is changing our lives, and I believe new uses of technology hold great promise for promoting acquisition of literacy. Studies have shown verbal gains in children who watched quality educational programming such as *Sesame Street*. Computer-based multimedia interactions and other new computer technologies are already making their way into preschools. Among educators there is a call to examine and better understand the role of "electronic meaning making" as an aspect of literacy learning.[3]

While it may seem contradictory to the AAP policy statement, I believe there is great potential for multimedia resources to have a positive impact on literacy as parents participate with their children interactively at home, creating and expressing meaning and literacy in electronic formats. In the future, new programming and new uses of technology may afford parents new opportunities to introduce their children to a world where Internet competency is important.

What should I do if I suspect my child may have dyslexia or another learning disability?

If your child has good thinking and reasoning skills but seems to have particular difficulties with the sound and spelling activities presented in each of the phase chapters, it may signal dyslexia. Early signs of dyslexia include extraordinary difficulties with pronunciation, rhyme, and spelling. Often children with dyslexia do not go through the normal early phases of spelling development and later display a conglomeration of the early phase strategies, such as mixing abbreviated spellings with awkward attempts and failure to replace early low-level strategies with correct spelling and higher-level strategies. Sometimes dyslexics can memorize correct spellings for a spelling test but later cannot transfer the correct spellings into their writing or recall the memorized spellings. Additionally, dyslexia runs in families. If other family members have been diagnosed with dyslexia, it increases the probability that a child may be at risk.

If you suspect that your young child is dyslexic, alert your pediatrician and request a referral for further evaluation. If your child is in school, find out your school district's procedure for referral and testing and request an evaluation. Do not wait. Early intervention in school is recommended for children at risk for dyslexia. Unfortunately, the way school districts handle dyslexia referrals varies widely: Some districts have excellent options for testing and follow-up, but others are limited. Parents may contact the International Dyslexia Association (http://www.interdys.org/) and the National Center for Learning Disabilities (http://www.ld.org) for information and resources. *Overcoming Dyslexia* by Sally Shaywitz is an excellent resource for parents wishing to gain a deeper understanding of dyslexia.

DIGGING DEEPER: FIVE PROFOUND QUESTIONS ABOUT AWAKENING LITERACY

In 1982, eighteen distinguished researchers from English-speaking countries throughout the world gathered in a symposium at the University of Victoria in Canada to investigate how children become literate without formal schooling. They were particularly interested in children who learned to read before entering school. Unfortunately, the symposium raised more questions than it answered and reportedly ended with a great deal of frustration and silence. No set of guidelines for parents or teachers emerged.[4] Perhaps symposium participants did not heed a caveat from the philosopher Isaiah Berlin, who has been reported to have said that the trouble with academics is "that they care more about whether ideas are important than whether they are true."[5]

While I have long wondered whether the theories of this gathering of academics sometimes blinded them from the truth, I've always been grateful for the fact that they raised important questions that have captivated me all these years. It's now possible to find practical answers to some of these questions. Parents are looking for such answers, and fortunately, much has come to light over the past twenty-five years regarding how children learn to read. Here's my best attempt, through synthesis of research, personal experience, and personal conviction, to give you answers to the really profound questions about early literacy.

Can children learn to read on their own?

No. Reading has to be taught.

Can children learn by imitating adults?

Yes. I believe that imitation, repetition, and memory reading are sometimes undervalued in current theory and practice, and that the work you do at home with informal reading instruction must not give imitation short shrift. The evidence for the importance of imitation is unequivocal: Babies learn by imitating, or "aping," their parents beginning at birth.

In this regard, the saying "Monkey see, monkey do" can be taken quite literally. In 1990, researchers discovered a special brain capacity in both monkeys and humans for imitating. They named the cells responsible for this phenomenon "mirror cells." Uniquely human mirror neuron systems in a part of the brain called the *insula* contribute to some of our highest levels of acting, thinking, and feeling. Mirror cells fire off when a child sees or hears an action and when she carries out the same action on her own. Humans are hard-wired for imitation, which is why a baby only a week old can watch his mother stick out her tongue and then imitate her. We are hard-wired for imitating the actions, intentions, and emotions surrounding reading behavior as well.[6]

What can and do adults do to introduce their children to literacy?

Read aloud and talk to your child, preferably beginning at birth. Encourage early drawing and writing. Create a joyful, literate environment at home, and respond to your child's natural curiosity and questions. Bond with your child through book sharing and other literacy activities—often.

How do parents enhance a child's ability and motivation to read?

Instilling children with an enthusiasm for reading is not always easy. Start by embracing literacy at home and making time for reading. Provide a responsive environment for your child, and think of it as fostering your child's search for meaning. If your child is struggling in school, don't wait. Intervene to get help now. Choose to go to the library even when your child is very young, and make it a habit. Give him choices when selecting books or literacy activities. Value your child's opinions and interests. Give him as many intellectually stimulating experiences as possible, including picnics, trips to the zoo, and family vacations to interesting destinations. But if you can't afford Hawaii, be assured that it's the everyday things that matter most: Take him with you on errands to the post office, the grocery store, and so on, and talk to him about everything in those surroundings, even if he is a baby and is not yet talking to you. Knowledge of the world is directly related to reading comprehension.

Literate parents certainly are more apt to raise confident readers than parents in a home where literacy is neither practiced nor valued. In any case, you must make time for literacy in your child's life and value literacy learning. If you truly feel you cannot provide the experience yourself, make sure that some other caregiver does.

Beyond these recommendations, celebrate and encourage your child's early attempts at writing. Recognize that writing is a key to early reading and that writing is one of the deepest modes of thinking—for beginners and adults alike. Remember that learning to write like an adult is much like learning to speak like an adult: It happens gradually over a long period of time with a lot of hypothesis testing and error making before perfect production. Respond positively, compliment often, and think before you insist upon adult-like correctness.

You won't build good literacy habits by putting your child down. We all learn from failure as much as we learn from success. In the words of Samuel Beckett, "Fail again. Fail better." This certainly applies to early spelling attempts. Encourage thinking, not error-free sentences. Remember that children who engage in writing before entering school are engaging in logical thinking, and the thinking and deep analysis they do with printed language during early writing will lead to their ability to read. The learning effects are cumulative—the more your child knows, the easier it is to learn more. Your child is learning how to learn.

Should all children read before school?

Children do not have to be reading independently before entering school, but they do have to be *prepared for success* with reading. Children who enter kindergarten without a cultural heritage enlightened by literature or with no exposure to the tools of literacy—books, paper, pens, and, in the twenty-first century, even digital literacy apparatus—are not well prepared. Children who have no appreciation for story telling, no knowledge of the letters of the alphabet, and no beginning awareness of the sounds in words are not well prepared for learning to read through formal instruction in school. These children are at risk for failure with reading, and that failure can impact the rest of their lives.

All children need literacy before school. Language is a uniquely human gift, and as this book has made clear, exposure to reading and writing at home before entering school enriches a child's early language learning and intellectual development. Preschool literacy contributes to a child's self-motivated quest to make meaning in life, to discover his or her world, to create new possibilities, to enjoy his or her highest potential, and to achieve understanding, insight, and self-fulfillment. Every parent should raise a confident reader.

APPENDIX

Special Memories and Keepsakes

You might like to create a Special Memories and Keepsakes Book to celebrate and remember all the stages of your child's literacy development. Follow the outline below and keep photos and mementos such as artwork, writing samples, anecdotes, and homemade books in a special notebook or album. Organize Special Memories and Keepsakes by phases following the approximate age expectations.

I've provided a complete template below for Phase 0, breaking the phase into several stages. Due to the wide normal variations in ages and attainment of skills beyond Phase 0, the templates for the later stages are minimal. Add to these by simply being creative and observing your child's literacy growth. You can use your computer to print out labels for a scrapbook, with photos mounted on the pages, or, if you enjoy being artistic, try using markers, special handwriting, and some of the scrapbooking tools that are now available to make your child's Special Memories and Keepsakes Book meaningful. Record the dates for special memories created during each of the phases, using photos and other items that tell the story of your child's growth as a reader and writer. For keepsakes that do not fit into a scrapbook format, such as your child's favorite books, you could decorate a cardboard box or purchase a keepsakes box.

Once you begin recording these moments, you will likely come up with all kinds of ideas on your own based on your child's unique experiences. For example, you can take a photo of your child showing how old she was when she first started writing letters of the alphabet. Have her hold up the completed piece in front of her chest, and take a close-up shot of her so that the letters she has written will be visible in the photo. Take another photo like this in six months, and you'll see how your child is changing—both physically and as a writer! You might also want to make a video recording of your child singing the alphabet song, or have someone hold the camera and record the two of you doing a read-aloud in each phase. Simply record those special moments in every phase for you and your child to celebrate and enjoy.

PHASE 0: SPECIAL MEMORIES AND KEEPSAKES FROM BIRTH TO SIX MONTHS

______________ (name) read me my first story on _________ (date). I was _____________ (days/years old).

Daddy's first time reading to me was on _________ (date). He read ____ (book title).

Mommy's first time reading to me was on _________ (date). She read ____ (book title).

My favorite book from birth to six months was ____ (book title).

I first smiled when Mom/Dad was reading ____ (book title).

I laughed when Mom/Dad was showing me ____ (an illustration).

I sat supported for the first time when Mom/Dad was reading ____ (book title).

I first cooed along with ____ (rhyme or chant).

I tried to explore ____ (book title) with my mouth.

Note: Some of the milestones listed here may actually appear later than six months of age. Every child develops differently, so it's important to be patient.

PHASE 0: SPECIAL MEMORIES AND KEEPSAKES FROM SIX TO TWELVE MONTHS

My favorite book from six to twelve months was ____ (book title).

My favorite rhyming book was ____ (book title).

My favorite caption book was ____ (book title).

I laughed when Mom/Dad showed me ____ (an illustration).

The first book I selected and brought to my parents was
________________________________ (book title).
My favorite lift-the-flap or gimmick book was
________________________________ (book title).
I loved reading about ________________________ (favorite subject: animals, trucks, trains, airplanes, flowers, etc.).
The first words I read were: ________________________.

PHASE 0: SPECIAL MEMORIES AND KEEPSAKES FROM TWELVE TO EIGHTEEN MONTHS

My favorite book from twelve to eighteen months was
________________________________ (book title).
Other favorites included:
____
________________ (book titles).
I loved reading about ________________________ (favorite subject: animals, trucks, trains, airplanes, flowers, etc.).
I learned to read some words: ________________________.
I loved to draw and write about: ________________________ (favorite subject: animals, trucks, trains, airplanes, flowers, etc.).

PHASE 0: SPECIAL MEMORIES AND KEEPSAKES FROM EIGHTEEN MONTHS TO TWO YEARS

My favorite book from eighteen to twenty-four months was
________________________________ (book title).
Other favorites included:
____
________________(book titles).
I loved reading about ________________________ (favorite subjects: animals, trucks, trains, airplanes, flowers, etc.).
I learned to read some words: ________________________.
I loved to draw and write about ________________________ (favorite subjects: animals, trucks, trains, airplanes, flowers, etc.).

SPECIAL MEMORIES AND KEEPSAKES FROM PHASE 1

My favorite book in Phase 1 was

________________________________ (book title).

Here are some books I can read from memory!

____

__________________.

I loved reading about __________________________ (favorite subject: animals, trucks, trains, airplanes, flowers, etc.).

I learned to read some words in this book:

________________________________ (book title).

I loved to draw and write about: __________________________ (favorite subject: animals, trucks, trains, airplanes, flowers, etc.).

SPECIAL MEMORIES AND KEEPSAKES FROM PHASE 2

My favorite book in Phase 2 was

________________________________ (book title).

Here are some books I can read from memory!

____

__________________.

I loved reading about __________________________ (favorite subject: animals, trucks, trains, airplanes, flowers, etc.).

I learned to read some words in this book:

________________________________ (book title).

I loved to draw and write about: __________________________ (favorite subject: animals, trucks, trains, airplanes, flowers, etc.).

SPECIAL MEMORIES AND KEEPSAKES FROM PHASE 3

My favorite book in Phase 3 was

________________________________ (book title).

Here are some books I can read from memory!

____.

I loved reading about ______________________________ (favorite subject: animals, trucks, trains, airplanes, flowers, etc.).

I learned to read some words in this book:
____ (book title).

I loved to draw and write about: ______________________________ (favorite subject: animals, trucks, trains, airplanes, flowers, etc.).

SPECIAL MEMORIES AND KEEPSAKES FROM PHASE 4

My favorite book in Phase 4 was
____ (book title).

Here are some books I can read independently!
____
____________________.

I loved reading about ______________________________ (favorite subject: animals, trucks, trains, airplanes, flowers, etc.).

I learned to read some words in this book:
____ (book title).

I loved to draw and write about: ______________________________ (favorite subject: animals, trucks, trains, airplanes, flowers, etc.).

NOTES

INTRODUCTION

1. Betty Hart and Todd Risley, *Meaningful Differences in Everyday Experience of Young American Children* (Baltimore: Brookes, 1996).

2. John O'Neal, "Early Repairs in Foundations for Reading," *New York Times*, October 4, 2006, A25.

1. NURTURE YOUR CHILD'S BRAIN AS IT GROWS INTO READING

1. Betty Hart and Todd Risley, *Meaningful Differences in Everyday Experience of Young American Children* (Baltimore: Brookes, 1996).

2. Lise Eliot, *What's Going On in There? How the Brain and Mind Develop in the First Five Years of Life* (New York: Bantam Books, 1999), 363.

3. Ibid., 458.

4. S. Shaywitz, *Overcoming Dyslexia* (New York: Alfred A. Knopf, 2003).

5. J. Richard Gentry, *Breakthrough in Beginning Reading and Writing* (New York: Scholastic, 2007).

6. Jill Stamm, *Bright from the Start: The Simple, Science-Backed Way to Nurture Your Child's Developing Mind, from Birth to Age 3* (New York: Penguin, 2007).

7. Stanislas Dehaene, *Reading in the Brain* (New York: Viking, 2009); J. R. Gentry, *Breaking the Code: The New Science of Beginning Reading and Writing* (Portsmouth, NH: Heinemann, 2006); E. Paulesu, J.-F. Demonet, F. Fazio, E. McCrory, V. Chanoine, N. Brunswick, S. F. Cappa, G. Cossu, M. Habib, C. D. Frith, and U. Frith, "Dyslexia: Cultural Diversity and Biological Unity," *Science* 291, no. 5511 (March 16, 2001): 2165.

8. Shaywitz, *Overcoming Dyslexia*.

9. National Institute of Child Health and Human Development, *Report of the National Reading Panel. Teaching Children to Read: An Evidence-Based Assessment of the Scientific Research Literature on Reading and Its Implications for Reading Instruction*, NIH Publication No. 00-4769 (Washington, DC: U.S. Government Printing Office, 2000).

10. Shaywitz, *Overcoming Dyslexia*, 79.

2. THE BRAIN-BASED FORMULA

1. Lise Eliot, *What's Going On in There? How the Brain and Mind Develop in the First Five Years of Life* (New York: Bantam Books, 1999).

2. Ibid., 341.

3. Ibid., 367.

4. Edmund Burke Huey, *The Psychology and Pedagogy of Reading* (New York: Macmillan, 1908).

5. William S. Gray, *Basic Readers* (New York: Scott, Foresman, 1929).

6. Rudolf Flesch, *Why Johnny Can't Read—And What You Can Do About It* (New York: Harper and Row, 1955).

7. National Institute of Child Health and Human Development, *Report of the National Reading Panel. Teaching Children to Read: An Evidence-Based Assessment of the Scientific Research Literature on Reading and Its Implications for Reading Instruction*, NIH Publication No. 00-4769 (Washington, DC: U.S. Government Printing Office, 2000).

8. Maria Montessori, *The Montessori Method* (New York: Schocken Books, 1964), as reported in Rudolf Flesch, *Why Johnny Still Can't Read: A New Look at the Scandal of Our Schools* (New York: Harper and Row, 1981), 119.

9. Delores Durkin, *Children Who Read Early* (New York: Teachers College Press, 1966).

10. Marie Clay, *Becoming Literate: The Construction of Inner Control* (Auckland: Heinemann, 1991), 105.

11. Marie Clay, *Observing Young Readers* (Exeter, NH: Heinemann, 1982).

12. See, for example, Carol Chomsky, "Write First, Read Later," *Childhood Education* 41 (1971): 296–299; Charles Read, *Children's Categorizations of Speech Sounds in English* (Urbana, IL: National Council of Teachers of English, 1975); J. Richard Gentry, "A Retrospective on Invented Spelling and a Look Forward," *The Reading Teacher* 54 (2000): 318–332.

3. FIND YOUR CHILD'S PHASE

1. Linnea C. Ehri, "Learning to Read and Learning to Spell Are One and the Same, Almost," in C. A. Perfetti, L. Rieben, and M. Fayol, eds., *Learning to Spell* (London: Lawrence Erlbaum Associates, 1997), 237–269; J. Richard Gentry, *Breaking the Code: The New Science of Beginning Reading and Writing* (Portsmouth, NH: Heinemann, 2006); J. Richard Gentry, *Breakthrough in Beginning Reading and Writing* (New York: Scholastic, 2007).

2. See discussion of J. Richard Gentry, "Early Spelling Strategies," *Elementary School Journal* 79 (1978): 88–92; J. Richard Gentry, "An Analysis of Developmental Spelling in GNYS AT WRK," *Reading Teacher* 36 (1982): 192–200; Donald Richgels, "Invented Spelling, Phonemic Awareness, and Reading and Writing Instruction," in Susan B. Neuman and Donald D. Dickinson, eds., *Handbook of Early Literacy Research* (New York: Guilford Press, 2001), 147–149.

3. Charles Read, *Children's Categorizations of Speech Sounds in English* (Urbana, IL: National Council of Teachers of English, 1975).

4. Gentry, "An Analysis of Developmental Spelling in GNYS AT WRK."

5. Ehri, "Learning to Read and Learning to Spell."

6. C. Snow, M. W. Burns, and P. Griffin, *Preventing Reading Difficulties in Young Children* (Washington, DC: National Academy Press, 1998); M. S. Burns, P. Griffin, and C. E. Snow, eds., *Starting Out Right: A Guide to Promoting Children's Reading Success* (Washington, DC: National Academy Press, 1999). Available online at http://www.nap.edu/html/sor/.

7. International Reading Association. "Learning to Read and Write: Developmentally Appropriate Practices," *The Reading Teacher* 52 (1998): 193–214.

8. Adapted from J. Richard Gentry, "You Can Analyze Developmental Spelling," *Teaching K-8* 15, no. 9 (1985): 44–45.

4. TEACHING READING IN PHASE 0

1. Lise Eliot, *What's Going On in There? How the Brain and Mind Develop in the First Five Years of Life* (New York: Bantam Books, 1999), 371.

2. Ibid., 352.

3. Ibid., 102.

4. Caroline Blakemore and Barbara Ramirez, *Baby Read-Aloud Basics* (New York: American Management Association, 2006).

5. Eliot, *What's Going On in There?* 216.

6. Ibid., 196.

7. Ibid., 389.

8. Ibid., 341.

9. Linda Acredolo and Susan Goodwyn, *Baby Minds: Brain Building Games Your Baby Will Love* (New York: Bantam Books, 2000), 159.

10. The following sources were consulted in compiling the Literacy Milestones Checklist: Acredoloo and Goodwyn, *Baby Minds*; Nell Duke Bennett-Ammistead and Annie Moses, *Beyond Bedtime Stories: A Parent's Guide to Promoting Reading, Writing, and Other Literacy Skills for Birth to 5* (New York: Scholastic, 2007); Blakemore and Ramirez, *Baby Read-Aloud Basics*; Eliot, *What's Going On in There?*; J. Richard Gentry, *Step-by-Step Assessment Guide to Code Breaking* (New York: Scholastic, 2008); J. Richard Gentry, *Breakthrough in Beginning Reading and Writing* (New York: Scholastic, 2007); J. Richard Gentry, *Breaking the Code: The New Science of Beginning Reading and Writing* (Portsmouth, NH: Heinemann, 2006). Deborah Wells Rowe, "Social Contracts for Writing: Negotiating Shared Understandings About Text in the Preschool Years," *Reading Research Quarterly* 43, no. 1 (2008): 66–95; Jill Stamm, *Bright from the Start: The Simple, Science-Backed Way to Nurture Your Child's Developing Mind, from Birth to Age 3* (New York: Penguin, 2007); Nancy D. Wiseman, *Could It Be Autism? A Parent's Guide to the First Signs and Next Steps* (New York: Broadway Books, 2006).

11. Eliot, *What's Going On in There?,* 373.

5. TEACHING READING IN PHASE 1

1. Barbara Peterson, "Selecting Books for Beginning Readers: Children's Literature Suitable for Young Readers," in D. E. DeFord, C. A. Lyons, and G. S. Pinnell, eds., *Bridges to Literacy: Learning from Reading Recovery* (Portsmouth, NH: Heinemann, 1991), 119–147.
2. Rebecca Treiman and V. Broderick, "What's in a Name: Children's Knowledge About the Letters in Their Own Names, *Journal of Experimental Child Psychology* 70 (1998): 97–116.
3. L. M. Justice, K. Pence, R. B. Bowles, and A. Wiggins, "An Investigation of Four Hypotheses Concerning the Order by Which 4-Year-Old Children Learn the Alphabet Letters," *Early Childhood Research Quarterly* 21 (2006): 374–389.
4. The following sources were consulted in compiling the Literacy Milestones Checklist: Linda Acredoloo and Susan Goodwyn, *Baby Minds: Brain Building Games Your Baby Will Love* (New York: Bantam Books, 2000); Nell Duke Bennett-Ammistead and Annie Moses, *Beyond Bedtime Stories: A Parent's Guide to Promoting Reading, Writing, and Other Literacy Skills for Birth to 5* (New York: Scholastic, 2007); Caroline Blakemore and Barbara Ramirez, *Baby Read-Aloud Basics* (New York: American Management Association, 2006); Lise Eliot, *What's Going On in There? How the Brain and Mind Develop in the First Five Years of Life* (New York: Bantam Books, 1999); J. Richard Gentry, *Step-by-Step Assessment Guide to Code Breaking* (New York: Scholastic, 2008); J. Richard Gentry, *Breakthrough in Beginning Reading and Writing* (New York: Scholastic, 2007); J. Richard Gentry, *Breaking the Code: The New Science of Beginning Reading and Writing* (Portsmouth, NH: Heinemann, 2006); Deborah Wells Rowe, "Social Contracts for Writing: Negotiating Shared Understandings About Text in the Preschool Years," *Reading Research Quarterly* 43, no. 1 (2008): 66–95; Jill Stamm, *Bright from the Start:*

The Simple, Science-Backed Way to Nurture Your Child's Developing Mind, from Birth to Age 3 (New York: Penguin, 2007); Nancy D. Wiseman, *Could It Be Autism? A Parent's Guide to the First Signs and Next Steps* (New York: Broadway Books, 2006).

6. TEACHING READING IN PHASE 2

1. Barbara Peterson, "Selecting Books for Beginning Readers: Children's Literature Suitable for Young Readers," in D. E. DeFord, C. A. Lyons, and G. S. Pinnell, eds., *Bridges to Literacy: Learning from Reading Recovery* (Portsmouth, NH: Heinemann, 1991), 119–147.
2. The following sources were consulted in compiling the Literacy Milestones Checklist: Linda Acredoloo and Susan Goodwyn, *Baby Minds: Brain Building Games Your Baby Will Love* (New York: Bantam Books, 2000); Nell Duke Bennett-Ammistead and Annie Moses, *Beyond Bedtime Stories: A Parent's Guide to Promoting Reading, Writing, and Other Literacy Skills for Birth to 5* (New York: Scholastic, 2007); Caroline Blakemore and Barbara Ramirez, *Baby Read-Aloud Basics* (New York: American Management Association, 2006); Lise Eliot, *What's Going On in There? How the Brain and Mind Develop in the First Five Years of Life* (New York: Bantam Books, 1999); J. Richard Gentry, *Step-by-Step Assessment Guide to Code Breaking* (New York: Scholastic, 2008); J. Richard Gentry, *Breakthrough in Beginning Reading and Writing* (New York: Scholastic, 2007); J. Richard Gentry, *Breaking the Code: The New Science of Beginning Reading and Writing* (Portsmouth, NH: Heinemann, 2006); Deborah Wells Rowe, "Social Contracts for Writing: Negotiating Shared Understandings About Text in the Preschool Years," *Reading Research Quarterly* 43, no. 1 (2008): 66–95; Jill Stamm, *Bright from the Start: The Simple, Science-Backed Way to Nurture Your Child's Developing Mind, from Birth to Age 3* (New York: Penguin, 2007); Nancy D. Wiseman, *Could It Be Autism? A Parent's Guide to the First Signs and Next Steps* (New York: Broadway Books, 2006).

7. TEACHING READING IN PHASE 3

1. Marie Clay, *Observing Young Readers* (Exeter, NH: Heinemann, 1982), 4.
2. Barbara Peterson, "Selecting Books for Beginning Readers: Children's Literature Suitable for Young Readers," in D. E. DeFord, C. A. Lyons, and G. S. Pinnell, eds., *Bridges to Literacy: Learning from Reading Recovery* (Portsmouth, NH: Heinemann, 1991), 119–147.
3. Mem Fox, *Zoo Looking*, illustrated by Candace Whitman (New York: Mondo, 1996).
4. Wylie and Durrell identified thirty-seven rimes that generated about five hundred easy-to-read words. See R. E. Wylie and Donald D. Durrell, "Teaching Vowels Through Phonograms," *Elementary English Journal* 47 (1970): 787–791.
5. The following sources were consulted in compiling the Literacy Milestones Checklist: Linda Acredoloo and Susan Goodwyn, *Baby Minds: Brain Building Games Your Baby Will Love* (New York: Bantam Books, 2000); Nell Duke Bennett-Ammistead and Annie Moses, *Beyond Bedtime Stories: A Parent's Guide to Promoting Reading, Writing, and Other Literacy Skills for Birth to 5* (New York: Scholastic, 2007); Caroline Blakemore and Barbara Ramirez, *Baby Read-Aloud Basics* (New York: American Management Association, 2006); Lise Eliot, *What's Going On in There? How the Brain and Mind Develop in the First Five Years of Life* (New York: Bantam Books, 1999); J. Richard Gentry, *Step-by-Step Assessment Guide to Code Breaking* (New York: Scholastic, 2008); J. Richard Gentry, *Breakthrough in Beginning Reading and Writing* (New York: Scholastic, 2007); J. Richard Gentry, *Breaking the Code: The New Science of Beginning Reading and Writing* (Portsmouth, NH: Heinemann, 2006); Deborah Wells Rowe, "Social Contracts for Writing:

Negotiating Shared Understandings About Text in the Preschool Years," *Reading Research Quarterly* 43, no. 1 (2008): 66–95; Jill Stamm, *Bright from the Start: The Simple, Science-Backed Way to Nurture Your Child's Developing Mind, from Birth to Age 3* (New York: Penguin, 2007); Nancy D. Wiseman, *Could It Be Autism? A Parent's Guide to the First Signs and Next Steps* (New York: Broadway Books, 2006).

8. TEACHING READING IN PHASE 4

1. Else Holmelund Minarik, *The Little Bear Treasury*, illustrated by Maurice Sendak, includes three complete books: *Little Bear*, *Little Bear's Friend*, and *Little Bear's Visit* (New York: HarperCollins, 1961).
2. Donald Richgels, "Invented Spelling, Phonemic Awareness, and Reading and Writing Instruction," in Susan B. Neuman and David K. Dickinson, eds., *Handbook of Early Literacy Research*, vol. 1 (New York: Guilford Press, 2003), 142–155.
3. Barbara Peterson, "Selecting Books for Beginning Readers: Children's Literature Suitable for Young Readers," in D. E. DeFord, C. A. Lyons, and G. S. Pinnell, eds., *Bridges to Literacy: Learning from Reading Recovery* (Portsmouth, NH: Heinemann, 1991), 119–147.
4. James Preller, *NBA Action from A to Z* (New York: Scholastic, 1997).
5. R. E. Wylie and Donald D. Durrell, "Teaching Vowels Through Phonograms," *Elementary English Journal* 47 (1970): 787–791.
6. Timothy Rasinski, "Making and Writing Words," http://www.readingonline.org/articles/words/rasinski.html (accessed October 11, 2009).
7. Parents may use a free tool on my website to find all the English words in a particular word family or all the English words that share a particular chunk, such as *–ash*. Go to JRichard Gentry.com and click "Links" on the homepage. Then click on "Find and Unscramble Words" under Free Tools.
8. The following sources were consulted in compiling the Literacy Milestones Checklist: Linda Acredoloo and Susan Goodwyn, *Baby Minds: Brain Building Games Your Baby Will Love* (New York: Bantam Books, 2000); Nell Duke Bennett-Ammistead and Annie Moses, *Beyond Bedtime Stories: A Parent's Guide to Promoting Reading, Writing, and Other Literacy Skills for Birth to 5* (New York: Scholastic, 2007); Caroline Blakemore and Barbara Ramirez, *Baby Read-Aloud Basics* (New York: American Management Association, 2006); Lise Eliot, *What's Going On in There? How the Brain and Mind Develop in the First Five Years of Life* (New York: Bantam Books, 1999); J. Richard Gentry, *Step-by-Step Assessment Guide to Code Breaking* (New York: Scholastic, 2008); J. Richard Gentry, *Breakthrough in Beginning Reading and Writing* (New York: Scholastic, 2007); J. Richard Gentry, *Breaking the Code: The New Science of Beginning Reading and Writing* (Portsmouth, NH: Heinemann, 2006); Deborah Wells Rowe, "Social Contracts for Writing: Negotiating Shared Understandings About Text in the Preschool Years," *Reading Research Quarterly* 43, no. 1 (2008): 66–95; Jill Stamm, *Bright from the Start: The Simple, Science-Backed Way to Nurture Your Child's Developing Mind, from Birth to Age 3* (New York: Penguin, 2007); Nancy D. Wiseman, *Could It Be Autism? A Parent's Guide to the First Signs and Next Steps* (New York: Broadway Books, 2006).

9. IS EVERYTHING ON TRACK?

1. The following websites were consulted in compiling the information in Figure 9.1: "Leveling Resource Guide," Scholastic, http://www2.scholastic.com/browse/article.jsp?id=4476;

"Reading Level Correlation Chart, UALR Arkansas Literacy Coaching Model," http://www.arliteracymodel.com/pdf/resources/040514_reading_level_correlation_chart.pdf; "Reading Level Correlation Chart," http://www.placonference.org/2008/handouts/1013_125Neef_Penny__116051_Mar03_2008_Time_014921PM.pdf; "Reading Grade-Level Comparison Chart," Harcourt Achieve, http://www.oema.net/lexiles/ReadingLevelComps.pdf.

2. American Academy of Pediatrics, "AAP Policy Statement," *Pediatrics* 104, no. 2 (August 1999): 341–343, http://aappolicy.aappublications.org/cgi/content/full/pediatrics;104/2/341 (accessed October 11, 2009).
3. D. J. Leu, Jr., and C. K. Kinzer, "The Convergence of Literacy Instruction with Networked Technologies for Information and Communication," *Reading Research Quarterly* 35 (2000): 108–127.
4. Hillel Goelman, Antoinette Oberg, and Frank Smith, eds. *Awakening to Literacy* (Portsmouth, NH: Heinemann Educational Books, 1984).
5. Michael Ignatieff, "Getting Iraq Wrong: What War Has Taught About Political Judgment," *New York Times Magazine*, August 5, 2007, 28.
6. Sandra Blakeslee, "Cells That Read Minds," *New York Times*, January 10, 2006, D1.

REFERENCES

Acredoloo, Linda, and Susan Goodwyn. *Baby Minds: Brain Building Games Your Baby Will Love.* New York: Bantam Books, 2000.

American Academy of Pediatrics. "AAP Policy Statement," *Pediatrics* 104, no. 2 (August 1999): 341–343, http://aappolicy.aappublications.org/cgi/content/full/pediatrics;104/2/341 (accessed October 11, 2009).

Bennett-Ammistead, Nell Duke, and Annie Moses. *Beyond Bedtime Stories: A Parent's Guide to Promoting Reading, Writing, and Other Literacy Skills for Birth to 5.* New York: Scholastic, 2007.

Blakemore, Caroline, and Barbara Ramirez. *Baby Read-Aloud Basics.* New York: American Management Association, 2006.

Blakeslee, Sandra. "Cells That Read Minds." *New York Times*, January 10, 2006, D1.

Chomsky, Carol. "Write First, Read Later." *Childhood Education* 41 (1971): 296–299.

Clay, Marie. *Becoming Literate: The Construction of Inner Control.* Auckland: Heinemann, 1991.

———. *Observing Young Readers.* Exeter, NH: Heinemann, 1982.

Dehaene, Stanislas. *Reading in the Brain.* New York: Viking, 2009.

Durkin, Delores. *Children Who Read Early.* New York: Teachers College Press, 1966.

Ehri, Linnea C. "Learning to Read and Learning to Spell Are One and the Same, Almost." In C. A. Perfetti, L. Rieben, and M. Fayol, eds., *Learning to Spell.* London: Lawrence Erlbaum Associates, 1997.

Eliot, Lise. *What's Going On in There? How the Brain and Mind Develop in the First Five Years of Life.* New York: Bantam Books, 1999.

Flesch, Rudolf. *Why Johnny Still Can't Read: A New Look at the Scandal of Our Schools.* New York: Harper and Row, 1981.

———. *Why Johnny Can't Read—And What You Can Do About It.* New York: Harper and Row, 1955.

Fox, Mem. *Zoo Looking.* New York: Mondo, 1996.

Gentry, J. Richard. *Step-by-Step Assessment Guide to Code Breaking.* New York: Scholastic, 2008.

———. *Breakthrough in Beginning Reading and Writing.* New York: Scholastic, 2007.

———. *Breaking the Code: The New Science of Beginning Reading and Writing.* Portsmouth, NH: Heinemann, 2006.

———. "A Retrospective on Invented Spelling and a Look Forward." *The Reading Teacher* 54 (2000): 318–332.

———. "An Analysis of Developmental Spelling in GNYS AT WRK." *The Reading Teacher* 36 (1982): 192–200.

———. "Early Spelling Strategies." *Elementary School Journal* 79 (1978): 88–92.

Goelman, Hillel, Antoinette Oberg, and Frank Smith, eds. *Awakening to Literacy.* Portsmouth, NH: Heinemann Educational Books, 1984.

Gray, William S. *Basic Readers.* New York: Scott, Foresman, 1929.

Hart, Betty, and Todd Risley. *Meaningful Differences in Everyday Experience of Young American Children.* Baltimore: Brookes, 1996.

Huey, Edmund Burke. *The Psychology and Pedagogy of Reading*. New York: Macmillan, 1908.

Ignatieff, Michael. "Getting Iraq Wrong: What War Has Taught About Political Judgment." *New York Times Magazine*, August 5, 2007: 26–29.

International Reading Association. "Learning to Read and Write: Developmentally Appropriate Practices." *The Reading Teacher* 52 (1998): 193–214.

Justice, L. M., K. Pence, R. B. Bowles, and A. Wiggins. "An Investigation of Four Hypotheses Concerning the Order by Which 4-Year-Old Children Learn the Alphabet Letters." *Early Childhood Research Quarterly* 21 (2006): 374–389.

Leu, D. J., Jr., and C. K. Kinzer. "The Convergence of Literacy Instruction with Networked Technologies for Information and Communication." *Reading Research Quarterly* 35 (2000): 108–127.

Minarik, Else Holmelund. *The Little Bear Treasury*, including three complete books: *Little Bear*, *Little Bear's Friend*, and *Little Bear's Visit*. Illustrated by Maurice Sendak. New York: HarperCollins, 1961.

Montessori, Maria. *The Montessori Method*. New York: Schocken Books, 1964.

National Institute of Child Health and Human Development. *Report of the National Reading Panel. Teaching Children to Read: An Evidence-Based Assessment of the Scientific Research Literature on Reading and Its Implications for Reading Instruction*. NIH Publication No. 00-4769. Washington, DC: U.S. Government Printing Office, 2000.

Neuman, Susan, and David Dickinson, eds. *Handbook of Early Literacy Research*, vol. 1. New York: Guilford Press, 2001.

O'Neal, John. "Early Repairs in Foundations for Reading." *New York Times*, October 4, 2006, A25.

Paulesu, E., J.-F. Demonet, F. Fazio, E. McCrory, V. Chanoine, N. Brunswick, S. F. Cappa, G. Cossu, M. Habib, C. D. Frith, and U. Frith. "Dyslexia: Cultural Diversity and Biological Unity." *Science* 291, no. 5511 (March 16, 2001): 2165.

Peterson, Barbara. "Selecting Books for Beginning Readers: Children's Literature Suitable for Young Readers." In D. E. DeFord, C. A. Lyons, and G. S. Pinnell, eds., *Bridges to Literacy: Learning from Reading Recovery*. Portsmouth, NH: Heinemann, 1991, 119–147.

Preller, James. *NBA Action from A to Z*. New York: Scholastic, 1997.

Rasinski, Timothy. "Making and Writing Words," http://www.readingonline.org/articles/words/rasinski.html (accessed October 11, 2009).

Read, Charles. *Children's Categorizations of Speech Sounds in English*. Urbana, IL: National Council of Teachers of English, 1975.

Richgels, Donald. "Invented Spelling, Phonemic Awareness, and Reading and Writing Instruction." In Susan B. Neuman and David K. Dickinson, eds., *Handbook of Early Literacy Research*. New York: Guilford Press, 2003, 142–155.

Rowe, Deborah Wells. "Social Contracts for Writing: Negotiating Shared Understandings About Text in the Preschool Years." *Reading Research Quarterly* 43, no. 1 (2008): 66–95.

Shaywitz, S. *Overcoming Dyslexia*. New York: Alfred A. Knopf, 2003.

Snow, C., M. W. Burns, and P. Griffin. *Preventing Reading Difficulties in Young Children*. Washington, DC: National Academy Press, 1998.

Stamm, Jill. *Bright from the Start: The Simple, Science-Backed Way to Nurture Your Child's Developing Mind, from Birth to Age 3*. New York: Penguin, 2007.

Treiman, Rebecca, and V. Broderick. "What's in a Name: Children's Knowledge About the Letters in Their Own Names. *Journal of Experimental Child Psychology* 70 (1998): 97–116.

Wiseman, Nancy D. *Could It Be Autism? A Parent's Guide to the First Signs and Next Steps*. New York: Broadway Books, 2006.

CREDITS

The author and publisher wish to thank those who have generously given permission to reprint material.

Figures I.1, I.2, I.3, I.4, 3.2, 3.3, 3.4, 5.1, 5.3, and 6.1 adapted from *Breaking the Code* by J. Richard Gentry. Copyright © 2006 by J. Richard Gentry. Published by Heinemann, a division of Houghton Mifflin, Portsmouth, NH.

Figures 3.2, 3.3, 3.4, and 5.1 adapted from *Step-by-Step Assessment Guide to Code Breaking* by J. Richard Gentry. Copyright © 2008 by J. Richard Gentry. Reprinted by permission of Scholastic, Inc.

Figures 3.5B and 3.6A adapted from "An Analysis of Developmental Spelling in GNYS at WRK" by J. Richard Gentry. From *The Reading Teacher* (36 [2] November 1982). Copyright © 1982 by the International Reading Association. Reprinted with permission.

Figures 3.5C, 3.6B, 3.6C, and 3.6D adapted from *Breakthrough in Beginning Reading and Writing* by J. Richard Gentry. Copyright © 2007 by J. Richard Gentry. Reprinted by permission of Scholastic, Inc.

Figure 3.7 adapted from "You Can Analyze Developmental Spelling" by J. Richard Gentry. From the May 1985 issue of *Teaching K-8 Magazine*, Norwalk, CT 06854. Reprinted with permission of the publisher, Early Years, Inc.

Figures 4.2 and 4.3 from *Zaner-Bloser Handwriting*. Copyright © Zaner-Bloser, Inc. Used with permission from Zaner-Bloser, Inc. All rights reserved.

Figure 6.3 from *Nursery Rhyme Time: Reading and Learning Sounds, Letters, and Words* by J. Richard Gentry and Richard S. Craddock. Copyright © 2005 by Universal Publishing. Reprinted by permission.

INDEX